"Deliver Us from
This Cruel War"

"Deliver Us from This Cruel War"

The Civil War Letters of Lieutenant Joseph J. Hoyle, 55th North Carolina Infantry

JOSEPH J. HOYLE

Edited by Jeffrey M. Girvan

McFarland & Company, Inc., Publishers

Jefferson, North Carolina, and London

Excerpts from the Joseph J. Hoyle Papers located in the Rare Book, Manuscript, and Special Collections Library, Duke University.

ISBN 978-0-7864-4757-2 (softcover : 50# alkaline paper)

LIBRARY OF CONGRESS CATALOGUING DATA ARE AVAILABLE

British Library cataloguing data are available

Front cover painting ©2010 PicturesNow; background excerpt of 1863 letter by Joseph Hoyle

Manufactured in the United States of America

McFarland & Company, Inc., Publishers
Box 611, Jefferson, North Carolina 28640
www.mcfarlandpub.com

To all those who have served and are serving to ensure
the liberty and freedoms we all cherish, especially
Charles J. Girvan (U.S. Navy)
Charles J. Girvan, Jr. (U.S. Air Force)
Harold "Butch" Wissner, Jr. (U.S. Army)
James Dowd (U.S. Air Force)
Craig Lawther (U.S. Army)

Table of Contents

Acknowledgments

As in all historical endeavors there are individuals and institutions that make it all possible. When I began researching and editing the Joseph J. Hoyle letters I received great assistance from many people. I would like to thank the archivists and librarians at the Rare Book, Manuscript, and Special Collections Library at Duke University for all their assistance in making available the letters of Joseph J. Hoyle and for providing permission to publish the Civil War portion of these wonderful correspondences. The fine librarians and student assistants that work in the manuscript departments at the libraries of the University of North Carolina at Chapel Hill, East Carolina University, and the Prince William County Public Library System, especially those at Independent Hill Neighborhood Library and the staff who diligently work in the interlibrary loan section. Also the curators and research assistants at the Museum of the Confederacy in Richmond, Virginia; and the historians at the Fredericksburg and Spotsylvania National Military Park in Fredericksburg, Virginia; the Gettysburg National Military Park in Gettysburg, Pennsylvania; the Petersburg National Battlefield in Petersburg, Virginia; and at the Richmond National Battlefield in Richmond, Virginia.

I also would like to thank my brother Greg Girvan for his assistance in editing and providing valuable additions and corrections to the manuscript. Colonel Dick Camp, vice president for museum operations for the Marine Corps Heritage Foundation, provided insight and referred sources for study of combat and combat motivation.

The time that was needed to research and write this book occasionally prevented me from sharing in family activities with my wife, Jodi, sons Jared and Joshua, and daughter Jocelyn. I was fortunate enough to have a supportive and caring family who encouraged me along the way as I finished this manuscript. For this, and for all they do to make everything meaningful, I am sincerely thankful. Finally, my thanks to my parents, Charles and Carolyn Girvan, who instilled in me from a young age the importance of history and education.

Preface

Although the Army of Northern Virginia, commanded by Robert E. Lee, is a well known fighting force and there have been many scholarly works written about all his principal lieutenants there is still relatively little known of the daily lives of the men who fought for this famed legion. To truly understand the impact of the frontline soldier one must read the letters and diaries written by the men who served in the ranks. Memoirs written years after the Civil War ended have value, but time can affect memory and sometimes individuals feel the need to justify or enlarge their actions for a particular audience. Therefore it is crucial to the understanding of the American Civil War to read and study the wartime letters and diaries of the fighting men who experienced the monotony of camp life as well as the horrific combat of a conflict that saw the birth of modern warfare.

The goal of this book is to provide a more thorough review of the wartime experiences of one frontline soldier who rose from the rank of Private to 1st Lieutenant and commanded troops in many significant battles like Gettysburg and Globe Tavern. Also, the publishing of Joseph J. Hoyle's Civil War letters will make his perspective of the conflict more accessible to scholars, as well as those who want to learn more about the individuals who participated in one of the most monumental events in the history of the United States.

I first came to read the Joseph J. Hoyle letters, which are kept at the Rare Book, Manuscript, and Special Collections Library at Duke University, while researching for my master's thesis on the 55th North Carolina for East Carolina University. I was aware that the young lieutenant had written several letters to North Carolina newspapers during the war to keep the local inhabitants apprised of the war effort and the exploits of his unit, Company F, 55th North Carolina. I wanted to find more first hand accounts of soldiers who had fought with the regiment and came across Hoyle's letters while researching the James K. Wilkerson Papers at Duke University. Once I read through the correspondences, which are primarily comprised of letters to his wife,

Sarah Hoyle, I knew that after I finished my work on the 55th North Carolina I would begin editing his papers for publication.

The letters, although edited for better understanding, have remained exactly as Hoyle wrote them, the only changes being the merging of some of the paragraphs for better readability and the removal of the dashes that were popularly used at the time instead of periods and commas. These style alterations were implemented only to assist the reader with the manuscript and enhance the flow of his writing.

This book is not a unit history of the 55th North Carolina or of Hoyle's Company F. My previous book, *The 55th North Carolina in the Civil War: A History and Roster*, published by McFarland in 2006, provides a more concentrated study of the regiment. Although the letters have been divided into chapters, which include an overview of the events and actions that the 55th North Carolina participated in, the narrative portions are designed only to offer the reader an overall understanding of what was happening in the war and with Hoyle's unit while he was writing his letters. The narratives are written to present the letters into a proper historical context, not to tell the whole story of the 55th North Carolina.

Joseph J. Hoyle was a combat soldier and fought in every major engagement that the Army of Northern Virginia participated in from Gettysburg to Globe Tavern. To provide a better study of the wartime experiences of Hoyle I felt an introduction to some of the scholarly works that focus on the common soldier of the Civil War would afford readers a basic understanding of the historiography of the subject and a short list of books that they may want to consult if they are new to the subject. For those already aware of the growing attention scholars have placed on the lives of frontline soldiers the reviewed titles will not surprise, but may encourage some thought and consideration for discussion.

Combat, after all, is the most trying aspect of the life of a soldier, and to gain an appreciation of what it was like to experience battle is essential to understanding the common fighting man of the Civil War. The second chapter of this book offers readers an overview of the experience of combat and soldiers' emotional responses to it. This section is not meant as a military history of the Confederate soldier, but only as a view of what it was like to march into battle during the Civil War.

The remaining chapters of the book contain the letters, which have been annotated to present insight into the life of Joseph J. Hoyle, to provide historical context of the period in which the correspondence was written, and to identify the many individuals Hoyle mentions in his letters.

As a historian, I enjoy the opportunity to completely immerse my thoughts into past events, and into the experiences of a man I found to be honorable and courageous. Finding out as much as possible about the people referred to throughout the letters, however, proved to be a challenge. Many of the men and women Hoyle mentions are not well-known historical figures. Throughout the correspondence there are mentions of prominent persons like Robert E. Lee, Jefferson Davis, and George B. McClellan, but these men, and the other renowned individuals referred to, were not known to Hoyle personally. The majority of the people mentioned are common soldiers, town folk from Cleveland County, North Carolina, and officers from his regiment. To discover who these people were I had to study the Federal Census records, county land and marriage records, military rosters and parole papers. One of the most helpful secondary sources for those trying to research Civil War soldiers from North Carolina is the multi-volume work *North Carolina Troops: A Roster*, published by North Carolina's Division of Archives and History. These volumes provide well written unit histories of all the regiments organized in North Carolina during the Civil War. But the invaluable parts of these works are the unit rosters. Not only have the fine historians working for the North Carolina Department of Archives and History in Raleigh, North Carolina, provided a comprehensive roster, but each soldier's entry is accompanied by a brief semi-biographical sketch that presents useful information on his wartime experiences.

The 55th North Carolina is a little known regiment that did not join Lee's famed army until after the spectacular victory at Chancellorsville but would be in the ranks of the Army of Northern Virginia from Gettysburg to Appomattox. The letters written by Joseph J. Hoyle during the war offer readers a glimpse of the daily life of one of Lee's frontline soldiers. Hoyle's insightful correspondence enhances our knowledge of what it was like to serve in one of the most renowned military units in American history, and his firsthand accounts of the battles of Gettysburg and the engagements that made up the Overland Campaign are useful for both scholars and novice researchers.

Introduction

Around two o'clock on the afternoon of July 3, 1863, Johnston Petti-grew, temporarily in command of Major General Henry Heth's division, ordered his men forward — in the words of 1st Lieutenant Joseph J. Hoyle, one of his company commanders — into the "very jaws of death." By the end of the unsuccessful attack, over 1120 Confederate soldiers lay dead on the field and more than 4020 others, some of whom would die later, were wounded.[1] Although a number of historians argue that the Army of Northern Virginia didn't lose its ability to win the war for the South until late 1864, many consider this fateful assault, popularly called Pickett's Charge, the Confederacy's final attempt at winning the war.

One of the forty-two Confederate regiments that participated in this final assault against the Federals at Gettysburg was the 55th North Carolina, a unit organized in the summer of 1862. The 55th, which had also fought on the first day of the battle, suffered approximately 375 casualties — more than half of its troops — during the fighting around Gettysburg. Most of the regiment's company commanders were either killed or wounded, and some companies, like Company F (also known as the South Mountain Rangers) were reduced to only fourteen men ready for duty on July 4, 1863.

In charge of Company F on July 3 was a relatively inexperienced twenty-five-year-old 1st Lieutenant named Joseph J. Hoyle. He had never fought in a major battle, and had been in the Confederate Army for only a little over a year. Although he and his men had engaged in combat, they had never been asked to charge across a mile-long field and assail a fortified position. Every soldier who stood in line for battle on Seminary Ridge that warm July afternoon knew that even if they succeeded in taking the Federal position, many of the men they had come to know and respect while serving together would not live to answer another roll call.

Just two days earlier, on July 1, 1863, the regiment had faced remnants of the Federal First Corps, including troops of the Iron Brigade, and had been bloodied by the relentless fire of some of the best soldiers in the whole Army of the Potomac. Yet still the Confederates had managed to win the initial stage of the engagement. Now, on the third day of this climactic battle, 1st Lieutenant Joseph J. Hoyle prepared to face the seemingly tireless enemy once again, hoping to experience the same triumph.

As is now known, the outcome of this legendary charge was devastating to the Army of Northern Virginia. Never again would General Robert E. Lee lead his troops in an invasion of the North. Although the war would continue for nearly two more years, the luster of the once indomitable Confederacy had begun to fade. Joseph J. Hoyle had not been there in July 1862 when this same army had pushed the Federals off the Peninsula between the York and James Rivers, nor had he been there when they routed a superior Army of the Potomac at Second Manassas near the end of August that same year. And though Lee's first invasion of the North had culminated in a tactical draw at Antietam on September 17, 1862, the Army of Northern Virginia had completely dominated the Federals at Fredericksburg in December and then again at Chancellorsville (May 2–4, 1863). But the fighting of July 3, 1863, stunned Lee's grand army, and with the recent loss of Vicksburg the Confederacy was reeling. Thus the army Joseph J. Hoyle now fought with was no longer the conquering force it had once been but, rather, a wounded collection of ragged troops whose vigor had begun to wane, even as their hopeful dream of ultimate victory remained intact.

Joseph J. Hoyle was born on April 14, 1838, amid tumultuous times in what is now Cleveland County, North Carolina. Throughout his lifetime the United States expanded by more than a third of its previous size, fought and won a war with Mexico, and had somehow remained united amid growing sectional disparity. Joseph was the first of five children born to Martin and Susan Hoyle.[2] Like many western North Carolina residents, Martin Hoyle was a farmer who owned a modest piece of land that fed his family and served his financial needs. The Hoyles' lineage can be traced to "Pioneer Peiter" Heyl, who came to America from Germany in 1738, aboard the ship *Robert and Alice*, which set sail from Dublin, Ireland, and arrived in Philadelphia on September 11. In accordance with a law established in 1727 that pertained to German immigrants, upon his arrival in Pennsylvania Peiter Heyl promptly took an oath of allegiance to King George II of England. After living in Pennsylvania for two years, Peiter Heyl migrated south in search of more land. He settled first in Frederick, Maryland, where he remained for several years. Yet, still discontent, Peiter and his wife, Catherine Dale, traveled farther south and purchased property in a part of Bladen County, North Carolina, that is now in Gaston County.[3]

Peiter Heyl had eight children. The eldest, Jacob Hoyl, was Joseph's great-great-grandfather. The Hoyl clan eventually spread throughout western North Carolina, Tennessee, and as far west as California. Jacob's son, Martin Hoyl (Joseph's great-grandfather), and a number of Peiter's descendants eventually settled in present day Cleveland County, where many of the Hoyles still live to this day.[4]

Cleveland County, originally spelled Cleaveland after Colonel Benjamin Cleaveland, a Revolutionary War officer who commanded troops at the battle of King's Mountain, was formed in 1841 from neighboring Rutherford and Lincoln counties. Over the years the county contributed its share of state political leaders and was a well known vacation spot for those who enjoyed the therapeutic qualities of sulfuric springs found in the area, especially Wilson Springs. With small family farms, few plantations, grist and saw mills dotting the landscape, a healthy social and economic community grew to a little over 12,000 residents by 1861. When the war finally began the county supplied fourteen companies of soldiers, totaling around 2035 fighting men; 93 of those fought with Company F, 55th North Carolina.[5]

Joseph J. Hoyle, one of those ninety-three, was married to Sarah A. Self on October 18, 1860. The war, throughout its four interminable, grievous years, would ultimately cut short this young couple's time together, interrupting what may have been a long happy life together.[6] But the time they spent with each other appears to have been filled with love and admiration.

Joseph began courting Sarah in 1858 while attending Rutherford Academy. With affectionate letters to "Dearest little Sallie," and "My charming friend," Joseph informed Sarah of his studies and his hopes and dreams of becoming a minister. The war, which had been raging for fourteen months beginning in April 1861, finally pulled Joseph away from his seemingly joyful life. The majority of the short time the Hoyles were married Joseph was away, encamped with his regiment or engaged in battle with the Federals in places Sarah had most likely never even heard of. However, the two remained close through a constant exchange of letters, which provides those interested in the Civil War, or any occasion that causes people to be parted, a glimpse of how, although separated by hundreds of miles, a young couple remained loyal and amorous. In times of trouble or sorrow, Joseph opened his heart to his wife, revealing his trust in their love and his faith in God. His concern for Sarah during his time away is evident in these letters. Joseph's consistent request for news from home and his opinions on how Sarah should respond to individuals and events exhibits a clear attempt to stay connected with his real life and not allow the war to engulf him.

Sarah Hoyle, if not typical, is an example of how the war could affect one individual. Of her six brothers alive when the war began, two died during the conflict, both from disease. Berryman Self, who served with Company G, 57th North Carolina, died of pneumonia shortly after joining the army. Lemuel Self, who enlisted in the 34th North Carolina, was captured near the North Anna River on May 23, 1864, and died from disease while imprisoned at Point Lookout Prison Camp in Maryland. Her remaining four brothers all served in the Confederate Army. William R. Self, the eldest, also served with the 57th North Carolina and was wounded three times in battle. He was eventually captured near Winchester, Virginia, on July 20, 1864, contracted smallpox in a Federal hospital and was later exchanged and released. Jacob Self, along with his two younger brothers, Isaac and Rufus, served with Joseph in Company F, 55th North Carolina. Jacob was sick for several months before being wounded and discharged in April 1864. Isaac was captured at Gettysburg in 1863 and spent the remaining years of the war in Fort Delaware Prison. Rufus was also wounded at Gettysburg and spent several months in various hospitals. After returning to duty sometime in 1865, he was captured near Sutherland Station, Virginia, and released at the end of the war.[7] In all, the war years were not happy ones for Sarah, or her family who sacrificed so much for the Lost Cause.

Education was part of Joseph Hoyle's life. He prided himself on his intellectual capacity and the effort he put forth to improve upon it. At Rutherford Academy Joseph was one of the top students in his class, gaining the opportunity to deliver a valedictorian speech to his fellow classmates. Upon finishing his studies Joseph obtained certification to teach in both Cleveland and Lincoln counties. He was endorsed to instruct students in algebra, arithmetic, chemistry, geography, grammar, Latin, logic, reading, spelling, and writing. After graduating Joseph began teaching, an occupation he would continue with until May 1862. Although there is no record of how effective Joseph Hoyle was as a teacher, there are, scattered throughout his papers dated before the Civil War, lesson plans, discourses in logic and arithmetic, chemistry and algebraic equations, and practice essays for his students to copy. There are also rules that the young instructor expected his students to adhere to; these included, for example, his high expectations concerning conduct and study and "no coughing" or "unnecessary talking or whispering" during class time.[8]

How much Joseph Hoyle enjoyed teaching is unknown, but when one looks at his lessons it is easy to discern that he put time and effort into his instruction. Also, there is enough information in his papers to quickly come to the understanding that above all he wanted to become a minister and devote his life to the Christian faith. His concern for the welfare of others is seen in his joining the Sons of Temperance in May 1860, and during the war he wrote often to his wife of the debilitating effects of drink and vice on the moral stability of his fellow soldiers. Throughout his letters, even during the darkest days of the war, Joseph Hoyle told his wife to remain faithful and trust in God. Although he wrote about many topics and concerned himself with worldly problems, Joseph Hoyle never strayed too far from expressing his strong faith and encouraging others to follow his example.

As the events of the 1850s pushed the country closer to civil war, Joseph Hoyle spent his days in the sometimes oblivious world of academia. Hoyle's letters tell us little of his feelings toward secession and the coming conflict. A letter from a friend, A. B. Hayes, who would himself soon volunteer to fight for the Confederacy, provides some indication. Hayes wrote to Joseph Hoyle shortly after the nation, or as many Southerners saw it, the North, elected Abraham Lincoln in the 1860 presidential election. Stating that a "fatal calamity" had befallen the country Hayes wrote, "I presume that you are strong for a disunion or secession of the South." Although Joseph's response is not known one can perhaps assume he supported the concept of secession from some of his earlier writings.[9]

During his time at Rutherford Academy, Joseph Hoyle wrote several essays on government. In one of these treatises Hoyle stated that he firmly believed in Thomas Jefferson's principle that revolution was not only necessary when a government begins to infringe on the rights of its citizens but the duty of everyone who loves and supports liberty and freedom. If Joseph Hoyle believed that the Republicans were a party bent on trampling Southern rights, then he probably would have supported secession, at least in theory.

The crisis of 1860, leading to eleven states seceding from the Union, had been simmering since the Constitution Convention of 1787.[10] Although North Carolina did not leave the Union until May 20, 1861 (five months after South Carolina and one month after the South fired on Fort Sumter), the Old North State had firmly supported the Southern cause during the previous decades and so joined as a staunch backer of the Confederacy. Sometimes derisively called the "Rip Van Winkle state" in the antebellum period, North Carolina remained a rural state well into the war years and after. By the early 1860s, only 2 percent of the state's population lived in towns, and only six of these towns had more than 2,000 residents. However, by the 1830s internal improvements made it possible for the interior of North Carolina to expand economically. The growth of railroads and the opening of vast new markets made farming in the Piedmont and western counties more profitable. This financial development helped unify the state, and although North Carolina remained a predominately agrarian state, these domestic improvements began its modernization.[11]

The plantation system, so well popularized as standard Southern living, was not a dominating institution in North Carolina. Less than one-third of the white families living in the Old North State owned slaves in 1860. A staggering 88 percent of these owned fewer than twenty, the nominal limit of the Planter classification. However, as modes of transportation progressed, cash crops became more marketable and slavery was on the rise in the state as the Civil War approached.[12]

Political activity in North Carolina, as in most states at the time, went hand in hand with the issue of slavery, although not as extreme in views as in the Deep South. At times in the 1840s the Whig Party contested for political power in the state, but the slave issue, among others, eventually brought the resurgence of the Democratic Party. Although North Carolina abstained from attending the Nashville Convention, which was the pro-secessionist response to the possibility of Congress passing legislation banning slavery from the newly acquired territories, Whigs in the state who supported the pro–Northern measures of the Compromise of 1850, like the admission of California as a free state, lost their seats in the Senate and House of Representatives. As concerns over sectionalism continued to grow throughout the decade preceding the Civil War, North Carolinians began aligning themselves more and more with the struggle for Southern rights.[13] Tension over slavery and the passage of the Kansas-Nebraska Act of 1854 finally overcame the Whig Party in North Carolina. The once mighty Democratic Party, although losing strength in the North, became, once again, the dominant political party in the Old North State. North Carolinians continued to support the expansion of slavery into the territories, but the threat of radical abolitionists from the North became the prevailing concern for many. The rise of the Black Republicans and John Brown's raid convinced many of the state's citizens that strong support for the South was their only alternative.[14]

Although many former Whigs and some unionist Democrats worked hard to keep North Carolina in the Union, events continued to persuade moderate citizens to follow the radical secessionist view. Abraham Lincoln's election in November 1860 and his call for 75,000 troops after the fall of Fort Sumter, which Governor Ellis referred to as a "high-handed act of tyrannical outrage," pushed a reluctant North Carolina into the arms of the Confederacy. Historian Victor Davis Hanson stresses the belief that men born and raised under the auspices of Western culture have a tendency to fight more devoutly when liberty is being threatened. The young men living in North Carolina at this time seem to support that thesis. As news of the convention's passage of the Ordinance of Secession spread throughout the state, sporadic celebrations erupted as many North Carolinians gladly welcomed the idea of a Southern Confederacy, but not all were so joyful. When hearing the news of the state's secession Unionist Jonathan Worth commented, "I think the South is committing suicide, but my lot is cast with the South and being unable to manage the ship, I intend to face the breakers manfully and go down with my companions." Those who felt only elation would ultimately undergo sorrow, as the state would suffer over 40,000 deaths throughout the war years, and countless wounded.[15]

Perhaps the martial spirit that eventually prompted young Joseph J. Hoyle to enlist in the Confederate army came from his ancestors. Family genealogy traces Hoyle ancestors serving under Frederick Barbarossa and Richard the Lion-Heart, and John Hoyl, Peiter's youngest son, fought during the Revolutionary War and is known to have been present at the battle of Kings Mountain.[16] Regardless, war came to Joseph J. Hoyle, and he would face the same horrors and bittersweet self-satisfaction that all men experience in battle. Although conscription had not yet taken effect in the South, he volunteered to fight. As the Conscription Act had been passed on April 16, 1862, the Confederate Congress had allowed a thirty day interval before enforcing it, to allow men the chance to freely join the army. This time may have motivated Joseph to join so he could avoid the mortification of being drafted, or he may have wanted to have a say in which unit he fought with, which he would not have had the privilege of doing if he were to be conscripted. However, being a teacher Joseph knew he was exempt from service and would not have been conscripted anyway, and at this time in the war he could not have foreseen the massive need for manpower the Confederacy would face in the coming years which forced the Confederate Congress to change the exemptions.[17] Most likely he decided that it was time to do his part to help his fellow North Carolinians win Southern independence. For whatever reason, Joseph J. Hoyle enlisted in the Confederate Army on May 10, 1862. He was mustered in as a Private, and served as Company F's commissary for six months until the position was abolished by regimental commander Colonel John Kerr Connally. He received a promotion to Sergeant on November 25, 1862, and finally 1st Lieutenant on May 11, 1863. He would see action during the battle for Washington, North Carolina, in September 1862, and subsequently throughout Lieutenant General James Longstreet's siege of Suffolk, Virginia, in April–May 1863. Next he would fight at Gettysburg, where he would be in command of his company, and Bristoe Station and continue to see action right through the Overland campaign in the summer of 1864, until being fatally wounded at Globe Tavern on August 18, 1864.

His career in the Army of Northern Virginia resembles that of most young men who gave their lives for their country and their fellow soldiers during the Civil War. His story, though common, is rarely fully understood because no one can completely know exactly what motivated him to fight or comprehend the sorrows he faced throughout his war experience. For instance we will never be able to know how the war changed Joseph J. Hoyle. Did he regard the death of fellow comrades the same way he had in 1862? Did the understanding of the killing and maiming he participated in alter the perception he once had for the world or for himself? For this reason, more than any other, the insight gained by reading the letters and diaries of combat soldiers and can help one appreciate their experiences. It is through the common soldier of the North and South that we learn the horrors of battle, the elation of victory and the sorrow of defeat. Although one can never truly identify with those who have actually been in combat simply by reading a book on the subject, the more we learn of the experiences of the ordinary soldier the closer we come to understanding the true essence of the war.

I HISTORICAL AND BIOGRAPHICAL BACKGROUND

1. Studies of the Common Soldier of the Civil War

"The soldier endures many hardships and privations"

A study of an individual soldier's letters greatly enhances our understanding of the Civil War and combat in general. By reading what combatants wrote to loved ones or friends almost immediately after the events is much more accurate than memoirs written years after the experiences occurred or from edited diaries that may or may not have been rewritten for a particular cause. Therefore the study of what a soldier wrote during the war is a lesson in what it was like to actually be on the battlefields or in camps or hospitals — in essence to live the experience, albeit vicariously through the eyes of another.

The American Civil War is a subject that has been written about more extensively than most other periods in American history. Practically every battle or campaign has been meticulously researched and reviewed. The major political and military figures have had studies, even multi-volume works, published about their lives and exploits.

In all of these studies published on the American Civil War the common soldier has been relatively ignored. However the past twenty years has seen a focus on the common people, including those who served on the front lines. In the thousands of pages of Civil War literature published by Civil War scholars, the life of the common soldier has remained in the shadows of the more celebrated characters and aspects of the conflict. Although the largest bodies of primary sources pertaining to the Civil War are the diaries, letters, and reminiscences of the common soldier, the study of these men has not been as abundant as works on campaigns and generals.

Hundreds of diaries and letter collections written by common soldiers of the Civil War have been published and many scholars have edited and enhanced these works with valuable commentary. These published sources have added to the study of the Civil War and have provided a view of what the common soldiers felt during the conflict. Many works published about the Civil War rely on these published and unpublished primary sources to prove or disprove popular beliefs about the Civil War, but the majority of these studies do not focus on the lives of Johnny Reb and Billy Yank.

In recent years three trends in Civil War historiography have become apparent: an increasing concentration on the war in the western theater, the tendency to focus on the psychological and intellectual aspects of the sectional conflict, and a growing interest in the common soldier who fought the bloody battles and paid the price for freedom. Within the last trend, several subdivisions have dominated the writings of Civil War scholars: the social history of the common soldier, combat motivation and experience, and the contributions and accomplishments of black soldiers. As the reading of letters written by a Civil War soldier is part of the study of the common fighting man who fought during the conflict it is fitting to first briefly review some of the published works centering on the experiences of soldiers. The works discussed in this chapter represent only a fraction of the books focusing on the common soldier of the Civil War that have been published and were selected to provide the reader with a basic understanding of the many facets and interpretations Civil War scholars have tried to convey.

In 1943, the late Bell Irvin Wiley, then teaching at what is now the University of Mississippi, published his social history of the common soldier of the Confederacy. *The Life of Johnny Reb: The Common Soldier of the Confederacy* set the standard for studies focusing on the lives of the average soldier. This pioneering study brought the life of the common soldier to the attention of Civil War scholars and the general public.[1]

The Life of Johnny Reb explores almost every feature of the Confederate soldier. Wiley bases all of his findings on published and unpublished letters, diaries, and reminiscences. The study is a social history and it describes the daily pattern of the Southern fighting man's life during the Civil War. Though he writes with admiration of the Confederate soldier, Wiley does not exclude the faults and weaknesses of Johnny Reb.

Several themes are evident in Wiley's work. His main objective was to present the life of the Confederate soldier as it was, not as tradition has made it. To accomplish this, the author based his narrative on primary sources, and whenever possible used the words of the soldiers themselves to describe the different aspects of their war experiences.

Wiley concluded that the average Confederate soldier was not well educated but showed courage and bravery in battle. Although the Confederate soldier went off to war with great excitement for adventure, his feelings toward the war soured as the years of war rolled endlessly on. Wiley also contends that the average Southern soldier did not really understand why the war was being fought and held no strong political or ideological sentiment.

Wiley asserts that the main reason Confederate soldiers continued to fight well, even after their initial excitement vanished, was primarily the fear of social ostracism. Johnny Reb was willing to endure the agony of battle because he was afraid to let his comrades down and did not want friends and family at home to become ashamed of him. Wiley contends that the fear of how the folks at home would feel if one showed any signs of cowardice was a strong motivation to continue the fight, but he also states that the home front did not influence how the Confederate soldier felt about the war.

In 1952, Bell Wiley published the companion volume to his study of the common soldier of the Civil War. *The Life of Billy Yank: The Common Soldier of the Union* is another wonderful addition to the historiography of the Civil War soldier.[2] Following the same methods and themes as *The Life of Johnny Reb*, Wiley describes the life of the common soldier who fought for the Union during the Civil War. The themes presented by Wiley in *The Life of Billy Yank* are not much different from those stated in his previous work on the Confederate soldier. Wiley argues that the average Union soldier was more educated than the Southern trooper but no more interested in the politics of the conflict than most Confederate soldiers. In fact, Wiley stresses that most Union soldiers were less concerned with the reasons for the war than Southern troops. Wiley also contends that the average Union soldier held deep prejudices towards blacks and Southerners, a point he claims was held by Southern soldiers towards Northerners as well.

In the concluding chapter of *The Life of Billy Yank*, Bell Wiley compares Johnny Reb and Billy Yank. His conclusions are that, though the two were slightly different, they shared many similarities. The two studies on the lives of Johnny Reb and Billy Yank by Wiley are still considered classics today. Wiley's work inspired many of his students to continue examining the Civil War from the lower ranks. Although the views of leading participants are very important for the overall understanding of the conflict, Wiley proved that the lesser known participants have something very interesting and vital to offer to the scholarship of the Civil War.

Wiley continued his research of the life of the common soldier and republished his two studies in 1978. Wiley himself states in the preface of the reissued volumes that although many more unpublished diaries and letters have surfaced since his first publication of *The Life of Johnny Reb* and *The Life of Billy Yank*, his conclusions have not changed. This reissuing of his works, however, did spark renewed interest in the study of the average soldier of the Civil War.

More recently, historians have integrated quantitative research methods into the study of history. This method found its way into several works on the Civil War. In 1970, Pete Maslowski published "A Study of Morale in Civil War Soldiers" in the *Military Affairs* journal.[3] Maslowski attempts to examine the Civil War soldier as *The American Soldier, Studies in Social Psychology in World War II* (1949) did with the GI of the Second World War.[4] His assessment of the Civil War soldier does not differ from Wiley's, but his call for historians to use scientific methods, especially quantitative analysis, influenced a generation of Civil War scholars.

The American Soldier, a four-volume study edited by Samuel A. Stouffer, is an influential work that brought the use of questionnaires and statistical analysis into practical use by Civil War historians. Many Civil War scholars in the last half of the twentieth century have mirrored the work of Stouffer and the other authors of *The American Soldier,* who hinted that the guidelines they used to write their multi-volume work may be applied to the study of soldiers in other wars.

Michael Barton applied this technique to examine the character of the common soldier of the American Civil War. *Goodmen: The Character of Civil War Soldiers* (1981) is a quantitative historical analysis of the character of the common soldier of the Civil War.[5] Barton uses quantitative data to determine the core values of the common soldier. Barton uses over 400 published diaries and letter collections, which are divided almost equally between Union and Confederate officers and enlisted men. He examined the diaries and letters and compiled how frequently certain words appeared in the writings of the soldiers. Words such as honor and bravery were tabulated to discover key concepts like individualism, freedom, equality, and morality. The author applies models from sociology and psychology to generalize these concepts.

Barton asserts that although most Civil War soldiers went to war with high moral standards, the monotony of camp life and pressure from peers caused many men to set aside their values. Gambling, drinking, and prostitution were rampant in most Civil War camps. Barton contends, however, that these flaws did not affect the overall character of the soldiers. He insists that most soldiers were self-denying and remained devoted to loved ones at home. The occasional pitfall did not necessarily imply that a soldier had bad character and low moral standards. In fact, Barton concludes that most Civil War soldiers continued to be very religious and actively sought God's intervention through prayers and acts of kindness. Barton declares that both the Northern and Southern soldiers' writings provided insights into their character but believes that Southerners were more open. According to Barton, Southern soldiers were more stylistic and expressive in their writings than Northerners, and hence provided more vivid accounts of their experiences during the war. Barton doesn't attempt to claim that the Southern character was better or worse than that of Northerners, but that Johnny Reb expressed his feelings and thoughts in a more readable fashion.

The information obtained from the study is notable; however, Barton does not add any new conclusions to the study of the average soldier of the Civil War. Barton's work adds statistical support to what Bell Wiley stated in his pioneering studies. Barton, who describes his work as a "quantitative sociolinguistic case study in historical psychological anthropology,"[6] does provide a vivid study of the character of the common soldier who fought during the American Civil War, but presents no new interpretations.

Toward the end of the 1980s several works appeared that focused specifically on the common soldier of the American Civil War. In 1988, two works examined the social aspects of the Civil War soldier. These studies, *Soldiers Blue and Gray* by James I. Robertson and *Civil War Soldiers* by Reid Mitchell, followed Wiley's method of focusing primarily on the diaries and letters of the soldiers themselves to tell the story. Although these works parallel Wiley's techniques and many of his conclusions, neither completely agrees with all of his findings.

James I. Robertson states in the preface to *Soldiers Blue and Gray* (1988) that the study does not "presume to be a replacement for the two Wiley compilations. Its intent is to supplement those works, not only with material which Wiley did not use, but also with reliance on a sampling of the post–1955 tidal wave of publications."[7] The tidal wave Robertson referred to is the mass of diaries and letters located and published after 1955. Robertson's main objective is simply to add a fresh view of the life of the Civil War soldier.

Robertson, like Wiley, allows the soldiers to tell their own history through narratives and quotations. Although the author's introductory remarks lead readers to assume his work is a modern retelling of Wiley's works, *Soldiers Blue and Gray* does not duplicate any previous research of the common soldier. Robertson does agree with Wiley's conclusions, but he does not reproduce any quotes or sources used by Wiley. By discussing the ingenuity of the Civil War soldier, Robertson offers a well-written supplement to Wiley's earlier works without retelling the same story. He relates how the troops developed several different recipes from a minute variety of foods and were able to construct lodgings out of almost anything. He also tells how soldiers spent most of their time in camp thinking of ways to relieve the boredom between campaigns. Letter writing occupied a large part of their free time, but Robertson affirms that above all else singing and playing music reigned supreme, and declares that the Civil War soldier sang more than any other American soldier ever has. Robertson also writes about the aftermath of the war, stating that because the war had made such a major impact in the lives of the men who fought in it, most soldiers learned to forgive but not forget. He does mention, however, that time healed many of the psychological wounds caused by the war and many Northern and Southern soldiers were able to meet years later at reunions and embrace as brothers.

Although *Soldiers Blue and Gray* is an insightful study of the Civil War soldier and is based on different sources, Robertson does not attempt to argue with any of Wiley's findings. The only difference found in the study is Robertson's opinion that Johnny Reb and Billy Yank were not diverse. Wiley concludes in *The Life of Billy Yank* that, though the Union and Confederate soldiers had many similarities, they clearly were two distinct groups. Robertson, on the other hand, paints a picture of Johnny Reb and Billy Yank that leaves the reader thinking there were no differences at all. This conclusion does an injustice to both the Union and Confederate soldier in that it distorts their culture and lifestyles.

Soldiers Blue and Gray partially succeeds in accomplishing what the author intended. The work does add a fresh view of the common soldier of the Civil War, but it does not submit any new findings to the historiography of the Civil War soldier. Robertson, except for the one difference mentioned above, does not present any new explanation or descriptions of the Civil War soldier. As one of Bell Wiley's finest students, James I. Robertson adds a fine supplement to his teacher's pioneering work.

The traumatic events of the 1960s were bound to affect many Americans, and historians were by no means immune to the emotional changes of the time. In this era of questioning the motives and reasons behind United States military actions, Civil War historians began to ask why the common soldier of the Civil War was willing to fight for such a length of time. One of the first historians to ask this question more in depth was Reid Mitchell. Mitchell, who states he has been described as a post–Vietnam historian, proclaims in the preface of *Civil War Soldiers* (1988) that some believe the Vietnam War may have distorted his views of the Civil War. These distortions were possibly brought on by the moral questions sparked by the Vietnam War.[8] Mitchell does not argue with this claim, but cites that he is also a post–Civil Rights historian, having attended a desegregated high school in New Orleans. The social changes that occurred in the United States and the world after the Second World War have brought many historians to believe history has been misinterpreted in that only one side has been examined. The Civil War is included in this belief and therefore several Civil War scholars have tried to tell the history of the conflict from a different perspective.

Mitchell's *Civil War Soldiers*, like the above-mentioned studies, uses the words of the soldiers to illustrate his findings. As in Robertson's *Soldiers Blue and Gray*, Mitchell's book examines both the Union and Confederate soldier in a single volume and is based almost completely on primary sources. Mitchell attempts to offer a meaning of the Civil War in hopes that understanding what the conflict meant to the generations living in the 1860s will aid our understanding of it today. The author writes the book with a simple but effective premise: he uses the diaries and letters written by Civil War soldiers to answer questions he would have asked them if they were alive when he was writing his book. Mitchell asked many of the questions the authors of *The American Soldier* did in 1949. "What did you think of your enemy?" "How did you feel about race and slavery?" "Why did you fight?"

Mitchell lets the soldiers answer these questions and many more by quoting or paraphrasing their comments. This method is successful in several ways. First, it allows the reader to gain an understanding of what the soldiers thought and felt about given topics. Also, it presents a clearer understanding of why these men fought and died for their beliefs. According to Mitchell, the majority of Civil War soldiers were farmers or sons of farmers. Family honor was a powerful incentive to continue the fight, and most volunteers had the support of family and friends. Mitchell also emphasizes that soldiers who remained in the army for three or more years lost their pre-war identities. The agonizing brutality of war and the excruciating hardship of everyday camp life changed the way most men saw the world. Mitchell suggests that soldiers from the North and South agreed that ultimately the overall cause of the war was American sin. Northern soldiers, who Mitchell claims committed more acts of theft and vandalism than Southerners, saw the conflict as a war against the Southern way of life. The burning and looting of plantations is simply described as an attack against Southern culture. Southerners on the other hand believed the Northern society to be wicked and malevolent. Civil War soldiers in general were able to commit savage acts of violence against their foes because they perceived them to be evil.

Mitchell disagrees with Robertson's conclusion that most Union and Confederate soldiers were similar. He describes the similarities between Johnny Reb and Billy Yank in the first half of his study, but the remaining pages focus on the differences between the two. Mitchell concurs with Wiley and Robertson that Union and Confederate soldiers shared a common American culture, but he implies that the two regions were separated by sectional identity. Billy Yank and Johnny Reb viewed each other as different. Northern soldiers felt superior to the sinful Reb and felt Southern culture was less civilized. In Mitchell's estimation both soldiers held a perception of themselves that was very different than their enemy. Mitchell's overall conclusions, however, are in agreement with Bell Wiley and James Robertson.

Mitchell again focused his scholarly research on the Civil War in *The Vacant Chair: The Northern Soldier Leaves Home* (1993).[9] As the title indicates, this study concerns only Union troops. As in his previous book, Mitchell bases his work mainly on the writings of the soldiers and allows them to tell the narrative. This study differs with other works that focus on the common soldier of the Civil War in that the author examines the role gender played in the conflict. Writing from the perspective of a feminist historian, Mitchell analyzes how soldiers tested ideas of masculinity and femininity even as the war reinforced those beliefs. Mitchell very successfully describes this concept throughout *The Vacant Chair*.

Mitchell posits that the autonomy many soldiers felt was their right as men was sharply curtailed by military life. No longer could they go where they wanted or do as they pleased. Military discipline transformed soldiers into a semi-childlike state, which shredded pieces of their manhood. At the same time, the high casualties of the war affirmed women's roles. Their roles as healer and comforter were magnified during the dreadful years of the conflict and women were made to feel that it was their patriotic duty to support their husbands, brothers, and fathers as they went off to war.

The Civil War also gave men the opportunity to prove their manhood on the battlefield. The chance to be warriors allowed many soldiers the opportunity to test their courage and bravery. Those who chose to remain out of the fight at the beginning of the war were ridiculed and called dandies by their friends and neighbors. To choose peace was considered by many as feminine and cowardly. Mitchell notes that most people believed real men would not be content staying at home.

Mitchell also briefly examines the relationship the soldiers had with political questions of the period. Mitchell's work introduced the presumption that Civil War soldiers were interested in political issues, and offered a different view than that of Wiley and Robertson. This concept is only briefly examined, but it is viewed more in-depth than in other works on the Civil War soldier. Mitchell does not challenge other conclusions expressed in Wiley's *The Life of Billy Yank*, but his focus on gender does add new areas of interest to the historiography of the Civil War soldier.

Another area Mitchell examines is the effect the home front had on shaping the political and behavioral attitudes of the Northern soldier. Other works dealing with common soldiers ignore the influence friends and family members that did not go off to war had on the men. Mitchell believes that the Puritan culture, which emphasized hard work and putting in one's fair share, influenced the way many Union soldiers felt. Culturally, soldiers were raised to believe in the wisdom of Northern civilization and the wrongs of Southern culture. Similarly expressed in more recent works by James M. McPherson and Earl J. Hess (mentioned below), Mitchell maintains that combat motivation was rooted in patriotism and ideas stemming from home and community. Family honor and the need to prove one's manhood were instrumental in motivating soldiers to remain in the fight.

The Vacant Chair is a fine study of how Northern culture affected Billy Yank, but Mitchell's intended or unintended omission of northern blacks and immigrants weakens the book's overall value. Many of the soldiers who fought for the Union during the war were considered immigrants and by the end of the conflict over 200,000 African Americans troops were in uniform.

As previously stated, beginning with Reid Mitchell's *Civil War Soldiers*, Civil War historians interested in examining the lives of the common soldiers began to ask why these men fought at all. This theme dominates James M. McPherson's study of the Civil War soldier, *For Cause and Comrades: Why Men Fought in the Civil War* (1997).[10] The title may lead the reader to believe that McPherson is only interested in answering this question, but his study goes much deeper. The main premise of the book is to determine why soldiers who fought in the Civil War were willing to endure the hardships of prolonged warfare. McPherson first posed this question in a series of Walter L. Fleming Lectures delivered at Louisiana State University in 1991. These lectures were later published in a book titled *What They Fought For, 1861–1865* (1994).[11] In both of these works McPherson challenges the well-established belief that Civil War soldiers held no strong convictions for the conflict and held no deep ideological or political beliefs about slavery, patriotism, and liberty. McPherson contradicts the findings of Bell Wiley and most other scholars of the Civil War soldier. Wiley believed that soldiers enlisted for profit or adventure, and remained in the fight because of pressures by other enlisted men. McPherson counters this conclusion and states that Civil War soldiers did hold strong political and ideological convictions and a need to see the conflict through. He enhances themes and conclusions introduced by Mitchell and Robertson and his research validates their findings.

McPherson examined over 1000 letters and diaries from an equal percentage of Northerners and Southerners. He also delineates three types of motivation: enlistment, combat, and sustaining motivation, and states that each category sustained its own force in pushing the soldier forward. The work displays a wide range of opinions and beliefs. McPherson agrees with Wiley and Mitchell that peer pressure was a powerful factor in combat motivation, but this was not unrelated to a complex mixture of ideology, duty, patriotism and honor. McPherson also argues that the need to prove one's manhood, as Mitchell contends in *The Vacant Chair*, was a major factor of combat morale. McPherson alleges that generally Civil War soldiers did not receive adequate training and were extremely weak in discipline. He also contends that most soldiers, as well as officers, were deficient in leadership skills. These conclusions concur with those of Paddy Griffith in his study of Civil War tactics published in 1989.[12] McPherson stresses that soldiers from the North and the South were fundamentally different in their attitudes toward the Civil War. Many Southerners believed they were fighting for states' rights, but they also wanted to defend their homes from the Northern invasion. Northern soldiers, however, felt they had been called to restore the Union and cleanse America of the sin of slavery. McPherson does not imply that all Union troops were abolitionists, but by war's end they had come to understand that the fundamental cause of the conflict was slavery.

Another theme McPherson puts forth in his work that is different from Wiley's and Robertson's studies deals with racial issues. In *For Cause and Comrades* McPherson expresses the opinion that by 1864, most Union soldiers broadened their conception of liberty to include blacks. This assertion is well supported in *For Cause and Comrades*, but is in contrast to Wiley's and Robertson's studies and to most works that focus on the black soldier. These works, which are described later in this essay, reveal that prejudice was at the heart of many Union troops well after the end of the Civil War.

Joseph Allan Frank's 1998 study of the Civil War soldier, *With Ballot and Bayonet: The Political Socialization of American Civil War Soldiers*, concurs with McPherson's work in that it places political values at the forefront of why the common soldier fought. Frank notes that "politics steeled men's souls and shaped their armies"[13] and that the American political tradition and the deep convictions held by enlisted men served as the most important motivational factor throughout the war. Like Mitchell in *The Vacant Chair*, he discusses the importance of the home front during the war and argues that it was the loved ones at home who helped encourage the men, yet he disputes Mitchell's conclusions that the home front forced its beliefs on the soldiers — that instead it was the soldier who influenced the people at home by demanding that those at home suppress dissidents who tried to undermine the war effort. He agrees that the political beliefs held by the Civil War soldier were sectional. Northern troops wanted to punish the Southern traitors and restore the Union. Most Union soldiers also supported emancipation but questioned the use of black troops. Southerners resented Northern aggression and the fact that Yankees were trying to impose their culture on the South. Most Confederate soldiers feared that the Northern concept of America would radically alter their society. Frank insists that soldiers from both sides understood what was at stake during the war and were keenly interested in the outcome of the conflict, disputing Wiley's and Robertson's claims that soldiers fought the Civil War for honor and glory alone.

In essence Frank's study echoes other works on the Civil War soldier in that it rests primarily on the letters and diaries of the actual soldiers. Like McPherson, Frank reviews the letters and diaries of over 1000 soldiers. He also follows Barton in that he uses social science categories to identify politically aware soldiers and then defines and classifies the men according to their political awareness. Although Frank's study implements sociological methods to analyze his data, the work is readable and informative and demonstrates that quantitative methods and the use of other disciplines can enhance the value of a study.

McPherson's and Frank's works have challenged the long held belief that Civil War soldiers did not fight for political or ideological reasons. They have successfully challenged the dean of the Civil War soldier, Bell Wiley, and enhanced views briefly submitted by Reid Mitchell. The social account of the Civil War soldier has been competently studied and the historiography has begun to increase. Although these social records presented much new insight into the lives of the common soldiers of the Civil War and nineteenth-century America, a complete understanding of the soldier had not been achieved. To fully understand a soldier one must examine the role combat played in his thoughts and actions. Most social histories that focus on the common soldier of the Civil War describe combat morale, but only briefly and not in any great detail.

Earl J. Hess, a Civil War scholar who has focused on the combat experiences of Northern soldiers in his study *The Union Soldier in Battle: Enduring the Ordeal of Combat* (1997), credits John Keegan and his book *The Face of Battle* (1976) with inspiring a generation of Civil War scholars to investigate the lives of the common soldier and his combat experiences.[14] Keegan's main objective, Hess states, was to "reconceptualize our understanding of the relationship between the soldier and the physical environment of the battlefield." To continue in the same vein, Hess also urges scholars of the Civil War to analyze the emotional and psychological impressions of battle on the common soldier and not the relationship to the physical aspects of battle.[15]

One of the first studies to show how combat and tactics affected the Civil War soldier is Grady McWhiney and Perry D. Jamieson's *Attack and Die: Civil War Military Tactics and the Southern Heritage* (1982).[16] In this study the authors examine how the Southern fighting man was more prone to offensive tactics because he was more chivalric than Northerners. This disregard of changing military tactics, especially the use of the rifled musket, led to the Confederates bleeding themselves to death throughout the war. McWhiney and Jamieson credit the Celtic heritage of most Southern Civil War soldiers with providing a strong foundation on which Confederate officers were able to order their troops into suicidal frontal assaults. The values and the culture in which the common Southern soldier was raised produced men willing to sacrifice all for the sake of honor and glory. The brave and honorable charge was, after all, the Celtic way of war.

Attack and Die is a clearly written ethnic study of the fighting spirit of the common Civil War soldier of the South. Applying the ethno-cultural analysis to the Civil War soldier does raise some intriguing questions, but the book fails to completely support the thesis that the culture and values of the South were the main factor behind Confederate military tactics and the soldier's willingness to fight to the death. The book, while providing helpful insight into the mind of the Southern fighting man, is more (as Hess stated) a study of combat emotion and psychology than battlefield experiences.

Battle Tactics of the Civil War (1989) by Paddy Griffith, exempt from being a thorough study of the common soldier, is mentioned here specifically because the thesis presented by Griffith counters that of McWhiney and Jamieson.[17] Griffith refutes the findings in *Attack and Die* by denying that the American Civil War was the first modern war. Instead, she believes the final Napoleonic conflict modernized warfare, a theory that disputes the assertion that the rifled muskets changed the face of combat. However, *Battle Tactics of the Civil War* does not present any new primary or secondary sources to disprove McWhiney and Jamieson's thesis. Griffith surmises that the battles fought during the Civil War were so deadly because the soldiers were ill prepared to handle such violent clashes, mainly due to lack of drilling and discipline. This argument is supported in McPherson's *For Cause and Comrades* and Joseph Allan Frank and George A. Reaves *"Seeing the Elephant": Raw Recruits at the Battle of Shiloh.*

Gerald F. Linderman's *Embattled Courage: The Experience of Combat in the American Civil War* (1987) analyzes the battlefield experiences of soldiers in the first two years of the conflict.[18] Linderman's thesis proclaims that courage was the central value shared by almost all soldiers and that all other thoughts and behaviors revolved around it. In contrast to *Attack and Die*, Linderman does not give ethnic and sectional beliefs credit for shaping the minds and actions of the Civil War soldier. Though Linderman's thesis is well supported and convincing, his conclusions are suspect because he examined the letters and reminiscences of only a select group of soldiers. The book solidly describes how courage affected the way soldiers felt and acted, but the small number of soldiers researched (approximately fifty highly educated and articulate upper-class men) weakens the overall support of the thesis. Linderman's view that the heroic culture of the Victorian age influenced these soldiers and that their idea of courage deflated as the war progressed is interesting, but the majority of troops were not from the pinnacle of society and had little education.

Embattled Courage also examines the introduction of the rifled musket into the war and how it changed the tactics of Civil War battles. Linderman states that the minie ball forced military commanders to forsake the heroic charge and revert to using trench and guerrilla warfare. The argument that the rifled musket revolutionized warfare is in agreement with McWhiney and Jamieson and is, of course, contrary to Paddy Griffith's views.

Not completely new to the study of the Civil War soldier, but covered more in depth in Linderman's work, is what happened to these men and their society after the war. Linderman speculates that the return of some two million men from the horrors of war must have transmogrified society as a whole. Linderman does not state specifically how the returning troops altered American culture; rather, he leaves the question for other scholars to ponder. Linderman reasons that when the soldiers returned to their homes, their values and perception of the world had changed and therefore they changed American beliefs as well. At first, soldiers were reluctant to discuss their wartime experiences. But in the 1880s they began to describe the gruesome details of battle, and finally people in the United States began to understand how terrible the war really was.

Joseph Allan Frank and George A. Reaves quickly expanded upon studies of combat experiences of the Civil War soldier in 1989. *"Seeing the Elephant": Raw Recruits at the Battle of Shiloh* attempts to present an in-depth analysis of the motivation, training, combat reaction, and responses to stress and fear of Union and Confederate soldiers during the battle of Shiloh.[19] The authors examine the relationship between human behaviors and combat focusing on the soldier, and assert that once combat was initiated, the rank and file took control. Frank and Reaves use quantitative and sociological methods to examine the letters and diaries of over 450 soldiers who had previously had little or no combat experience. The authors contend that most soldiers lacked discipline and training. Frank and Reaves also stress that during combat soldiers were full of excitement, but that once the rattle of rifle and musket fire had ceased they experienced emotional anguish and depression. These conclusions concur with those expressed by McPherson in his work *For Cause and Comrades.* The authors of *"Seeing the Elephant"* claim that duty to fellow soldiers was a primary element of combat motivation for the Civil War soldier. Many other motives pushed raw recruits into remaining engaged in battle, but the excitement of combat and duty to friends were, according to Frank and Reaves, the main factors. *"Seeing the Elephant"* is one of the first studies to take a comprehensive approach to combat morale in the American Civil War.

In the modern era, combat has been described as a traumatic event in the lives of young men unfortunate enough to experience it. Eric T. Dean expresses this belief in his work *Shook Over Hell: Post-Traumatic Stress, Vietnam, and the Civil War* (1997).[20] Dean's work introduces the effect battle psychosis had on the Civil War soldier. Dean describes the effects that post-traumatic stress disorder (PTSD), a new clinical term for battle fatigue, had on Civil War soldiers. Called hypo or the blues during the sectional conflict, PTSD has not been attached to other combat studies focusing on the Civil War. Dean bases his views on the Vietnam soldier mostly on secondary sources, but his conclusions of the Civil War soldier are primarily supported by original research. Dean concludes that, for the most part, the common soldier of the Civil War suffered more than recent combat veterans. The misery of nineteenth century warfare is described in good detail throughout Dean's book.

The most interesting themes portrayed in *Shook Over Hell* focus on the actual feelings and emotions most Civil War soldiers probably felt during combat. Bell Wiley states in his studies of the common soldier of the Civil War that Southern soldiers were able to achieve great feats of bravery on the battlefield. Dean agrees with this conclusion, but does not attribute it to any sectional or ideological reason as asserted in *Attack and Die* and *The Vacant Chair*. Dean convincingly argues that miracles of valor were obtained simply because during combat soldiers experience a rush of adrenaline to their brains. This adrenaline rush has, as Dean states, an almost narcotic effect on the soldiers and enables them to do things on the battlefield they never thought possible. Once combat had ceased and the adrenaline flow stopped soldiers experienced depression and emotional anguish. This conclusion is supported in *"Seeing the Elephant"* and in Earl J. Hess's work, *The Union Soldier in Battle: Enduring the Ordeal of Combat.*

No studies focusing solely on the combat experiences and motivation of Civil War soldiers had appeared after *"Seeing the Elephant"* until Earl J. Hess published *The Union Soldier in Battle: Enduring the Ordeal of Combat* in 1997. Hess's book has brought attention once again to the combat experiences of the common soldier of the Civil War. In his work, Hess follows Keegan's theme of including the relationship of the physical environment of the battlefield and the soldier. The main purpose of Hess's work is to examine how the Northern soldier was able to deal with combat.

Hess disputes Linderman's position that soldiers of the Civil War were unable to master the emotional and psychological effects of war. Hess notes that the Northern soldiers mastered their reactions to combat and were not victims as Linderman states. He clarifies how Union troops developed a sense of military professionalism. Northern soldiers acquired confidence and competence after repeated combat. As troops mastered the technical aspects of battle, their fears subsided and they were able to face battle with a sense of calm and ease. Hess does not suggest that all Northern soldiers were able to master the psychological effects of combat, but the majority did. Hess's work is more convincing than Linderman's study for several reasons. Unlike Linderman, Hess analyzes the letters and diaries of a wide range of soldiers from different socioeconomic backgrounds. Also, the majority of Linderman's primary sources were published diaries and reminiscences that had been rewritten in the postwar years. Hess agrees with McPherson that such tainted sources do not always provide an accurate account of how a soldier felt about the war.

In all of the studies published that pertain to the Civil War soldier, the story of the black soldier has been relatively forgotten. Although Bell Wiley's stirring works on the Civil War soldier did mention African American troops, he and most other scholars did not analyze their contributions in depth. Wiley did, however, state in the introduction of the 1978 edition of *The Life of Billy Yank* that he regretted not being able to include the history of the black Union soldier in his previous work. Some 200,000 black soldiers wore the blue uniform during the Civil War, and as recent studies have shown, thousands of black men fought and aided the Confederacy in some capacity. Their story, like many misunderstood events in history, has remained in the background of Civil War history. Although the story of black troops is beginning to find its way into Civil War studies, it was the period immediately after the war that saw the first studies of black soldiers and their contributions to the war effort. William Wells Brown's *The Negro in the American Rebellion* (1867), George W. Williams' *A History of the Negro Troops in the War of the Rebellion, 1861–1865* (1888), and Joseph T. Wilson's *The Black Phalanx: A History of the Negro Soldiers of the United States in the Wars of 1775–1812 and 1861–65* (1888) were overviews of the roles black troops played in the Civil War.

While these works appeared in the postwar period, it was not until 1953 that another major study was published that focused on the black soldier of the Civil War. Several works appeared in the 1950s that explored the contributions and actions of black soldiers during the Civil War. Bruce Catton, James G. Randall and other prominent historians brought renewed interest in the Civil War in post–World War II America. Also during this time, many historians began to view history in a new light. Instead of studying events and people from the top, they viewed the actions and contributions of the less notable participants. In this inspired time of examining different aspects of well-known historical events, some scholars of the Civil War chose to focus on the African American view of the conflict.

Benjamin Quarles' *The Negro in the Civil War* (1953) launched a resurgence in the study of the significance of black soldiers in the Civil War.[21] Quarles' work sets out to prove that black troops were active participants in the war effort. He describes the black soldier's attempt to gain recognition and respect from the white military establishment, an effort that was rebuffed until emancipation became a clear war objective. In *The Negro in the Civil*

War Quarles examines five engagements in which black troops participated. The main thesis of the work is that black soldiers contributed to the war in a positive and valuable manner. Quarles supports this premise well throughout his study. Among the evidence Quarles provides is how successfully black troops handled themselves during combat. He states that one of the major factors preventing President Lincoln from enlisting black soldiers was the common belief that they would flee at the first sound of gunfire. Quarles effectively dismisses this claim and describes the audacity and courage displayed by many black troops throughout the remaining years of the Civil War. Quarles also succeeds in detailing the cost many black men paid for their freedom, disputing the belief that black people were freely given their liberty during the Civil War. Quarles is successful in proving his claim that the use of black troops during the Civil War was an important factor in Union victory. Bell Wiley seconds this assertion in the introduction to the 1978 republished edition of *The Life of Billy Yank.*

The Negro in the Civil War is a competent study of the role of black troops in the Civil War, but the main focus of the work is to examine how emancipation and influential political leaders pushed for the use of black soldiers. The study is an excellent view of the reasons that resulted in the decision to enlist black men to fight for the Union but does not give the black soldier his needed view as Bell Wiley's works did for white soldiers.

The Sable Arm: Negro Troops in the Union Army, 1861–1865 (1956), by Dudley Taylor Cornish, is another interesting book that examines the role of the black soldier in the Civil War.[22] Cornish observes the evolution of the use of black troops from laborers to fighting men. The work is seen today as the classic study of the black soldier of the Civil War, but it does not provide an in-depth view of the soldier. As with Benjamin Quarles' work and later studies such as James M. McPherson's *The Negro's Civil War: How American Negroes Felt and Acted During the War for the Union* (1964), Cornish's study is mainly concerned with the political and social issues that led to emancipation and the use of black troops. Although several aspects of the soldier's life are mentioned, these studies do not offer a good view of the black fighting man. The inner conflicts and everyday life of the black soldier have yet to be examined in-depth, thus not offering the reader a sense of what soldier life was really like for black men during the Civil War.

One reason for the lack of scrutiny of black soldiers is the fact that an estimated 70 percent of black soldiers were illiterate. With less written documentation it is difficult for historians to provide an accurate account of the feelings and attitudes of many black soldiers. Many firsthand accounts and diaries written by black troops during and after the Civil War have been discovered in recent years and have led to more study and research.

Freedom's Soldiers: The Black Military Experience in the Civil War (1982), edited by Ira Berlin, is one of the first studies to use these newly located sources.[23] It is the second in a series of works that attempts to determine how black American life was transformed during and after the Civil War. The well-documented study examines patterns of recruitment and enlistment of black soldiers, and views the struggles for equality that occurred in the United States Army and Navy during the conflict. This investigation of racial conflict follows the same conclusions made by Quarles and Cornish in their studies of black troops.

Several sections of *Freedom's Soldiers* examine how the war affected the lives of many of the black men who fought for the Union. The war gave many former slaves and free blacks the opportunity to travel and see the nation. Their experiences were broadened and the war provided many black soldiers with the opportunity of viewing the world from a position of dominance. Although black soldiers rarely were promoted past the rank of private, they had greater control of their own destiny and marched with pride past their former homes of bondage. Free blacks were also able to function in an important role and gained confidence in the knowledge that they were helping restore the Union. *Freedom's Soldiers* also examines several general aspects of black Civil War soldiers that Bell Wiley viewed in his works on the common white soldier. These areas include camp life, military performance, and health conditions. The book also reviews postwar experiences of black soldiers very much in the same methods that Gerald F. Linderman and Earl J. Hess did in later years with respect to white troops. *Freedom's Soldiers* is a well-written documented account of the black soldier of the American Civil War. It is considered by several historians, including James M. McPherson, as the standard work to begin with for any scholar interested in studying the black soldier of the Civil War.

Joseph T. Glatthaar examines the relationship between black soldiers and their white commanders in his 1992 study *Forged in Battle: The Civil War Alliance of Black Soldiers and White Officers.*[24] Glatthaar agrees with the position of Dudley Taylor Cornish that the study of American military history is more social and political history than martial in character. In his work Glatthaar examines the attitudes and experiences of the black soldiers and also analyzes the relationship between the colored troops and their white officers. He uses official records, memoirs and unpublished manuscripts to describe the attitudes and beliefs of black soldiers during the Civil War. His conclusions about these topics do not differ from those mentioned in *Freedom's Soldiers*. Where Glatthaar breaks from previous works that focused on the black soldier is in his breakdown of the racial ideology of the colored troops and the white officers. This concept appears in other works, but comparing and contrasting the attitudes of white officers with black soldiers is new. Glatthaar reports that racial tensions and ideology were as dangerous a threat to the Union as to the Confederate Army. As found in the works of Quarles and Cornish, discrimination and injustice were central themes in *Forged in Battle*. Glatthaar's assertions that black troops paid a price for their freedom and displayed remarkable courage under fire is also in agreement with Quarles and Cornish. Even though a strong relationship developed between many white officers and their black soldiers, as *Freedom's Soldiers* attests to as well, these social ties collapsed after the conflict ended. Glatthaar's work, although lacking in explaining the influence religion and community had on many black soldiers, which prevents the work from offering a better view of the black soldier, is a good study of colored troops during the Civil War. As with *Freedom's Soldiers* and *The Sable Arm*, *Forged in Battle* brings the black soldiers into the thoughts of historians but fails to provide a well-rounded perspective of the black soldier. This failure however, it may be argued, possibly stems from the lack of availability of primary source material which would have given these historians the necessary facts to base larger conclusions upon.

A controversial aspect of the historiography of black Civil War soldiers is discussed in two recent works published in the *Journal of Confederate History Series*. When one considers the Civil War as a fight to end slavery, it is hard to conceive that many black Americans would have willingly supported the Confederacy. As more sources are discovered and existing ones studied more keenly, set historical truths are cast aside and new beliefs established. This is the case of black soldiers who willingly fought for the Confederacy.

Historian Leonard Haynes commented, "When you eliminate the black Confederate soldier, you've eliminated the history of the South."[25] Richard Rollins, editor of *Black Southerners in Gray: Essays on Afro-Americans in Confederate Armies* (1994), investigates the statistical evidence that proves black troops were active members in Confederate armies.[26] Rollins also discusses the many Confederate monuments located throughout the South that are dedicated to loyal black Americans who aided with the Confederate war effort.

Richard Rollins states in the opening essay of *Black Southerners in Gray*: "To imagine the Confederate armies without black Southerners in their ranks is to perpetuate the historical myth of the South as a compartmentalized society. It ignores the real relationship between blacks and whites in the Old South, as well as the role and experiences of a small but significant portion of black Southerners in the Confederacy." Rollins writes that the question is not if black Southerners actively participated in the Confederate armies, but what they did and how they contributed to the war effort that is important.[27] *Black Southerners in Gray* examines the contributions black soldiers made to the Confederate war effort and views the actions they were engaged in. The essays revolve around three basic categories of how black Southerners served and bore arms for the Confederacy. Black Southerners were servants, private individuals, and served in units that were made up mostly or entirely of black soldiers. The documented evidence cited in the study supports this assertion and proves that unlike the Union Army, the Confederate Army did not segregate its ranks.

Another theme evident in *Black Southerners in Gray* is the lack of political ideology as a source of motivation for black soldiers. The work clearly asserts that black soldiers were less interested in political intentions and more concerned with family matters. Most black troops understood that their freedom hinged on Union victory. During the conflict black soldiers fought for the freedom of their families, and free blacks participated in combat in the hope that after the war they and their family members would be treated like equals and not second-class citizens. This reference to family and community ties is different from Joseph T. Glatthaar's work *Forged in Battle*, which ignores the role of community and family in the black Union soldier's motivation to fight.

The second study to examine black Confederate soldiers is *Forgotten Confederates: An Anthology About Black Southerners* (1995), edited by Charles Kelly Barrow, J.H. Segars, and R.B. Rosenburg.[28] *Forgotten Confederates* breaks from *Black Southerners in Gray* in that it mainly focuses on the black Confederate soldier and not just black servants and laborers. Following the same methodology as *Black Southerners in Gray*, *Forgotten Confederates* is a collection of essays that examine the role of black soldiers in the Confederacy. As in the work edited by Richard Rollins, *Forgotten Confederates* confirms that the black Southern community was very influential in shaping the values and actions of many black Confederate soldiers. Also, *Forgotten Confederates* sets forth the thesis, as does *Black Southerners in Gray*, that black men actively participated in the Confederate armies for one or more of three basic reasons. Blacks who fought with or aided the Confederate armies were protecting their own economic or social interest, or for the excitement and adventure of war. The study also asserts that many of these men considered themselves Southerners and fought for the South.

These two studies have provided a step for further historical research into the lives and actions of black Confederate soldiers, but they fail to provide an overall assessment of black soldiers as the works of Bell Wiley did for white soldiers.

One of the most recent studies that details the black soldier is Noah Andre Trudeau's *Like Men of War: Black Troops in the Civil War, 1861–1865* (1998).[29] Trudeau attempts to fill the gap left by other historians of black soldiers of the Civil War by publishing a comprehensive view of the black soldier. The author does not accomplish this goal, but he does provide an excellent addition to the historiography of the black Civil War soldier. *Like Men of War* is the first comprehensive study of all of the engagements black Union soldiers participated in. The work is a fine overview of the contributions and sacrifices made by black Union troops. Trudeau stresses the belief that black soldiers fought with courage and bravery, but he does not overstate their achievements. Unlike Quarles and Cornish, who in an attempt to correct the lack of scholarship on black soldiers did not discuss the failures of many black troops, Trudeau openly describes success and failure.

Trudeau concludes that black troops were effective soldiers and were willing to die for the right to be considered citizens. An interesting analysis made by Trudeau is his contention that black regiments were led by committed and sometimes-gifted commanding officers, but weak generals administered the divisions and corps they were assigned. These corps and divisional commanders consistently used black troops as laborers and did not trust their fighting quality. Trudeau also points out that even at the army level, officers that did not believe Negro troops could fight led black soldiers. Benjamin Butler and William T. Sherman are two commanding officers Trudeau describes as flawed in their understanding of the fighting spirit of the black soldier.

Like Men of War adds much to the historiography of the black Civil War soldier. As do most works on the subject, in his concern for the Union soldier, Trudeau has provided a study that attempts to offer a comprehensive view of the contributions of the black Union soldier in battle. Although these recent studies have done much to enhance our knowledge and understanding of the black Civil War soldier, they have submitted as many questions as they have answered. These fine studies only prove that more intense research into the black soldier of the Civil War is necessary.

To date, the most abundant sort of works published focusing on the Civil War soldier have been social histories. These studies have focused on the general, everyday events of the soldier, but the historiography has shifted in recent years to answering specific questions. Beginning with Reid Mitchell's *Civil War Soldiers*, historians started to ask why these soldiers were willing to endure the hardships of a long war. The move to combat motivation, though slightly reviewed in the social history works as well, has dominated the historiography of the Civil War soldier during the last decade. Combat motivation has always been a part of studies focusing on the common soldier of the Civil War, but Earl J. Hess's *The Union Soldier in Battle* has opened the door to more precise military aspects and motivation. His work has also made it clear that such detailed studies must continue and be applied to the Southern soldier as well.

The need to examine black Civil War soldiers has also begun to root itself into the minds of Civil War scholars. *Like Men of War* by Noah Trudeau put forth many unanswered questions that need to be discussed and completed. No serious study of combat motivation as it applies to black soldiers of the Civil War has been published. This gap must be filled in order to fully understand the Civil War soldier.

James M. McPherson's *For Cause and Comrades* is perhaps the most important and influential addition to the historiography of the Civil War soldier to appear in recent years. McPherson's recommendation that Civil War scholars avoid reedited diaries; memoirs and reminiscences will perhaps take the study of the common soldier closer to the real truth than has been done in the past. His book and the books of Joseph Allan Frank and Earl J. Hess have put forth convincing revisions of Bell Wiley's past studies and perhaps will usher in a new approach to the study of the lives, attitudes, and beliefs of the common soldier of the Civil War, which begins with the study and reading of letters and diaries written by soldiers during the war years. Therefore the reading of Joseph J. Hoyle's letters will enhance the reader's understanding of what it was like to fight in Lee's Army of Northern Virginia, and because, for the most part, these letters cover the months after Southern dominance on the battlefield it adds to the overall view of the common Confederate soldier, one sometimes overlooked by scholars of the South's most well known fighting force.

2. Lieutenant Joseph J. Hoyle in Combat

"The shock of battle"

Joseph J. Hoyle was a farmer and schoolteacher before enlisting in the Confederate Army at the age of twenty-four. Although he may have read military theory by classic theorists like Karl von Clausewitz and Antoine-Henri Jomini, perhaps even classic histories written by Homer, Thucydides, and Caesar, he had never been in a battle and therefore knew nothing of the death and carnage he would experience for the remaining years of his shortened life. Why Civil War soldiers, particularly Southern soldiers, fought well or performed poorly in battle may always remain a matter of speculation for historians. McWhiney and Perry D. Jamieson put forth the thesis that the Celtic heritage of most Confederate fighting men made them fierce warriors, and John Hope Franklin expresses the idea that Southern culture, which was more prone to violence than Northern society in the antebellum period, produced soldiers more prepared for battle than the Union troops.[1] However, Bell Irvin Wiley expressed the belief that Johnny Reb and Billy Yank were quite similar in every respect, a view shared by many scholars, including James I. Robertson and David Herbert Donald.

After arriving at Camp Mangum Joseph J. Hoyle began living the life of, and learning exactly what it meant to be, a soldier in the Confederate Army. Most volunteers were completely ignorant of military life and training. The companies of the 55th North Carolina spent their time drilling for four hours a day, practicing marching in close order, and performing guard duty. This drill time would have most likely been spent in small squad or company formation. This repetition of marching and learning how to handle, load, and fire their rifles would, their superior officers hoped, prepare each man to act effectively in battle.[2]

The man responsible for training the raw recruits of the 55th North

Carolina was Lieutenant Sidney Smith Abernethy, a veteran soldier who had served with the 30th North Carolina during the first year of the war. Joseph wrote to his wife about the many hours spent parading around the practice field and the tediousness of drill combined with long periods of inactivity that was enough to drive some soldiers to rowdiness and hard drinking. Confederate soldiers, not known to be as obedient and stalwart as their Yankee counterparts, tended to have an adverse relationship with their officers. But the men of the 55th seemed to respect Lieutenant Abernethy.

Napoleon believed that the first qualification of a soldier is fortitude. Fighting men must be able to stand up to the rigors of campaigns and battles and learn to live with little comfort. To enable raw troops like Hoyle to endure the severity and privations of the life of a soldier they first must undergo extensive training and drill. Not only will this prepare men physically for the fatigue and hardships campaigning requires, but it will train their minds to think and act like soldiers. Even after the campaigning seasons ended Civil War soldiers returned to a daily regimen of drill to keep fit and to ensure discipline and unit cohesion.[3]

The close order drills implemented by the officers and NCOs had many benefits for new recruits like Hoyle. Not only did the parade ground maneuvers build discipline, but it also made those unfamiliar with military life feel like soldiers. These drills helped build unity and instill a sense of pride in the unit. Also, the repetitious preparation made many actions necessary on the field of battle a conditioned reflex so that the soldier would be more effective and waste little time thinking about how to react. Although John Keegan stresses the belief that close order drill removed the individualism of the common soldier and reduced the fighting man of the gunpowder age into a mere mechanical device, these training techniques achieved the desired effect by making men more prepared for combat and more effective when engaging the enemy. Green troops first experiencing combat needed the touch of fellow soldiers that close order formations provided. Veterans understood that the confusion of battle made staying in line of battle almost impossible, but inexperienced men saw the breaking of structure as an indication that all was lost.[4]

As stated above the training Civil War soldiers were immersed in built an *esprit de corps* among the forces in a particular company or regiment. This spirit gave the men an emotional bond that made the men of the unit better combat troops because their performance in battle reflected upon the status of their unit. This at times manifested itself into competition between individual divisions, brigades, regiments, or companies. An example of this type of unit pride occurred during the battle of Gettysburg. On the first day of the battle after the 55th North Carolina had pushed remnants of the First

Corps back toward McPherson's Ridge the regiment's commanding officer, Colonel John Kerr Connally, was wounded while carrying the unit's battle flag in an effort to motivate his men forward. When asked by another officer if he was severely wounded Connally responded, "Yes," but was more concerned with his regiment surpassing fellow brigade regiments in valor and honor, stating, "Don't let the Mississippians get ahead of you."[5]

It was not unusual for the young colonel to defend the reputation of his regiment. In April 1863, during the siege of Suffolk, Virginia, when the courage of the 55th was questioned Connally stepped forward to inform the officers responsible for the remarks that he would hold them accountable for their insinuations. The youthful colonel returned to his regiment and informed his staff of the accusations and his response. He then explained that the 55th North Carolina's second in command, Lieutenant Colonel Maurice T. Smith, would join him in challenging the two Alabama officers who had made the remarks to a duel. The colonel then notified the rest of his staff that if he and Lieutenant Colonel Smith fell mortally wounded or were so badly injured that they were unable to continue every officer on the staff was expected to carry on until the honor of the regiment had been restored. Smith, a devout Christian, abstained for religious reasons, but the rest of the staff agreed. The second in command's decision, which was respected by the men, for he had shown courage in battle and was not deemed a coward, led to Major Alfred H. Belo taking his place. The next morning Connally and Belo, accompanied by their seconds, met their adversaries in an old field about a mile from the 48th Alabama's camp. The weapons of choice were double-barreled shotguns for Connally and Captain Terrell, and Mississippi rifles for Belo and John Cussons.[6]

The duel between Major Belo and Cussons was first to start. At the given time both men fired their rifles but missed their mark, Belo's shot putting a hole in the hat of his counterpart. Cussons asked the major if he was satisfied to which Belo answered no. The rifles were reloaded and the two officers fired another round. Belo's shot missed again, but Cussons grazed his opponent's neck. As they prepared for a third round Captain E. Fletcher Satterfield, who would be cut in two by an artillery shell at Gettysburg on July 3, 1863, and who was acting as Colonel Connally's second, rode up to the two officers and explained that an agreement had been reached. Thankfully for both sides no one had been seriously injured.[7]

The unit pride instilled in the hearts and minds of the individual soldiers was also a testament to the closeness of the fighting men serving within its ranks. Compatibility impacted how men behaved on the battlefield.[8] In the American Civil War many of the men who served with each other were close friends or in some cases family members. It was not unusual for fathers to fight with sons or brothers to charge the enemy lines side by side. Joseph J. Hoyle served with many close friends as well as cousins and several of his wife's brothers. To fall short of doing one's duty effectively meant failing the very people they loved and admired as well as letting their fellow comrades in arms down.[9] Civil War regimental companies, North and South, were raised in neighborhoods of larger cities and small towns and communities. Most of the soldiers fighting with a particular company, such as Company F of the 55th North Carolina, were friends and neighbors. They fought side by side with individuals they probably knew all their lives so they realized performing in a cowardly manner meant their whole community would hear of their actions. Comradeship was probably for most soldiers the primary reason they endured the carnage of the battlefield. The sense of being with men who would lay down their lives for their fellow men in arms was uplifting and provided enough morale to carry most through the unimaginable awfulness of war.

However, being motivated to march into the horrors of battle required more than just the pressures of peers and fellow soldiers. For many soldiers, perhaps even Joseph J. Hoyle, the war was the greatest event of their lives and they just knew they had to join up and fight. Although most of this early adventurous mentality was absent from those who joined armies after 1861, many soldiers still believed in glory or what Wilfred Owen would later referred to as the "old lie" *Dulce et decorum est pro patria mori.*[10] The war presented the opportunity for men to test their manhood, to answer the question, "How would I stand up to the test of battle?" Many learned that even if they could will themselves to stand against enemy rifle fire and the shells and canister rounds of artillery they could not conquer fear, but hope only to control it long enough to do their duty as soldiers.

Religion was another factor that enabled men to endure the carnage and insanity of combat. The chance that death waited just around the next stream or path in the woods had a profound effect on many soldiers. Historian Drew Gilpin Faust asserts that if religion was a fundamental concept in the hearts and minds of most Southerners it was "of greatest importance to the common southern soldier," who faced the possibility of imminent death quite often.[11] Men who before the war rarely would have considered themselves pious in any terms began to attend prayer meetings and ask for the protection of God's hand. However, even though religion for some provided a supporting factor that made them effective combat troops, as Hoyle's letters attest, many soldiers found the freedom from home and the carefree restraints of army life too hard to resist.

Joseph J. Hoyle was a religious person, as anyone reading his letters will readily come to understand. This devotion to Christianity perhaps enhanced his combat motivation and may have made him more willing to take personal risk. Many men who believed in life after death were courageous and focused in battle because they believed God would protect them. In the religious thinking of the day, to question death was to question the wisdom of the Almighty and therefore a sin.[12] This is not to say that those who believed in a higher being were never fearful of being wounded or killed in battle but that their beliefs enabled them to endure combat better than those who shared no such conviction. In fact, the lack of faith shown by many soldiers bothered those inclined to believe in God. They did not think themselves superior, but were truly worried about the salvation of their fellow soldiers. Hoyle was no exception. In his letters he often refers to those whom he believes are not as pious as he and pities them because they have not seen the light. For him the belief in the salvation of Jesus Christ is the ultimate duty of every man and he firmly believed his life had purpose. Trusting in God was all he could do in times of extreme peril, and time and again Hoyle credits his survival in battle to God's protection.

Joseph J. Hoyle, fighting near McPherson's Ridge and in the Railroad Cut on July 1, 1863, knew nothing of the struggle for Culp's Hill or the fight for Little Round Top on July 2. Unless he happened to hear some of the key events from reading newspapers or from a soldier who had participated in the fight, most likely he went to his death without knowledge of the facts. Soldiers are usually not aware of grand strategies or even to what effect their success in taking a certain location will have on the outcome of a battle. They know what they have been ordered to do and even if their commanding officer provides some sense of overall reason for their attack or defense in a pre-battle speech the only thing they know for sure is that their fellow fighting men are relying on them to do their duty. In failing to fight effectively they are letting their comrades down and that is the most overriding factor pushing them on.

As Hoyle first experienced battle he underwent an "intense emotional ordeal." Staying alive became the primary thought of soldiers as they came under fire from enemy rifles and artillery. What was it like to face death marching toward those who wanted him dead? Being a civilian-turned-soldier Joseph had little knowledge if any of what to expect. The anxiety and fear of the unknown experience may have seemed overwhelming. The first evidence of battle many inexperienced men saw were the wounded troops streaming back from the front. Once engaged the fact that advancing sometimes meant stepping over fallen comrades was disheartening to many young soldiers. Despite the presence of hundreds of men the battlefield is a lonely place; the emptiness and remote atmosphere is hard for one to imagine.[13] How would he face combat? Would he retreat at the sound of the first shot? These and many other questions probably raced through his mind as he formed into line of battle with his fellow soldiers of Company F.

Once engaged in combat the fictional accounts of valiant men fighting in an organized manner disappear literally into clouds of smoke and dust. The romantic books of war many of the soldiers read in their youth did nothing to prepare them for the reality of combat. The two-rank formation infantry line of battle moved forward with a step or two separating the two ranks. Behind the lines the company lieutenants and other NCOs acted as file closers to keep the men in pace. These officers, Hoyle being one for many of the battles, were to keep order and prevent confusion. This, however, did not always work once shells and bullets began raking the formations. Commands, which were delivered by voice or bugle, were at times hard to hear because of the constant firing of rifles and cannons and the screams of wounded or dying men. Many units, therefore, relied on the use of the regimental colors to lead men where they needed to go — this being one reason color-bearers were targets for enemy sharpshooters. John Keegan asserts that "inside every army is a crowd struggling to get out." Panic and flight were always on the minds of officers who understood the need for discipline and order.[14]

Combat is a total assault on one's senses. The acrid smoke from the firing of rifles and cannons burned the eyes and nostrils of men while they coughed to clear their lungs of the suffocating putrid air. The dust kicked up by vast numbers of men, wagons, and horses mixed with the thick lying smoke to make sight difficult. The noises deafened the soldiers as rifles were discharged within inches of their ears, and the constant artillery blasts made communication and concentration almost impossible. The unbelievable loudness was more than anything these men had experienced in their lives before the war. The confusion brought on by the weapons and movement of men and horses led many companies astray and frustrated even the most amiable of officers. The physical terrain of the battlefield also disrupted formations and limited the field of vision for officers and soldiers.[15]

Other smells, as well as the taste of the battlefield, were also hard to endure. The stench of the men sweating from the heat and days of marching and the decay from dead animals or even dead soldiers made men sick. The pungent smoke left a sulfuric taste in the mouths of the fighting men as well as their own sweat and blood. But the sights that greeted their eyes as the combat raged on brought many courageous men to tears of agony and sorrow. The spectacle of the mangled and dead or dying bodies of their fellow soldiers, and at times their best friends — or even fathers, brothers or sons — was too much to handle. That in time most men who experience combat become accustomed to these sights is in itself a sad testament of war.[16]

Throughout Joseph J. Hoyle's letters one will find references to the death or wounding of friends and family. How much this affected the young lieutenant, or how the sickening sound of bullets or fragments of artillery shells or canister ripping into the flesh of fellow comrades played on Hoyle's emotions is hard to know definitively, but as the conflict seemed to go on forever more of these kinds of morbid facts found their way into his letters.

The reality that war means having to kill other men was a fact that most of the soldiers in Hoyle's company were not particularly prepared to accept. These men understood what they had been called to do, but the actuality of performing the task remained remote in their minds until the task was set before them in battle. Although seeing their friends mutilated beyond recognition or killed outright on the battlefield caused some men to act out with vengeance, participating in mortal combat was not easy to endure. Lieutenant Colonel Dave Grossman, who has studied the effects of killing on soldiers, asserts that it is an "intimate occurrence of tremendous intensity." Men in combat are at first concerned over the act of taking the life of another human being, but the killing in time of battle can happen so fast the action is more of a reflex than a conscious thought and the hours of training and drill taking over. The realization that they have ended the life of one of their enemies can be exhilarating. The adrenaline rush can become addictive to the point that the soldier never feels sorry for killing and desires nothing more than to keep annihilating the enemy. But the majority of men's thoughts quickly turn to remorse and revulsion once the rage of battle has ended and they have had time to think of their own actions. This remorse and revulsion can stay with them for the rest of their lives. Close proximity to enemy combatants in most Civil War battles made acceptance and understanding of the unnatural act of killing even more difficult. The average soldier rationalizes the need to eliminate the enemy and accepts it as an aspect of war; those who do not or cannot handle the death and bloodshed that has become part of their life begin to suffer from what is today known as post-traumatic stress disorder. For Civil War soldiers this was too often an effect of war that was not understood much at the time.[17]

The physical demands placed on Civil War soldiers and the lack of supplying these men with adequate necessities like food, water, and shelter were also factors that greatly impacted the men and their combat effectiveness. There were times when Hoyle and his fellow South Mountain Rangers of Company F, 55th North Carolina, marched 15 to 20 miles before being thrown into the whirlwind of battle. The actualities of war, such as fatigue, hunger, and thirst, all had an adverse effect on the fighting men of both armies during the Civil War. Lack of adequate shelter left men dirty, lousy, and at times susceptible to the elements. Physical and mental exhaustion left soldiers intensely weary and at times unable to function. Of course these strains on the body weakened the immune system leaving many combatants from both armies out of action. Dysentery, diarrhea, and other aliments were commonplace in the unhealthy environment these men lived in every day. It does not surprise most scholars of the Civil War to know that more fighting men died of disease during the war than in combat.[18]

Battle after all is, as John Keegan argues, a "moral conflict" requiring the willingness of two opposing forces. For a resolution to occur one side must be demoralized and then possibly physically destroyed. The losing side may eventually engage in battle again even multiple times — modern warfare has seen less and less of climactic battles like Waterloo — before the final outcome comes to fruition. History teaches that seldom will one engagement end the differences between warring parties and the Civil War is no exception. So although most battles do not follow the definition asserted by John Keegan as "something which happens between two armies leading to the moral and then physical disintegration of one or the other of them," they are still defined as a battle. The one intrinsic feature is the human element. For though every battle is different in scope and consequence it is the interaction of individuals that makes it unique. The study of battle is also the study of fear and how individuals react to the supreme test of character. Therefore the study of men in combat is essential to understanding battles and to fully comprehend war as a human endeavor.[19]

To gain an understanding of how the realities of war and the nature of combat were experienced by Joseph J. Hoyle, a view of his experiences during the battle of the Wilderness will provide some insight. The Overland campaign, in which the battle of the Wilderness was fought on May 5–6, 1864, brought a change to the type of warfare that had been the norm during the first three years of the Civil War. The honorable conduct of most officers and front line troops began to transform into a brutal, hard-handed total war aimed at not only destroying the enemy's will to fight, but also obliterating the civilian population's resolve to support the war effort and the physical infrastructure that enabled their opponent to resist. The Wilderness also began a period of fighting that was unlike the previous years when weeks or even months would separate battles. With the arrival of Ulysses S. Grant to the Eastern Theater, Lee finally faced an adversary who understood the characteristics of modern warfare and how to effectively implement a policy of total war to achieve ultimate victory. As the newly appointed Federal commander informed a young reporter for the New York *Tribune* who was preparing to travel to the nation's capital on the morning of May 6, 1864, as the second morning of fighting had begun in the Wilderness, "If you see the president, tell him for me that, whatever happens, there will be no turning back."[20] The more determined Grant was to defeat the Army of Northern Virginia, the more the great Southern general was prepared to stand and fight. Joseph J. Hoyle and his comrades of Company F, 55th North Carolina, were caught in the vortex of the hell these two supreme antagonists were preparing to unleash in Northern Virginia. The encounter in the Wilderness would be the first engagement in a series of battles that would cost the Army of Northern Virginia nearly 35,000 men and eventually lead to the surrender of Lee's once grand army at Appomattox.[21]

In his memoirs written years after the Civil War had ended Grant described the ferocious combat fought in the Wilderness by asserting that "more desperate fighting has not been witnessed on this continent than that of the 5th and 6th of May." The battle, like so many Civil War engagements, began without the commanding officers of either army desiring the commencement of hostilities. It started on May 5 as Lee moved to counter Grant's advance through the dense wooded area covered by thick underbrush and briers known locally as the Wilderness. The Confederates knew the terrain better than the Federals and Lee hoped the vegetation would undermine Grant's superiority in numbers and eliminate the use of mass artillery to even the odds. The commander of the Army of Northern Virginia ordered Lieutenant General Richard S. Ewell to advance his corps east along the Orange Turnpike and Lieutenant General A. P. Hill's Third Corps, which included the 55th North Carolina, to follow the Orange Plank Road in the same direction.[22]

On the morning of May 4, 1864, Brigadier General Joseph R. Davis's brigade, temporarily under the command of Colonel John M. Stone, commander of the 2nd Mississippi, began marching east toward Fredericksburg. Henry Heth's division was in the vanguard of Hill's Third Corps as they advanced along the Orange Plank Road. After nearly a twenty mile march the brigade halted for the evening near New Verdiersville, located near Mine Run. The next morning Hoyle and the rest of the 55th North Carolina were on the march again as Heth's division continued east toward the Wilderness.[23]

As he marched Hoyle may have had many thoughts on his mind, but the irrepressible anxiety of a forthcoming battle must have heavily outweighed trivial matters. Even though he may not have been privy to the intelligence his division commander, Major General Henry Heth, had received of Federal advances from General Lee or known the division's objective was to capture and hold the Brock Road located in the midst of the heavily wooded Wilderness, the young lieutenant most likely still knew a battle was imminent. The fear and apprehension brought on by the understanding that soon his life would be in danger from enemy fire was not new to Hoyle. He had, after all, led his company at the battle of Gettysburg and marched toward the

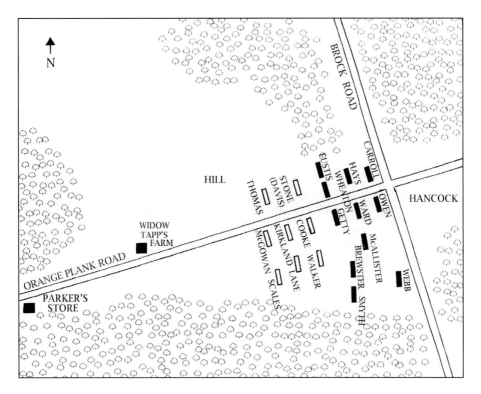

Hill's corps on the Orange Plank Road, May 5, 1864.

seemingly impregnable Union line on July 3, 1863, but every battle brought new unknown horrors and the possibility that this may be his last.

Unaware that the Union high command had ordered Brigadier General G. W. Getty and his division of Sedgwick's corps to move south and take up position on the Orange Plank–Brock Road intersection until Major General Winfield Scott Hancock's corps arrived in strength, Heth's men continued moving east in hope of gaining their objective with little or no resistance. Converging in front of them however, were 17,000 Federals. With 6,500 fighting men on hand Heth's men were outnumbered almost three to one.[24]

Around 1:00 P.M. Heth's skirmishers encountered Getty's troops near the Brock Road, but after probing the Federal lines the advance guard realized the Union troops were there in force and retreated to inform their commanding officer. Lee had ordered Heth not to bring on a general engagement until the entire Army of Northern Virginia was on the field of battle. Heth, having helped bring on the battle of Gettysburg by ignoring similar orders, most likely felt an overwhelming sense of duty to follow his commander's wishes to the letter. He informed his brigade commanders to hold their positions until he had received word from General Lee. He was prepared to attack the Federal lines with his whole division if he was ordered to do so, but the Northern forces attacked before his message asking for permission to attack reached Lee.[25]

Joseph J. Hoyle and his fellow South Mountain Rangers made their way through briars and thickets that were so dense that their uniforms were torn and their flesh lacerated by the jagged underbrush. Colonel Stone had deployed his brigade on the left side of the Orange Plank Road with the 55th North Carolina positioned in the right center of the line of battle with the 26th and 42nd Mississippi regiments on the extreme left. The 1st Confederate Battalion and the 2nd and 11th Mississippi regiments were on the immediate right and left of the North Carolinians.[26] The men had established their line on the crest of a small hill and quickly went to work setting up fieldworks to shield themselves from enemy fire. The 55th North Carolina's regimental historian, Charles M. Cooke, described the location of his unit as being "in a dense forest of small trees." He went on to describe the position of the regiment in his history.

> The hill in our front sloped gradually to a depression or valley which was a few yards wide, and then there was a gradual incline on the opposite side until it reached a point of about the same altitude as that occupied by us, about 100 yards from our line.[27]

Around 3:30 in the afternoon of May 5 the Federals launched their attack against Heth's division. The Confederate skirmishers were pushed back to the Rebel lines as the Union troops relentlessly advanced. Because of the thick vegetation the Federals, under command of Brigadier General Henry Eustis, were able to advance to within 100 yards of Stone's men before being noticed. The terrain made it hard for the Union soldiers to form into battle lines and the constant Confederate fire raked their formations. The battle near the Orange Plank–Brock Road junction continued for more than three hours. Four Federal divisions continued to hammer Heth's fatigued and desperate troops, but relief did not come.[28]

As the Federals began firing on Hoyle's line he must have had a sense of exhilaration as the adrenaline flowed through his veins. The almost overpowering anxiety he felt as he and his fellow comrades waited for the assault was gone, and his mind was free to focus on the present situation. The instinct to survive and the memories of previous engagements had taught him to think like a soldier and prepare to repel the Union onslaught. The denseness of the Wilderness kept the smoke from the constant rifle fire close to the ground where the soldiers were. Hoyle probably found it difficult to see and breathe as the already dark field filled with thick smoke. The noise throughout the battle was deafening as thousands of rifles discharged and pelted trees and human flesh. The cries of agony from wounded and dying men also made it difficult for soldiers to hear much of anything let alone orders from their officers.

Part of Hoyle's duty as an officer was to keep his men in formation and to prevent them from retreating. He knew from past experience that if a few men ran for the rear others would follow believing the order to withdraw had been given or that their lines had been overrun. Panic could cause a mass of men fleeing from the front lines and expose the flanks of fellow companies. But the Federal assault was like nothing he had ever experienced before. At Gettysburg his men were usually the attackers, and even when they were in a defensive position in the railroad cut on July 1, 1863, the attack from Colonel Rufus R. Dawes's 6th Wisconsin and other supporting Federal units lasted only a fraction of the time. On this day the Union commanders continued to send wave after wave of assaults, no less than seven attacks, and the ferocity of the combat grew more intense as time went by.

As the hours passed by more and more of the men in Company F of the 55th North Carolina fell dead or wounded from the incessant Union fire. Some of Hoyle's closest friends were hit and their cries for water or for someone to assist them to the rear probably tore at his heart. The maddening thoughts of vengeance may have raced through his mind as he continued to stand and perform his duties. The fighting became desperate as more fresh Federal troops poured into the field in front of Colonel Stone's brigade.

The hours of intense fighting were wearing down the men of the 55th North Carolina as well as all of Stone's forces. The extreme fatigue and thirst physically and emotionally drained the men to their breaking point. Lieutenant Hoyle may have walked the lines of his company encouraging his men to keep a steady stream of fire and continue to resist the irresistible Federal tide. As darkness approached visibility, already severely limited from the thick underbrush and smoke, was becoming impossible, but the Federals continued to attack. The men had been firing and reloading their weapons for hours and were low on ammunition. The thought that soon the Union troops would completely annihilate every man in the command went through the mind of at least one officer of the 55th North Carolina. Some drastic measure would have to be taken to hold the line.[29]

Colonel Stone called for an impromptu council of war with his line officers to discuss the brigade's options. Being a junior grade officer Lieutenant Hoyle was most likely not called to this conference, but he would have been informed by his commanding officer, Lieutenant Colonel Alfred H. Belo, whose brother Henry Belo of Company H had been killed during the battle, of its outcome.[30] The men would fix bayonets and charge the Federal position. Joseph Hoyle's reaction to this news is unknown, but he had fought in enough battles to know this was a death sentence for him and the men in his company. They had held off seven attacks from a vastly more numerous enemy throughout the afternoon and evening. Now his brigade, well below half strength by this time in the battle, would be no match for the Federals.

As the message made its way through the ranks the men of Stone's brigade prepared to advance. Lieutenant Colonel Belo ordered that the 55th North Carolina's battle flag be held high and kept well to the front as the men charged the Union lines. Hoyle may have had time to pray and think of his wife and the life he would never share with her before the order to advance was sounded. But at the last possible minute relief finally came and the order was countermanded. Brigadier General Edward L. Thomas's Georgia brigade had arrived and relieved Stone's battered and exhausted men. Joseph J. Hoyle had been granted a reprieve.

The 55th North Carolina suffered over 60 percent casualties; Hoyle's Company F lost over 50 percent. The unimaginable scene that Hoyle saw that night is almost indescribable. Dead and dying Federals lay stacked in front of the Confederate defensive line. The loud, incessant cries of wounded and dying men pierced through the darkness making sleep difficult. The search for friends was complicated by sharpshooters on both sides, which made movement difficult. The fetid smell of smoke still lingered in the air and the fires, which had ignited in certain areas during the exchange of rifle shots, continued to engulf wounded men who were unable to escape being burned to death.

The dread of battle would not remain out of Hoyle's thoughts for long. Lieutenant General Grant, sensing the weakness of Lee's lines along the Orange Plank Road, ordered an attack on that front early the next morning. Almost half of the Union force converged on A. P. Hill's shattered lines as exhausted Confederates tried to make a feeble stand. Many of A. P. Hill's men were asleep when the Federal onslaught began. Little if any effort had been made that night to reform and reinforce the Rebel defenses. Worn out from the previous day's battle the men of the 55th North Carolina who could sleep through the disturbing noise of that night had given in to tiredness and collapsed shortly after being relieved. This was the experience of the men in the 55th North Carolina during the morning of May 6, 1864, as the Union forces pushed into their lines and forced a mass retreat. Many of them would quickly reform, but most, including Hoyle, were kept in reserve. The dire situation, which at first seemed like the end for Hill's entire corps, was finally restored and the Federals were forced to fall back to their lines. The two days of fighting in the Wilderness had cost Grant 18,000 men and Lee some 11,000. The death and carnage had been astonishing.

The fighting that began on May 5, 1864, unleashed some of the war's most sustained and horrific fighting. Grant continued to pound and pursue the Army of Northern Virginia for the rest of the summer of 1864, until Lee was finally pushed back into a defensive line around Petersburg and Richmond. Joseph J. Hoyle continued to fight alongside of his fellow comrades through the battles around Spotsylvania Court House, Cold Harbor, the North Anna River, and Petersburg. Eventually however, the young God-fearing lieutenant would suffer a severe wound during the battle of Globe Tavern on August 18, 1864. Like so many of his friends and fellow soldiers, he too would die young, succumbing to his wounds on September 1, 1864. The specter of death that he had seen in so many battles finally succeeded in overtaking him just as he so often feared it would.

II LETTERS

3. Duty in North Carolina, May–September 1862

*"Let us look forward to a time
when we will enjoy each others love"*

Throughout the latter half of March and into May of 1862, men living in North Carolina began organizing companies of troops to join the Confederate Army. Although many had thought the war would be short, the Federal invasion of the North Carolina coast and Union advances in Virginia and the West forced Confederate leaders to recruit more men. To compel Southern men to enlist, the Confederate Congress passed the Conscription Act of 1862, which made all able-bodied men between the ages of eighteen and thirty-five eligible to be drafted into the army for three years, or the duration of the war. Certain exemptions from conscription infuriated many soldiers and citizens alike. With the knowledge that they would be forced into the army, many Southern men began to enlist before they were drafted in order to have a say in which companies they could or would join.[1] Although Joseph Hoyle does not state this anywhere in his letters, the draft may have been what prompted him to volunteer.

In Cleveland County, Peter M. Mull, who had previously served in Company K, 1st North Carolina Infantry Regiment, was appointed Captain of what would become Company F, 55th North Carolina State Troops on April 1, 1862. One of his first recruits was Joseph J. Hoyle, who enlisted on May 10, 1862, and shortly thereafter traveled by train with other new recruits to Raleigh, North Carolina. Upon arrival, the men were quickly transferred to Camp Mangum, several miles west of the state capital. The men recruited by Captain Mull were joined by nine other companies raised throughout the Old North State and organized into the 55th North Carolina State Troops Regiment on or about May 16, 1862. Company F, which became known as the South Mountain Rangers, was mustered into the Confederate Army on May 30, 1862.[2]

49

The majority of the men who fought with the South Mountain Rangers were farmers or farm laborers in their mid-twenties with no combat experience. Although most of the soldiers who served with Company F were from Cleveland County, there were men from Burke and Catawba counties as well.

Once the men arrived at Camp Mangum they began training to become soldiers. They spent many of their waking hours drilling, performing guard duty, and participating in dress parades to practice marching. This loose organization of men soon learned to be part of a military unit under the tutelage of Lieutenant Sidney Smith Abernethy, who had previously served with the 30th North Carolina, and now served as the regiment's drillmaster.[3]

Although the majority of soldiers who became members of the 55th North Carolina in May 1862 were inexperienced, there were several men who had seen at least limited action earlier in the war. The commanding officer of the 55th North Carolina, Colonel John Kerr Connally, had previously served with the 21st North Carolina State Troops Regiment, and had been at the First Battle of Bull Run. Connally had attended the United States Naval Academy before the Civil War and had served as a Captain with the 21st Having longed to command his own regiment for years, Connally proved to be a good disciplinarian and an effective leader.[4]

Another of the regiment's field officers who had experienced combat before joining the 55th was Major James S. Whitehead. Whitehead had been a lawyer before the war and served as a private with the 10th North Carolina. In 1861, the 10th North Carolina had been assigned to assist with the protection of coastal forts in North Carolina. Whitehead was taken prisoner when the Federals captured forts Clark and Hatteras in August 1862. After being paroled, Whitehead returned to Pitt County, North Carolina, and helped raise a company of men that eventually joined the 55th. After serving briefly as Captain of Company E, Whitehead was promoted to Major but died in August 1862 of disease.[5]

Alfred Horatio Belo, who also served as a Captain with the 21st North Carolina, joined the 55th as assistant quartermaster in November 1862 and would eventually become the unit's commanding officer. Like Connally, Belo aspired to command his own regiment and traveled to Raleigh in May 1862. Noting his experience and initiative, Governor Henry T. Clark assigned Belo the task of assisting with the training of new volunteers and conscripts. After serving at this post for several months, Belo was assigned to the staff of Brigadier General Robert F. Hoke, and sent to Winchester, Virginia. In November he was reassigned to the staff of the 55th North Carolina, which at that time was stationed in Petersburg, Virginia. Belo proved to be an effective officer and in time moved up the chain of command to lead the entire regiment.

His tenure as commander of the 55th lasted only five months, but during that time he earned the respect and admiration of his men.[6]

While at Camp Mangum, the men of the 55th North Carolina were well fed and well trained. Camp life became quite monotonous at times, but the soldiers found unique ways to entertain themselves. After spending a month drilling and becoming accustomed to army life, the regiment was ordered to move east. On June 27 the 55th North Carolina received orders to move to Camp Campbell, seven miles west of Kinston, North Carolina. Before departing, a hundred members of the regiment were sent to Raleigh to obtain muskets. The following day the men of the 55th boarded rail cars and began their journey east.[7]

In an effort to save Richmond from the threat of Major General George B. McClellan's advancing Federal army and remove enemy troops from Virginia, General Robert E. Lee proposed to take back the initiative. Lee believed a strategic offensive would achieve both these goals and allow his army to win victories that would take the South closer to independence. In order to proceed he would need troops from North and South Carolina to be sent to reinforce his men. As North Carolina regiments that were protecting the Atlantic coastline were sent north, newly formed units, like the 55th, marched east to take their place.[8]

While at Camp Campbell the men in the 55th North Carolina continued to drill, suffered from disease, and prepared for an attack from the Federals. Early in the war Union military leaders realized the importance of controlling the Albemarle, Pamlico, Core, and Bogue sounds located in eastern North Carolina. If these sounds were under their control, the Federals could effectively hold sway over one-third of the Old North State. This would enable the Federals to threaten the Wilmington and Weldon Railroad, a primary rail line running south from Richmond, Virginia.[9]

In August 1861, the Federals, under the command of Major General Benjamin Butler with a naval detachment under the command of Commodore Silas Stringham, succeeded in capturing forts Clark and Hatteras, which protected North Carolina's numerous inlets. These victories gave the Union forces control of the inlets to the Pamlico Sound. In February 1862, another Federal expedition, this time under the command of Major General Ambrose E. Burnside and Commodore L. M. Goldsborough, captured several Confederate positions on Roanoke Island, and within weeks Federal forces had gained control of North Carolina ports for 150 miles up and down the sounds.[10]

Major General Burnside had planned to move into the interior of North Carolina with a strike toward the railroad hub in Goldsboro, which could seriously have threatened the Confederacy's ability to supply its army. However, Major General George B. McClellan's Peninsula campaign required

Burnside's attention and he was sent to Virginia, leaving Major General John G. Foster in command of the Department of North Carolina.[11]

Major General Foster immediately began solidifying his position and sent detachments into North Carolina to reconnoiter the topography of the area and keep the Confederates at bay. It was during one of these reconnaissance missions that the 55th North Carolina received its baptism of fire. After spending several months participating in the defense of the coast, including playing a minor role in the Confederate attack on Washington, North Carolina, in which Joseph Hoyle saw action, the 55th was ordered to move to Petersburg where the unit was placed on provost duty.[12]

* * *

Camp Mangum
Near Raleigh,
May 15th, 1862

My Dear Wife:

This will inform you that we are here at camp.[13] Leaving Lincolnton on the 13th, after a three hour ride we arrived at Charlotte. This was a very disagreeable ride owing to a want of accommodation in seats. We remained at Charlotte until about 7 O'clock P.M. when we took the train for Raleigh, when we arrived a little after sun up next morning, having traveled all night. We had very excellent seats in this ride, and it would have been a very interesting ride if it had not been night. We lost one of our boys on the way (Mr. Goodson), but he came up yesturday evening.[14] A very serious accident occurred directly after we arrived at Raleigh. On dismounting from the train, some fifteen or twenty of our company went up into the water-House to get water, when the loft broke down immediately over the mouth of the well, injuring several, two so badly (Crow & Elmore) that they were sent to the hospital.[15] It seems marvelous that none of them fell into the well. Wm. Craig's hat fell into the well, though he escaped uninjured.[16] After some delay at Raleigh we moved up here to camp, about 4 miles from the city.

We were employed yesterday evening in putting up our tents and enjoyed a good nights rest last night, which you can appreciate from the fact that we had slept very little for the two preceding nights. The rain is pouring down this morning, though we have a very good tent cloth, which affords us effective shelter. Rob't Self & Jacob Gales are sick this morning.[17] I was very unwell yesturday which I attribute to loosing so much sleep; but I feel as well as usual this morning. Jacob & Isaac are well this morning.[18] I will write you again in a few days. Let my folks know that I am well. Pray for me. Your affectionate husban

J.J. Hoyle
Mrs. S.A. Hoyle
Knob Creek, N.C.

Camp Mangum, Wake Co., N.C.
May 17th, 1862

My Dear Wife:

I again embrace an opportunity of writing you a few lines. I am not very well. I have a very bad cold, though I am still able for duty. I feel that it is very hard to be parted from you though since it is the decree of fate, I will endeavor to bear it. I trust that the good Lord will take care of you; and soften all your sorrows. Into his hands I resign you. To day is the first day that we have drilled since we have been here. We are getting our tents and affairs fixed up pretty well. The following are our messmates[19] J.R. Willis, John Cline, Isaac and Rooker, Robert & Solomon Willis, Julius Kenedy, Jesse Cook and Wm. Self.[20] We have hired Robert Willis and Isaac to cook for us. Our camp is very lively. The boys sing a great deal. We have taken up prayer every night. Some few are complaining. We have tolerably good water. The war is very little talked of here in camp; so little so that we forget for what purpose we came here.

Reports say that the yankee gunboats are in 9 miles of Richmond. A terrible battle will no doubt be fought there soon.[21] I neglected to tell you of my good fortune as I came through Lincolnton. A very generous lady made me a present of a bible. She is unknown to me. God bless her. Pray that the good Lord will soon deliver us from this cruel war; and permit us to return home again. Though we are absent in body, yet we are joined in heart. Pray for me. Yours in hope,

J.J. Hoyle

Give my love to your father and mother, and brother. I have not an opportunity now to write them separate letters. Direct your letters to Raleigh, Camp Mangum, N.C.
Care Capt Mull[22]

Camp Mangum, N.C.
May 23rd, 1862

My Dear Wife:

I received your letter a few minutes ago, and you can not imagine what joy it has gave me. Oh how it raised my heart to read a few lines from one whom I know loves me and the little hair braid inside, dear Sarah you are so kind. But this is not all. I feel your love is with me. I know you heart is near mine, though we are many miles apart. Dear Sarah, God will take care of you. Love him with all your heart. Love him more than you love me for He is the great giver of all good.

I find myself moderately well this morning. I feel better this morning than I have since I arrived here. I enjoy camp life tolerably well. Of course I would rather be at home with you, but since my country demands it, I will have to be content to stay here. But pray that the war may end, so that we may all return home again. We have prayer in our tent every night. We are trying to serve the Lord the best we can, though there is so much disturbance that it is a hard matter to compose one's mind. We drill four hours a day, besides dress parade and guard duty.[23] We have plenty to eat. We have flour, meal, bread, bacon, beef, peas, and rice.[24]
John Willis and Patterson Bigham came in this morning. But I must close for the present.[25] Write soon. Your loving husban,

J.J. Hoyle

S.A. Hoyle

When you send letters by mail direct them thru

J.J. Hoyle

Company —* 55th Regt N.C. Troops

Camp Mangum, Raleigh, N.C.

Care Capt Mull

You will please excuse this short letter. As soon as I get a favorable opportunity, I will write you a more lengthy letter. There is so much noise an confusion about here that it almost runs one crazy, some are singing, some are playing, some are suffering, some are fiddling, and every thing else that you could think of.

But I am getting somewhat used to it.

* Not yet known[26]

Camp Mangum near Raleigh,
May 30th, 1862

My Dear Wife:

I grasp my pen this morning to drop you a few lines. I am tolerably well, and I hope these lines may find you well. I received your kind letter through Mr. Brindle, and I read it with much interest. You can not imagine what emotions heaved in my breast on reading your devoted letter. I do thank the Lord for giving me such a good wife. And I can safely say that I never knew what it was to be separated from a loving wife before. Yes, dear Sarah, I would give all I possess in this world to get to come back and live with you again. But such is the decree of this cruel war that we must be separated for a while, though I hope we will be permitted to enjoy each others company again in this world, yet if these hopes be frustrated, let us look forward to a time when we will enjoy each others love in a brighter world than this, and, thank God, there will be no parting there.

I think of you a great deal, and often I feel the tears running fast down my cheeks. I feel that your affectionate heart is near mine and though you are many miles away, yet I can feel your love. Oh that the Good Lord may take care of you. Love him with all your heart and pray to him to take care of your loving husban. I pray for you much. The Lord has promised to answer faithful prayer, then let us take courage, and pray with faithful hearts and the Lord will hear us. We fare as well here as soldiers could expect.

We have a tolerable civil company, the civilest, I believe, in the regiment. We have prayer in two or three of our tents every night, and regimental prayer every morning and evening. The mode of regimental prayer is as follows; the whole regiment is drawn up in three sides of a square, each man then places his right hand under his left elbow and raises his hat with the left hand, the minister then stands in the open side of the square, and pronounces the prayer.[27] I will come home at the time of the quarterly meeting at Bethlehem, if I can get off, But I fear I can not get off; for orders have been read that no more furloughs will be granted. This is hard, but we have to abide by it. I have no important news. A great battle is expected at Richmond every day. They have moved a great deal of property from Richmond to Raleigh. President Davis has sent his family to Raleigh.[28] I do fervently pray that the war may be speedily brought to a close. We sent you and your mother some soda; and I sent you some candy. I received a letter from Lemuel the other day.[29] He is well; he wants to come to our company. But I must close. Write often. Your loving husban till death.

J.J. Hoyle
Co. F. 55 Regt N.C. Troops.
Care Capt Mull

Camp Mangum, N.C.
June 4th, 1862

My Dear wife:

I seat myself this morning to drop you a few lines. I am well except a cold. I have had two or three sick brushes since I have been here; and I would have come home last week but I could not get a furlough. The colonel will not give any man a furlough, sick or well.[30] I expect we will leave here before long. I did want to come home before we left, but I reckon there will be no chance. I have been appointed company comissary.[31] This office excuses me from drill and guard duty. The great battle has took place at Richmond, but we have received no news of the final result yet.[32] The last dispatch says our men had the better yet. The slaughter is immense on both sides. May God grant us the victory, and with it, a speedy termination of this cruel war! I still hope the good Lord will permit me to return to the fond association of my dear wife again. Let us trust it all to the Lord, for he will do right. A very sad misfortune occurred in our company last night. Two men lost their pocket-books. One contained about $40; the other only a few dollars. It is thought they were stolen. The measles have made their appearance in our company. Joel Hoyle has had them several days.[33] We have also some other slight sick cases.[34] Enclosed I send you forty dollars, which you may dispose of as follows: 1. keep as much as you want for your own use; 2. Pay mother, if she will take it; 3. lift that note I gave your brother Lemuel; 4. Pay the balance to Berry.[35] Be sure and have him give credit on the note. Write to me soon. As ever, your affectionate husban,

J.J. Hoyle
Mrs. S.A. Hoyle

Camp Mangum near Raleigh
June 5th, 1862

My dear wife:

I take a few moments this morning to drop you a few lines. I am well and I hope these few lines may find you enjoying the same blessing. Camp life begins to seem a little easier than it did at first, yet I long to come back and live with you again. There is no place like home sweet home. It seems to me it has been almost a year since I left you, yet your memory still has a place nearest my heart.

O that the war would close. That we might all be permitted to return to our homes again. This is my constant prayer. We have a great deal of rainy weather; and it is very cold, as well as wet, this morning. I have no idea when we will leave here, we have no arms yet.[36]

We have no late news from Richmond. It seems curious that we cannot get any more news. Some think it is not a good sign; though at last accounts our men had the better of the fight. I tried for a furlough this morning, but could not get it. I think I will get one next week, but I fear I cannot get home in time for the quarterly meeting. I sent you forty dollars by Silas Proctor, and I want you to write to me as soon as you get it.[37] Our chaplain seems to be a very fine man, he preached twice for us last Sunday.

He is a Baptist.[38] I will want a pair of cotton breeches when I come home. But I must close. Write to me often, and write all the news you can. As ever, your loving husban

J.J. Hoyle

Mrs. S.A. Hoyle

If you could send us a few sweet cakes &c. by James Willis, they would be thankfully received. I want you to preserve all my letters.

The following letter was printed in the June 16, 1862, Raleigh newspaper *Spirit of the Age.*[39]

Camp Mangum, June 11.

Mr. Editor: This will inform the friends of the "South Mountain Rangers," that we are still at this place, and probably will remain here a few weeks, as we have not been armed yet. The health of our regiment is not good.(The measles and mumps are raging among us. But there has been but one or two deaths in the regiment that I am aware of.[40] Our Chaplain is a kind affectionate gentleman, and labors strenuously for the spiritual welfare of this regiment. May his labors be crowned with abundant success. While we are upon the tented field, we ask an interest in the prayers of our friends at home. Especially do we beseech our Christian brethren and class mates to remember us at a throne of grace. We are here surrounded by almost every influence which tends to divert our minds from serious meditation, and we need divine grace to sustain us. Ah! when I view the deteriorating influences of camp life, my heart heaves a sigh, and I implore the good Lord to cover our heads till his wrath be passed over. Friends, we beseech you, pray for us and our afflicted country till the Lord's wrath be turned away and the dark clouds of war and oppression give place to the genial rays of liberty and peace.[41]

J.J. HOYLE

Co. F, 55th Reg. N.C.T.

During the last several weeks of June through July 17, Joseph Hoyle was home on sick leave. On June 27, 1862, the 55th North Carolina received orders to move from Camp Mangum to a site near Kinston, North Carolina. During the evening of the 28th and through the morning hours of June 29 the regiment boarded railroad cars and traveled east to Kinston. The 55th North Carolina reached Camp Campbell, located seven miles west of Kinston, by nightfall on June 29.[42] The new camp was described by some of the men, including Private Hoyle, as unhealthy and the "drinking water unfit to drink." Included in the following set of letters is one to the *Spirit of the Age*, in which Hoyle describes his regiment's new camp. Although the new site wasn't as pleasing to the men as Camp Mangum, the overall health of the regiment began to improve.

Camp Campbell
July 20, 1862

My Dear wife:

I embrace this opportunity of dropping you a few lines, to let you know that I am well as common. I have a severe cough yet, but I think I am stouter than when I left home. I arrived here last Thursday night (17th day), and found all our boys doing well. The reason I did not get here sooner was, I did not take the cars at Lincolnton till Wednesday. When I arrived at Lincolnton, after leaving home on Monday, I met Capt. Mull, and he requested me to stay in Lincolnton till the Cleveland conscripts came to see if I could not get some recruits to our company.[43] Accordingly I staid till Wednesday and got five recruits, but I had to give four of them up at Charlotte; so I brought one (John Elmore)[44] on to the company. It did not cost me any thing to go, because I was taking recruits.

We have a very pretty camp here among the long-leaf pines. We can get tolerably good water by going a good ways after it. We have wells in the camp but the water is bad. Our company is healthy. We have but two on the sick list this morning, and they are going about. Two negroes were shot at Kinston last Friday. They had been out recruiting for old Burnside, and were taken by our men.[45]

We have no important news; every thing is very still. It is thought that McllelIand is reinforcing, and our generals are preparing to meet him if he attempts to advance again. Several Regiments have been sent from here toward Richmond, lately.[46] Some men think that the war will close before long. I pray that it may. And that I may be permitted to come home and live with my dear wife again. Love the Lord dear wife with all your heart, and you will find comfort.

I paid my tax as I passed through Lincolnton. It was five dollars. I borrowed the money from Wash Hull so you will pay him five dollars. Isaac has got well again. As I have not time to write your father a letter, you can let him read this one.

Write to me soon. Pray for me. As ever, your loving husban

J.J. Hoyle
Mrs. S.A. Hoyle
Direct your letters to
Kinston
Camp Campbell

55th Regt N.C. Troops
Care Capt. Mull

The name of our camp is changed from camp Johnston to camp Campbell.

The following letter was printed in the July 28, 1862, issue of the *Spirit of the Age.*

Camp Campbell, near Kinston, July 24, 1862

Mr. Editor: Through your kindness, I wish to communicate a few words to the friends of the 55th Regt. N.C.T. now in camp at this place. We occupy a very pretty encampment on the Atlantic and N.C. Rail Road, among the long leaf pines. (We have as good water as we could expect for this country. Our rations have proven sufficient thus far, and on the whole, this place seems to be better adapted to our well being than at Camp Mangum. The heath of the Regt. is comparatively good. The South Mountain Rangers are all on foot. One of our Lieutenants (Newton) has resigned on account of ill health, he says.[47] We do not expect an attack here, although such an event is possible. Should the invader come, we will show him North Carolina pluck.

J.J. Hoyle

Camp Campbell
July 25th '62

Dear wife:

I seize this opportunity of writing you a few lines to let you know that I am well, and I hope these lines may find you well. I have nothing of importance to write, except we have very warm weather and rain plenty. A few are sick in our company, though none dangerously.A great many persons think that peace will be made before long, and we have some indications that point in that direction if they be true. But we can only know the certainty by waiting. May the Lord's good time be at hand, when this cloud of war shall pass from us. Let me exhort you to continue to rely upon the Lord. He is able and willing to give you comfort. I hope I will get home to enjoy your company again. But if it is my lot to die while I am from you, I hope I will meet you in heaven where parting is no more. But I must end this short letter, as Isaac is ready to start to Goldsboro and I am to send this with him. As ever your loving husban.

Dear wife, as I failed to send this with Isaac, I will write you a few more lines. We do not know whether we will have to leave here soon or not. Our regiment are not all armed yet. Drilling goes very hard these hot days. Though I get short of it, except I want to. I have drilled one half of a day since I have been here. We get enough to eat but no more. We get fresh beef and mutton three times a week. We also get a few molasses, and wheat for coffee. We can buy some fruit but have to pay high.

Lieutenant Newton has resigned his office; and I expect we will have a big election for another lieutenant. I expect we will have six or eight candidates. I will be in the ring.[48] _____ I made that long mark because I had to lay down my pen and way out some meet for the cooks. Dear Sarah, it seems like a long time since I left you, though it has not been two weeks yet. Though many miles separate us. And we cannot see each others face. Yet, never dying love unites us, And we will meet at last. Your loving husban
My loving Sarah   J.J. Hoyle

---

12. O'clock   Kinston, N.C.
                                                                              July 27, 1862
Dear wife:

I seize this opportunity of dropping you a few lines. I am well. We were hurried off yesterday about 1.0'clock PM from our camp to meet the Yankees who were said to be advancing on Kinston. We drew our arms and then immediately hastened through the sand and the dust. We plodded on, and about 6.0'clock, arrived at Kinston, a distance of about 8 miles. Several of our boys gave out on the way. I came very near giving out myself, but I tuffed it out. We took up camp here at Kinston with nothing but the broad canopy of heaven for a cover; for we brought neither tents nor blankets with us. Nothing but our clothes and arms. About dark, and before we had got any thing to eat, it commenced raining. The regt was then ordered to get shelter where ever they could. I was at the depo at this time drawing provisions for our company. When I got back to the company, all were gone to hunt shelter but three or four, and we immediately hustled off to find shelter. By hard work we got into a negro hut (Lieut Hull[49] among us). We remained here till this morning. I did not sleep any scarcely. We expected to have to march on this morning toward the Yankees but we are still here. Some say we will go no further, and others say we will. But I have no more paper. God willing, I will write you soon again. Pray for me. Yours as ever,

                                                                              J.J. Hoyle

                                                                              S.A. Hoyle

I can not write as sadisfactory as I want to now. I will give you a better understanding in my next.

Camp Campbell
Aug. 1st, 1862

Dear Wife:

I seat myself this evening to drop you a few lines. I am in usual
health, though somewhat tired, for I have been very busy this evening. I
hope these lines may find you well. We returned to our camp this evening,
and I am very glad of it. We had been gone one week, as you will see by
reference to my last letter (written at Kinston) I will give you a meager
description of this our first trip against the Yankees. On the night of the
25th July, our camp was thrown into excitement by orders being issued to
be ready to march at ten minutes warning. But this excitement soon died
away and the boys went to bed again. In the morning we had a jolly laugh
about the bustle of the night; for we all thought that the orders had been
given just to try us; but, in reality they were in good faith. Nothing more
was said about us leaving till about one O'clock P.M. (26), when we were
ordered to fall in line. Arms, cartridges &c. were then given us, and we
were immediately marched off, taking nothing with us but our arms and
the clothes we had on and (some of us) canteens. This being the colonels
orders. At the first sitting out I did not know that we were to leave the
camp. We took the road toward Kinston, and I soon learned that we were
going to meet the enemy who was advancing on Kinston. All our boys
seemed in good spirits at the prospect of a fight, and to tell you the truth, I
felt cool and very willing to meet the foe. So we plodded on at quick time
through the sand; but we soon began to jade, and occasionally one would
be seen falling out of ranks into the fence corner. I felt very much like
falling out myself, but by hard enduring, I held out. Four or five gave out
in our company. About 6. O'clock, we arrived at Kinston and took up
camp for the night. Our camp was in an old field, with nothing to shelter
us from the approaching rain. About dark it commenced raining when
every man made for shelter. I was at the depot drawing provisions and
when I came back all were gone except a few: every place was crammed
full, and we found shelter in a negro kitchen. I never thought I would have
to stay in a negro hut, but I tell you I was glad of the chance this time; for
it rained tremendious. I had to sit up all night; for the house was crammed
full.[50] Next morning we expected to have to leave, but we did not. We
staid here till Friday (Aug 1st) when we were ordered back to camp. The
regiment left in the morning, but I was detailed to take charge of our baggage &c., so I staid till evening and came up on the train. We almost feel
like we were like we were at home again since we arrived at our camp. We
got nothing to eat while we were at Kinston but bacon and hard bread
except we bought it. Our pickets brought in four yankee prisoners while

we were at Kinston. The yankees came up to Trenton, 20 miles below Kinston, but went back again.[51] The yankees also took some of our cavalry. But so much for our first trip against the yankees.

I received a letter from you day befor yesterday. I was very glad to hear from you. I hope I will be permitted to return and spend the balance of my days with you. But if we never meet here any more let us look forward to a glorious meeting above. I know you will pray for me, yes, and I believe the good Lord will answer your prayer. But I must close for this time. Write often. As ever your loving husban,
S.A. Hoyle   J.J. Hoyle

Tell Rook that Isaac will sell his watch if he can.

Camp Campbell
August 14th, 1862

My dear wife:

I received your kind letter yesterday by Rooker, and was very glad to hear from you, as I always am. I am well at present. I have enjoyed better health since I came back than I did at camp Mangum, though we have endured a great many more hardships. The health of our company is not very good. Four are at the hospital in Goldsboro and several sick here at camp. I will not take time to give you another account of our trip against the yankees, as I gave you one in my last account in the Spirit of the Age. We are now at camp, but we do not know how long we will stay here. We may be ordered out to meet the enemy any day. May the God of might go with us!Another fight is expected about Richmond.[52]

I do pray that the Lord's good time may soon come when the war will close! Let us pray for it earnestly. I hope I will be permitted to come home and spend the evening of my life with you. How it makes my heart beat to think of living again with my dear Sarah; but alas! I may never be allowed this privilege. I may never see you more, dear Sarah, on this earth, but blessed be the Lord for the hope of meeting in heaven. I try to serve the Lord with my whole heart, and it does me so much good to think that my dear wife is doing so too.

Dear Sarah let us wean our love from earth and fix it on heaven. I do want to feel that I am wholy given to the Lord, and I want my dear Sarah to have perfect happiness in the love of Jesus. For this I pray continually. Let much of our thoughts be about meeting in heaven. There we will be permitted to enjoy each others love and company forever. No war can separate us there. O let us look forward to this happy time.

Dear Sarah, I should be very glad to see you, but I do not know when

I will get the opportunity; for even sick men can not get furloughs. I want you to write to me every week, for I am so glad to hear from you. Write how my hogs are doing, and all about my affairs. I stated to you in the first letter I wrote you that, I paid my tax as I passed through Lincolnton; but you never wrote whether you got that letter or not. The potatoes and sweet bread you sent us was thankfully received. I eat that red yam myself and thought of the dear little hand that hoed it, all the time.(Your Loving husban.

J.J. Hoyle

I learn that Berry and Will are ordered to Richmond.[53] I have received one letter from Sherrill since I came back.[54] He came through the battle safe. I was glad to hear that you had got my likeness. Give my best respects to Terrisa and all the rest.[55] If you can get me a pair of shoes made you may do so after a while. I will need a pair in a month or two.

Camp Campbell
Aug, 22nd '62

My Dear wife:

I take the pleasure this evening of dropping you a few lines. I am well at present, and I hope these lines may find you well. The health of our company is not good. Every thing seems quiet about here now, but there is no telling how long it will stay so. We may receive marching orders at any time. But if it is our fortune to get into a battle, I hope the Lord will shield us from harm. Do not be too uneasy about me, but trust it all to the good Lord. Pray in faith and the Lord will hear you. I have hope that we will meet again on earth, and oh how my heart throbs to think of meeting you again face to face. But, Dear Sarah, we cannot tell what the future has in store for us. It may be that the most of our troubles are over, and it may be they are just commenced. But let us hope for the best. Let us not make troubles before we come to them. I do sincerely pray that the Lord will give you sufficient grace to bear up under all your trials. Dear Sarah, be my good little wife as you have always been. I have not received any letter from you this week yet, I hope you will not fail to write.—I have no war news worth relating.

I am, as ever, your loving husban.

S.A. Hoyle   J.J. Hoyle

I received a letter from William R. Self yesterday. He and Berry and Calvin and Amsey Bast, and some others want to come to our company.[56] We are fixing out transfers for them today, and they will get to come if their general will sign their transfers, but that is doubtful. They are at Richmond now. The letter gives no news but the papers say Mcllelland is drawing off his forces below Richmond. He is aiming to make a break from some other direction. From appearances, another bat. He may be expected somewhere about Richmond. My own opinion is that the yankees do not intend to make an attack upon us here, but have been merely making feints in this direction, to draw troops from Richmond. But they have failed in this. I expect the storm will break loose somewhere before long. May God grant us complete victory and speedy peace.

J.J. Hoyle

Camp Campbell
August 31st 1862

My Dear wife:

Your kind letter was received yesterday, and I was very glad to hear from you. Dear Sarah I often think how lonesome you are; and feel so sorry that I cannot be with you. All that is dear to me on earth would I freely give up for the enjoyment of your companionship again. Dear Sarah we can now tell how much we love each other. O what would you not give to have me back with you again? I know you would give all the world did you posses it.

Dear Sarah it does me good to think that though we are many miles apart, yet we are joined in heart. Let us hope and pray that the happy time is near at hand when I will be permitted to return home again. No body knows what it is to be separated from home and loved ones but those who have to try it. I am trying to live right, and am happy to say that by God's grace I have been able to withstand all the evil influences which are prevalent in camp. We hold prayer meetings at our tent every favorable night; some interest seems to be manifested in it and, I hope it may turn out for good. Our company is still sickly. The mumps have made a new start among us. Five of our men have them now, among them are John and Henry Cline, and Wade McClurd.[57] Isaac is not well this morning. Rook is staying in a hospital tent near by. He is about like common. I know he ought to have a discharge but it is hard to get one here. I intend to talk to Capt Mull today about his case. The 54th regiment left here for Petersburg night before last. We do not expect that we will have to leave. But we would be rather weak handed if the yankees was to come upon us now, as there is but one regiment of infantry here now. I want you to write me whether you received this letter and other piece of writing I sent you by McClurd or not. I am not needing any more clothes just now, but will want some after a while. I will let you know when I want them. Our elec-

tion for lieutenants has not come on yet and I do not know when it will. The capt. Told me if there was any chance, he would have me in. I have drilled the company several times lately. But I must close for the present. Write every week, and write all the news you can. Your loving husban
S.A. Hoyle   J.J. Hoyle

Hope in the Lord and pray much; for the Lord will hear faithful prayers. Remember your kind husban in prayer. I continually ask the Lord to take care of my dear wife while I am gone. Write how you are all getting along at Saint Peters.[58] Give my love to all the family. <u>Remember me.</u>

The following letter to Lemuel Self, Joseph Hoyle's father-in-law, was sent to Sarah Hoyle along with the above letter.

Dear Father in-law:
I take the pleasure of dropping you a few lines, informing you that I am well, and I hope these lines may find you well. I have enjoyed good health since I returned to camp; except a bad cough which has not finally left me yet. We are getting along very well here now. We have not had any march in some time. There is considerable sickness in the regiment. The 17th regiment arrived here last night, and have put up tents to-day. Reports say General Pope is retreating before old Stonewall Jackson. General Stewart (cavalry) made a break upon Pope's army a few days ago, and entirely routed him. Our side took a good many prisoners. They got General Popes two horses, his saddle and bridle, sword, and uniform coat.[59] The federals are said to be giving back also in the west.[60] And viewing the whole, our armies are in a very prosperous condition now. I pray that God may so continue our success that our northern foe may see the impractibility of his design and be constrained to give us a speedy peace. Write whenever you can. As ever, your affectionate Son in law,
Lemuel Self   J.J. Hoyle

Camp Campbell
September 1st, 1862
Dear wife:
I take the pleasure of writing you a few lines. I am well as usual. I have been washing my shirt and breeches this evening. I thought I never could learn to wash, but I do not find it as hard a job as I expected. I find I cannot pay for every thing; so I concluded to wash for myself. We have to pay high for the fruit, watermelons, &c. that we get here. I do not buy many of them, and one reason is I cannot afford it. If a person would buy

every thing he sees and wants here his wages would not pay his expenses. We hear no talk of any yankees about here now. We have not had to take any marches in several weeks and I hope we may not have to take any more. But there is no telling when we may have to start. May the God of battles ever go with us. We have a great many reports here. Sometimes we have news that gives us hopes of a speedy peace; then directly we have a contrary report; and so it goes. I still have hopes that the good Lord will soon give us peace again. Let us trust the Lord and he will not forsake us. As ever, yours in hope
S.A. Hoyle   J.J. Hoyle

Camp Campbell
Sept. 12th 1862.

My Dear Wife:

I received your kind letter by Mrs. Cline a few hours ago, and was very glad to hear from you, as I always am. I expect you will be uneasy because you did not receive any letter last week; But the reason was I had not the chance to write. We left camp on last Wednesday week, the day after Rooker left and marched till Friday evening, when we halted about 10 miles from Washington, N.C. There we rested till 10. O'clock in the night, and then started to attack the yankees at Washington. We traveled till about day light when we arrived at the town and the battle commenced immediately. Some of our men backed out the first fire, but the balance of us charged into town, the balls whistling all around us, and some getting shot down. We succeeded in running the yankees out of town, but they commenced shelling us from their gun-boats, and we had to retreat. The battle lasted near three hours. Our loss does not exceed thirty five in killed, wounded and missing. Capt Mull was badly wounded in the left breast. Samuel Young of our company is missing.[61] All the rest of our company came through safe. Andrew McClurd had a hole shot through his coat sleave and breast, though it never touched the flesh.[62] It was a very fright-ful time, but I felt perfectly calm all the time. I did not feel frighted in the least. In fact I never thought that a bullet would hit me. The good Lord kept me from harm, to whom be all the praise. You will see a full account of the affair in the Spirit of the Age. We arrived to camp again last Tuesday having been gone seven days and marched 130 miles. The march was very hard. The news is very cheering from all our armies now. Our forces have crossed the Potomac and are making toward Washington City.[63] I pray God will so bless our arms with success as to speedily bring our enemies to terms of peace. I received the handkerchief you sent me and be sure it came in a good time; for I was out of one. I sincerely pray that the good Lord will grant you your request and return me to your fond embrace again. This is my utmost desire on earth, that I might be priviledged to return and live with my dear wife again.

Dear Sarah pray in faith and God will hear you. You wrote like you was afraid I would not come home if I should get the chance. Dear Sarah, you need not fear of that I want to come home as bad as you want me to come, and be assured if I get the chance I will come. But I fear there will be no chance till the war ends. The 51 regt. arrived here today and also a Regt. Of cavalry passed on to Kinston. There may be something in the wind, but we know not what. Pray that the Lord may protect us. I should be very glad to see you, but alas we are far apart, though we have one consolation we are joined in heart.   Yours in hope,
S.A. Hoyle   J.J. Hoyle

I almost forgot to tell you I was well. One happy thought still cheers my heart, that I shall again meet my loving wife on earth, and enjoy the sweet blessings of her delightful company. O deny me not this one desire. All other earthly good I _____ would give to secure this my only hope of earthly bliss. Remember your loving husban Dear Sallie.

The following letter was printed in the September 15, 1862 issue of the *Spirit of the Age.*

Camp Campbell, near Kinston, Sept. 10, '62.
Mr. Editor: A brief account of the late affair at Washington, N.C., by a participant, may prove of some interest to at least some of your numerous readers. For the satisfaction of the friends of our (55th) Regiment, I will give a brief detail of our march, &c. On the 2d inst., we were drawn up in line, when Col. Connelly announced that he wanted 200 men from the regiment "*to fight,*" and that he wanted them to volunteer.(Nearly all stepped out as volunteers for the intended service. Two companies of 100 men each were then formed and placed under the command of Capt. Mull and Capt. Smith, respectively. We then had orders to cook three days rations and prepare to march early next morning. Accordingly, on the morning of the 3d, we took up the line of march, accompanied by two companies of 100 men each from the 17th regiment and the commanded by Capt. Norman of the 17th, directing our course towards Greenville. On the evening of the 4th, we passed through Greenville, crossed Tar River and directed our course down the river toward Washington, which we learned,

was the object of our expedition. On the morning of the 5th we were joined by 150 men from the 8th N.C., making our force 550 men, all told. On we hastened, till about 4 o'clock, P.M. when we halted in about 7 miles of Washington. There we were joined by about 200 cavalry. About 10 P.M., we set out for the attack, taking a circuitous route in order to surprise the enemy. We marched on till full day-break, when we reached the edge of town. Our advance immediately attacked the outer guard and drove them in. This first fire from the guard confused the greater part of our men, and consequently they became disorganized; but after some time, the greater part were rallied and advanced into town. The fight now commenced in earnest. The yankees were concealed in lots and cellars, from which they shot at our men. Their batteries, which were so planted as to sweep the streets, now opened upon us, but with little effect, as the shot generally passed entirely over our heads. (But prior to this, our cavalry had made a charge into town, and drove the yankee cavalry (500) entirely out. Capt. Tucker's company was most conspicuous in this dash. Finally we succeeded in driving the enemy to his gunboats, except at one battery. We have taken five pieces of his artillery which were turned upon him with effect. The gunboats had commenced their old trade of shelling and as our men were in no condition to do further execution we retreated, carrying with us the cannon we had taken. Our loses in killed, wounded and missing does not exceed 35, over two-thirds of whom are wounded and missing. The enemy's loss was evidently much greater, including 12 prisoners. Report says 150 killed. Had it not been for the panic that arose among our men, our success would have been complete. The following is a partial list of the casualties in the 55th Regiment.[64]

> Co. F.— Capt. Mull badly, if not mortally wounded. Missing —
> Samuel Young.
> Co. C.— Killed, W.B. Weaver. Wounded T. Mitchen, in the arm.
> J.P. Roach, in the thigh. Missing, B.M. White.
> Co. D.— Missing, Thomas Greene.[65]

Captain Mull was wounded while gallantly leading his men against one of the enemy's batteries. His loss is very severely felt among the men of his Company to whom he had endeared himself very much. We returned to camp on yesterday, having been gone seven days, and marched 130 miles. The trip cost us a great deal of endurance and suffering, yet our men bore up with fortitude commendable of the noble cause in which we are enlisted.

J.J. H****
Co. F 55th Reg N C T

Five miles below Kinston, N.C.

Sept 18th, 1862.

My dear wife:

I am well at present and I hope this may find you well. We are on the march again. We left camp yesterday morning, and came here till last night, and have remained here all day to-day. We do not know when we will leave or where we will go to. Some say we will take up winter quarters somewhere down here; Others think we will attack Newberne (I do not think so). But we privates never know what we have to do till we get into it. Our pickets extend about 20 miles below here. So you see we are not very near the enemy yet, but a days march would take us there. We have orders to cook 2 days rations this evening, and it may be we will move someway to-night or to-morrow. I trust the good Lord will be with us and shield us from harm.

Dear Sarah, it makes my heart very sorry when I think how we are separated, but I pray continually that God will privilege us to meet again on earth, and spend the remainder of our days together. Yet dear Sarah, this is the only earthly good I desire, yet if it is not his will to grant us this desire, I hope we will enjoy eternal happiness in heaven. This is our only safe hope. Let us live Christians. It does me good to think that we are united in Christ. I believe the good Lord suffered your guardian angel to come near me last night as I lay sleeping on the ground: for I had such a sweet dream about you.(As ever, yours in hope.

S.A. Hoyle J.J. Hoyle

This is written very badly as I have a bad chance to write. I have nothing to write on but my cartridge box.

The following letter was printed in the September 22, 1862, issue of the *Spirit of the Age.*

National Repentance.

All governments are swayed by the hand of Providence; for we are taught in Holy writ, that *'the powers that be are ordained of God.'* The Old Testament contains sufficient instances, in connection with the history of the Jewish nation, to convince any man that God fundamentally directs the political concerns of man. This being admitted, it follows, as in the case of individuals, that God confers blessings or curses upon a nation, as it gives obeisance to His laws, or spurns his holy teachings.

This being established as a standard, it is easy to trace out the primary cause of our present difficulties.

God saw the oppression of our forefathers and delivered them from the yoke of tyranny. He gave their country nationality, and by His blessings, out of the western wilds a vigorous and promising nation was built up. It was permitted to add attainment to attainment, till it equaled if not excelled the most renowned nation of the eastern continent. Now in all this, God had a design, and that design was none other than that for which He created man — that His name might be glorified. All His designs are ultimately in furtherance of His grand design for the salvation of the human race. But unfortunately for our once happy nation, it thwarted the design of its creation. — With celebrity, came arrogance and pride; with wealth, came cheating and defrauding; with honor came depraved ambition with its retinue of evils. The crimes of our nation became "great," and its sins "very grievous." So He determined to scourge us for our iniquities, and justly entailed upon us this cruel war, with all its horrid consequences. His righteous judgments are visited upon us.

Now as His wrath burns against us on account of our sins, and as he holds the hearts of men in His hands, it follows that our deliverance must come through His agency alone. But God cannot, consistent with His attributes, deliver us from this scourge of war, while we continue in that course which brought it on us.

We must repent! Yea, we must bow down in *sack cloth and ashes. Repentance, humiliation* and *reformation* can only bring the approving smiles of a righteous God upon our young Confederacy; and these will as surely bring them, as cause produces effect. The teachings of the Bible confirm this proposition at every point.

Now we are prepared to ask the question: Have we indeed repented, as a nation? True, we have made some show of national repentance, but have we as a people humbled ourselves in heart? Have we cast off all idle amusements and worldly pleasures, and besought the Lord with sincerity of heart in our behalf? In a word, I ask, have we repented as a people, in the full sense of the word?

Look at the corrupt cravings of depraved humanity, in the form of fraud, speculation, cheating, &c. Look at the arrogance and pride conspicuous in all our cities and towns. Look at the corrupt aspirations of hell-born ambition; look at the great amount of wickedness prevalent among our soldiers; and then answer if we have bowed down in the dust of true repentance?

Will a righteous God deliver us while we continue in these things? We have no promise that He will yea, we have no hope, based upon the Bible, that he will.

I earnestly entreat every man and woman to earnestly consider from whence our deliverance must come, and the means, on our part, to be used in procuring it.—The matter earnestly commends itself to every individual in the Confederacy.

"At thy rebuke, O God of Jacob, both the chariot and horse are cast into a dead sleep. Thou, even thou art to be feared; and who may stand in the sight when once thou art angry."

Read the eighth chapter of Deuteronomy.

J. J. H****,
Co. F, 55th Regt. N. C. Troops.

---

5 miles below Kinston,
Oct 2nd, 1862.

My Dear wife:

I take the pleasure of dropping you a few lines this evening to let you know that I am well at present and I hope this may find you well. We left Trenton yesturday morning, and after a hard days march reached here last night. The yankees were advancing on Kinston and we were ordered up here to help keep them back; but they have gone back now. We expected the yankees would beat us here and thus cut us off, but they did not. We have a report this evening that we are ordered to Virginia, but I do not know how true it is. We have a first lieutenant appointed over us by the Col. He is a perfect stranger to us, and every body is perfectly mad this evening.

Dear Sarah we have seen some hard times for the last two weeks, but I have endured it all very well. I trust in the Lord that he will speedily deliver us from this war. Let us love him with all our hearts and all will be well with us. I would be very glad to see you and enjoy the sweet smile of my dear little wife and more. But if I am not permitted to enjoy this, I trust I shall enjoy your sweet communion in the world above. I did not receive any letter from you last week. If we do go to Virginia I will write to you immediately. Do not send me my closes yet awhile without you think you will not have a chance to send them after a while. Yours in hope.

S.A. Hoyle   J.J. Hoyle

---

4. From Petersburg to Suffolk, October 1862–May 1863

"We have been in the heat of battle"

The 55th North Carolina arrived in the vicinity of Petersburg, Virginia, on October 4, 1862, bivouacking about four miles from the city. The regiment spent most of the month of October drilling, building breastworks, and repairing roads to ease the movement of Confederate artillery. On occasion, intermittent Federal shelling from nearby gunboats forced the soldiers to take cover, but they were quickly able to continue their work.[1]

During this time the unit was not assigned to a brigade but placed under the authority of Major General Samuel French, who commanded the Department of North Carolina and southern Virginia. On October 29 the regiment was ordered to relocate their camp, which they had named Camp French, in honor of their new commander, west of Petersburg near the Model Farm. French placed the 55th in charge of performing provost duty in the city, which at times proved hazardous to those ordered to keep the streets clear of drunks and shirkers.[2]

Disease incapacitated a good number of the regiment's fighting men throughout the winter months. Mumps, pneumonia, typhoid, and smallpox were just some of the ailments that weakened the overall strength of the 55th during its time near Petersburg. The lack of winter clothing may have attributed to the ever-growing number of men who were unable to perform their duties due to sickness. In mid–December, Adjutant Henry T. Jordan wrote a letter to the *North Carolina Standard* describing the harsh conditions his fellow soldiers were experiencing and pleaded for the families of these men to send as much as possible. Although North Carolina would be known as one of the Confederate states that kept their troops well clothed, it is apparent that during this time of the war at least some North Carolina regiments were not receiving the necessary supplies.[3]

The men in the 55th North Carolina spent most of the remaining months of that winter drilling and performing provost duty in Petersburg. By the beginning of February, the regiment finally received winter clothing. However, not having been paid since October, many men were forced to sell their newly arrived garments to make money to purchase other necessities and to support their loved ones at home.

By the end of February, the unit was relieved of its provost duty and ordered to protect a ford across the Blackwater River. The men spent some time establishing Camp Green, located near Franklin Depot. The soldiers had no tents, but were able to construct shanties to help protect them from the elements. As the days passed into March, the colder weather began to subside and the 55th North Carolina was reassigned to the brigade of Brigadier General Joseph R. Davis, the Confederate president's nephew. This assignment became permanent at the end of March.[4]

The regiment's move was in accordance with the Confederate concern that the Federals were planning a move against their forces in southeastern Virginia. The officials in Richmond took notice when Major General Burnside and his IX Corps were moved to Newport News. Burnside and his 15,000 men began their move on February 7. This shifting of troops caused a panic in the Confederate capital, because many officials believed this move to be similar to McClellan's Peninsula Campaign. President Davis and his advisors had no way of knowing that this move was simply an attempt by President Lincoln to alleviate tension between Burnside and Major General Joseph Hooker, who replaced Burnside as commander of the Army of the Potomac on January 25, 1863. With the arrival of the IX Corps, the Federals had some 36,000 troops stationed in southeastern Virginia, which meant the Confederates were outnumbered three to one. If the Federals made a move on Petersburg or invaded North Carolina, the scant Southern forces in the region would be unable to stop them.

To counter the Union's possible plans, General Lee ordered Major General George Pickett's division to Richmond and instructed Major General John Bell Hood to have his force prepared to move if the Federals made any advance toward Petersburg or Richmond. Lee then ordered Lieutenant General James Longstreet to take command of the Department of Virginia and North Carolina. By mid–March Longstreet's attention was focused on gathering supplies from North Carolina and southeastern Virginia. These much needed provisions would help feed Lee's hungry army in the months to come.[5]

In addition to collecting supplies, Longstreet began contemplating a move to recapture Suffolk from the Federals. He believed if the Confederates could successfully take the city, the Confederates could expand their foraging parties into the land around the Chowan and Blackwater rivers, which were rich with bacon, saltwater fish, and corn. This would also bottle up the

Federals in Suffolk, and therefore protect Petersburg and Richmond.⁶ Longstreet's siege of Suffolk directly engaged the 55th North Carolina and forced
the unit into its first experience under heavy fire. The campaign not only
honored the 55th, but also paved the way for many future engagements. Colonel Connally's official report confirms his belief that the regiment's performance deserved praise.

> I have the honor to state that in compliance with Special Orders, Numbers 3,
> Headquarters French's Command, dated April 17, three companies from my
> regiment marched on Friday night, the 17th, to Norfleet's house, on the
> Reed's Ferry road, and on Saturday morning, the 18th, reported to Major
> Shumaker for duty, as specified in the order. The fort intended for the recep-
> tion of the two 32-pounder rifled pieces which my regiment was to support
> not having been completed, a detail of 60 men was, by order of Major Shu-
> maker, made from the three companies to finish it. This having been done on
> Saturday evening, the 18th, the guns were placed in position during the night.
> On Saturday night, the 18th, I moved with the seven remaining companies of
> my regiment to Norfleet's house, and some time during the evening commu-
> nicated with Major Shumaker, who advised me to place 4 men and a corporal
> at Le Compte's house, 4 men and a corporal at Reed's Ferry, 4 men and a
> corporal at a point nearly equi-distant between Le Compte's house and the
> ferry, and a company at Moore's house to support the three points men-
> tioned. He also advised me to place a company near the gate at the entrance
> of the field in which the battery of 32-pounder pieces was situated to support
> it. In addition to this advice I received an order from General French in exact
> accordance with the major's advice, except that the company placed at
> Moore's should be placed at Le Compte's house. In posting my men I obeyed
> General French's ordered to the letter except as to placing a company at Le
> Compte's house. This I did not do because Major Shumaker told me that he
> was thoroughly acquainted with the posts mentioned, and that it was better
> to place the company at Moore's, which I did. On Sunday evening, the 19th,
> Colonel Cunningham rode up to my quarters some time between 4 and 6
> o'clock and told me in substance — I do not remember his language — that
> General French wished me to support the batteries. The order was general,
> and I immediately ordered Lieutenant-Colonel Smith and Major [A. H.] Belo
> to go and ascertain the position of the batteries, the number of men necessary
> for their support, the ground to be occupied by the support, and to report to
> me as early as possible. They had not been gone more than an hour or an
> hour and a half when I heard loud cheering in the direction of the river. A
> few moments afterwards an officer (I know not who) rode up and reported
> that Stribling's battery had been charged by the enemy and captured. I imme-
> diately ordered my regiment under arms, left one company at Moore's house
> to support the three posts mentioned above, two companies at the gate
> referred to support the battery of 32-pounder pieces, and with the seven
> other companies proceeded as rapidly as possible to the house nearest Strib-
> ling's battery, which was in the fort known as the Old Fort. There I came up

with Captain [L. R.] Terrell, General Law's assistant adjutant-general, with
two companies from the Forty-eighth Alabama Regiment. I inquired of the
captain what he was doing there, and learned that he had been sent by General Law with the two companies mentioned to relieve the two companies
which were in the fort when it was captured. He stated that he had arrived
too late — that the fort had been taken before he could render assistance. I
had never been to the fort, knew nothing of its position or the grounds
around it, and asked Captain Terrell if he could give me any information
concerning it, telling him that I intended to charge and retake the guns. He
stated that he had been to the fort and knew all about its position; that it was
situated on a point of land extending down to the river and that there was a
deep ravine or marsh in its front over which my men could not possibly
charge. In addition to this the fort was defended by six gunboats — three
above and three below — and two land batteries across the river. In intended
to charge and retake the fort, if possible, but upon learning its position and
defense from Captain Terrell knew that it would be worse than folly to make
the attempt. Wishing, however, to ascertain if it was still occupied by the
enemy I moved up to within some 500 or 600 yards of the fort, formed line
of battle, and ordered the men to lie down. I then ordered Lieutenant-Colonel Smith, with two companies deployed as skirmishers, to advance until fired
upon, then to fall back upon the regiment. He had not advanced more than
50 or 60 yards before he was fired upon by the enemy's skirmishers, and, as
ordered, fell back. The fire of my skirmishers discovered to the enemy the
position of the regiment, when they opened upon me a heavy cross-fire from
the six gunboats and two batteries. I immediately withdrew my regiment out
of range of their grape-shot, and, thinking they would probably advance with
the intention of capturing the battery of 32-pounder pieces in my rear,
formed a second line of battle about half a mile from the Old Fort, threw forward skirmishers under command of Major Belo, and, although shelled from
the gunboats, awaited patiently the enemy's advance until, I suppose, about 1
A.M., when General Law came up and told me that I was too far in advance
and to fall back upon the skirt of woods some quarter of a mile in my rear;
also to draw in my line of skirmishers. I obeyed General Law's orders. this, as
stated above, was about 1 o'clock. At daylight, or very soon thereafter, General Hood came up and placed me under command of General Robertson,
with whom I remained until near sundown, when I was ordered by General
Hood, through General Robertson, to rejoining my brigade. General Law not
attempting to retake the fort during the night of the 19th, and General Hood
not attempting it on the 20th, establishes the fact that the attempt would
have been injudicious, and that I was fortunate in meeting with Captain Terrell, whose statement relative or its position and defense alone prevented my
making it. It will be seen, major, from this report that I did not have any
men in or near the fort when it was captured; that it was attacked so soon
after Colonel Cunningham left me that I could not possibly have placed men
in position for its support; that when captured two companies from General
Law's brigade were moving forward to relieve the two companies which were

in it, and that I moved with all possible dispatch to recapture the fort, had it been possible. As I was the commanding officer on the field at the time, I deem it my duty to give Captain Terrell's statement concerning the action of the two companies under his command, which was that all the men in the two companies deserted him except nine. I do not know the names of the nine men who remained with the captain or I would give them, thinking they deserve favorable notice. The fire upon my regiment, as you may well imagine, was very heavy indeed, yet both officers and men received it unflinchingly and with veteran-like steadiness. Lieutenant-Colonel Smith, Major Belo, and Adjt. [H. T.] Jordan behaved with the utmost coolness and gallantry. I had 10 men wounded (1 mortally) and 1 man missing, supposed to have been killed.[7]

Joseph Hoyle received a promotion to Sergeant on November 25, 1863. He spent Christmas Day away from his loving wife, Sarah, but was delighted to see her when she visited him at the regiment's camp in January.

Joseph Hoyle was well liked and well known in his company. On March 11, 1863, he was elected 1st Lieutenant. With Captain Mull still suffering from the wounds he received at Washington, Hoyle was in command of Company F most of the time until his death. He received a furlough in February and spent more time with his wife and family. This would be the last time Sarah saw him alive.

The following letter was written by Joseph Hoyle on October 5, 1862. The original is not among his letters. However, a typed version is included and was used for this book. Who retyped the letter and when is not known.

Petersburg, Va
Oct. 5th 1862

My Dear wife:

I hasten to drop you a few lines to let you know that we have arrived here. We left camp Campbell evening before last and arrived here yesterday about 12 o'clock. We will pitch camp three or four miles from the city. The regiment moved out here last evening but I was detailed to take care of our baggage which is still at the old fort. We will get it hauled into the camp this morning. Petersburg is a large place and much of interest may be seen here though we have not had a chance to go about the city. I received a letter from [_____] He helped a [frightened?] [_____] That was well after hrs before [_____] when we first began to fight and this army came through [_____] I have no war news of interest to tell. I hate this bloody strife many soldiers [have died?] since I received your letter. John Mull was [or was not?] very glad to read it, but I must close this [and send?] your letter to a post.[8]

As ever your loving husban,

J.J. Hoyle
Sarah Hoyle

Direct your letters to Petersburg, Va with a request to forward.

The following letter was printed in the October 6, 1862, issue of the *Spirit of the Age*.

Trenton, N.C., Sept 28.

Mr Editor:— The 55th N.C.T. now occupies quarters at this place. We left camp Campbell on the 17th, and after some delay on the road arrived here on the 23d. All has been quiet since we came here; though an attack was anticipated a few nights since — we lay under arms all night. Our pickets report the enemy closely confined to Newbern. It is not for me to say how much force is about here, but should the enemy come out, I guess he will find somebody watching. Col. Connolly and staff made a reconnoisance in the direction of Newbern yesterday. When within about six miles of Newbern, they came in contact with the yankee pickets, charged them and drove them some distance, when a well constructed fence, built for the purpose, arrested their further progress. The enemy took several deliberate fires from behind this obstruction at our heroes, but without effect. Part of the pickets were said to be negroes. This was a daring exploit, and will teach the wretches what they may expect, should they come beyond their fortifications. The health of our regiment is not good.— All our sick (nearly) have been sent to the hospital at Goldsboro and Raleigh. As a specimen of our condition, I will state that our Co. (F) numbers 76, and only 32 report for duty. We hope our friends will not forget us in their supplications at the throne of mercy. Remember our beloved, yet bleeding country, also. God will hear faithful prayer.

J.J. H****,
Co. F, 55th Reg., N.C.T.

Camp French, near Petersburg, Va,
Oct 8th, 1862

My Dear wife:

I take the pleasure of dropping you a few lines, informing you that I am well at present. We landed at Petersburg last Saturday, but I was detailed to stay with the bagage and did not get out to the regiment till Sunday. Our present camp is about 4 miles from Petersburg. There is no

likelyhood of an attack here, but we may be marched off to meet the
enemy at any time. The yankees are said to have a large force at Suffolk
about 60 miles from here, and an idea prevails that our forces will attack
them.[9] We heard firing all morning this morning in the direction of the
city Point. It was, probably, the enemy's gunboats in James River. They
come up the James river every now and then and throw a few shells at our
batteries. I visited Petersburg yesturday. It is fare ahead of all places I ever
seen. I cannot give you any account of it here. General Petigrew's brigade
(5 regiments) is at this place. I went over to the 26 regiment to-day, and
found A.B. Hays, my old schoolmate.[10] Of course we were very glad to see
each other.

Sarah, I have to mourn the loss of my dearest friend. R.M. Sherrill
died at Richmond on the 8th of Sept. You know he was my dearest friend,
and well he deserved my most worth affections; for he was among the cho-
sen noble young men. I feel that his place cannot easily be filled. Sarah, I
loved him as a brother, and I hope to meet him on the shores of eternal
bliss. I trust his soul is gone to rest. Sarah, I know you will not think that I
mean he was nearer to me than you are. I count you nearer to me than a
friend. You are my loving wife, the nearest earthly object to my heart.
Hence you are not included under the name of friend. You are more than a
friend. I hope the Lord will take care of you, an fill your dear little heart
with his holy love. I pray continually that he will permit us to meet and
spend the remainder of our days together, this is my only earthly desire.
But dear Sarah, if we are denied this privilege, I trust we are certain of a
better one, and that is of meeting in heaven. Let us love the lord with our
whole heart and He will do all that is good for us. I would like to come
home and see you but there is no chance to get a furlough now. I do not
want you to send me any clothes yet, for I cannot carry them if we have to
march. If you have me a pair of boots or shoes made, you may send them
by Dr. Osborne. We drew $10 a piece of our money the other day, and will
draw about as much more in a short time. If you need any money I want
you to let me know it. Write how you are getting along for money and salt.
I hope you will not neglect to write. Direct your letters to Petersburg, Va.
&c., I rec. a letter from L.S. Self a few days ago, he was well. The following is his address. I have lost his letter in coming here. As ever your loving
husban,
S.A. Hoyle   J.J. Hoyle

Though many miles apart, yet we are joined in the heart. My wife to me so
dear, is far from my sight yet I feel her love so near, and can say all is
right. Dear Sarah Remember me Till we meet again.

Camp French, Va.
Oct 17th, 1862

My Dear Wife:

I take the pleasure of dropping you a few lines this morning, inform-ing you that I am well at present, and I hope this will find you well. I received your kind letter by Rufus and read it with pleasure, for you must know that it makes my heart glad to receive a letter from you.[11] I would be glad if you could make your letters longer. Dear Sarah, write just what you would talk to me if I was there by your side while you are writing. I would be more than glad to see you and talk with you, but there is no telling when I can get an opportunity to come home. There is no chance for a furlough. The col. Tried to get a furlough for himself for only 2 days and could not get it. So you see there is no chance for a private. The pants you sent me fit me <u>jam up</u>, except they are a most too tight around the waist. You did not know how much I have fattened. I am a great deal fleshier now than when I left home. The cloth, I think is the prettiest jeans I ever saw. Every body here praises it. The nice letters you set upon the waist is also worthy of comment. I feel truly thankful to the good Lord for giving me such a kind and loving wife, and I am truly sorry that I have to be parted from her that I love the most of all earthly objects. Dear wife, I do pray that the good Lord will privilege us to meet before long. O that this cruel war would close. Dear wife, we are joined in heart, yes joined in christ and we will one day join in presences. O how it cheers my heart to think of meeting my dear Sarah. Dear wife, I cannot write as I fell. My heart is with you. Take care of it.

Dear Sarah, all is quiet about here. Our time is taken up in drilling and working on fortifications. I expect we will take up winter quarters here, if nothing takes place to prevent it. We fare just tolerably well here. We get meat and bread, and a little rice to eat, and not very plenty of that. We have nothing but branch-water to use. We have been digging a well, but we came to a marl bead and had to quit it. Every thing is very high here. Sweet potatoes are $4 per bushel, apples 30 or 40 cts per dozen and every kind of nick nack very high. Dear Sarah dont fail to write, and write long letters. I remain, as ever, your loving husban,

S.A. Hoyle   J.J. Hoyle

Petersburg, Va.,
Oct. 31st., 1862

My Dear Wife:

I received two letters from you yesterday, and was very glad to hear from you. I was sorry to hear that you do not get my letters regularly, for I have written every week. I am happy to inform you that I am well, except some biles on my legs. I have fattened up a great deal. If you could see me, I do not know whether you would hardly know me, but I guess you would soon find me out, at any rate, I would like to come home and see. We are now camped in the edge of Petersburg, about one mile south of the Weldon depo. We came here yesturday. I expect we will stay here this winter. We have very good houses here to stay in and if we stay here this winter, I think we will live very comfortable as soldiers. Our Regiment will have to act as provost guard in the city.

Dear Sarah, I know you do not want to see me more than I want to see you and whenever I can get an opportunity I will certainly come home. The exemption bill does not cover my case. It does not apply to persons now in service.[12] But there is a chance for me to get off any how, and I wrote to you and your father in my last letter how to proceed. You will have to get up a petition there asking the Secretary of War to detach me from the army for the purpose of tending my mills, stating that otherwise they will be subject to stop, and get the people to sign it and send it to the Secretary of War at Richmond. It would be best for you to send it here to me first, and I can have it sent on. You would do well to take a copy of it so if the one you send should get lost, you will still have one. This should be attended to at once. If your father and the people want me to come and tend my mills. I am willing to come, if I can get off in this way. If not I am willing to stay in the army. I am as willing as any other man to fight for my country; and although I desire nothing more ardently than to come home and live with you again and will certainly do so if an opportunity affords, yet I feel like I ought to stay with my fellow-soldiers, and shear my fate with theirs.

Dear Sarah, we have some very good news this morning, and I ardently hope it will come to pass. Northern papers state that England and France will soon make a requisition on Lincolns government for a cessation of hostilities, and if this is refused, they will recognize the Confederacy.[13] This news is said to have come from official sources. If this takes place, I think it will be the beginning of a peace, at least. Dear Sarah, sometimes I think that the good Lord will privilege us to meet before long. Let us hope and pray for it; for the Lord has promised to hear faithful prayer. I received a letter from Wm & Berryman yesterday, they were under marching orders but they know not where. This is our day to draw provisions, so I must close for the present. As ever, your loving husban,
My loving wife, S.A. Hoyle, Forever thine   J.J. Hoyle

Give my best wishes to all, and especially to your father and mother. I sent you a few needles and stamps, write whether you received them or not. Isaac and Rufus are well. Isaac is on guard duty in town and Rufus is gone with a wagon after a load of fodder. Eli Newton has joined our co. as a private.

Petersburg, Va.,
Nov. 7th, 1862

My Dear Wife,

I take the pleasure of writing you a few lines, informing you that I am well and I hope this will find you well. I have a very bad chance to write today, and my letter will necessarily be short. It has been snowing all day and the ground is covered several inches now and it continues to snow. We have a house to stay in but it has no chimney yet, but we have fire in it today any how, and the smoke has nearly put my eyes out. When we get chimneys to all our houses, we will have very comfortable quarters. But we have to be on guard every third day and sometimes every other day. I will have to go on guard in town tomorrow. This will be my first time, and I expect it will be a very cold time. The reason I have to do guard duty is, that the Col. Has abolished the company commissaries, imposing that duty on the Orderly Sergeant. I have no news of interest. I do hope this cruel war will soon end and we may all get home again. Sweet home! If any body in the world knows the worth of home, the poor soldier does. Imagine the weary sentinel, as he plods his lonely post in the freezing snow. How hard is his lot. I know you will not fail to pray for us. Sarah, I have such a poor chance, that I cannot write like I want to. There is a talk that we will get furloughs to come home after a while. Our regiment will stay here this winter to guard in the city, and it may be some of us will get to come home. I would like for you to come down and see me. Now will be a good chance for you to come if you want to, as we will be certain to stay here. Uncle Peter Mull has wrote for his wife to come, and said I should write for you to come along.[14]

Dear Sarah, I should be very glad to see you. You can write to me about it in your next letter. If you come or get a chance to send it, I want my overcoat. I renewed my subscription to the Spirit of the Age, and directed to have it sent to your name. So I suppose it will come, after this, in your name. I am getting so cold that I will have to close. Pray the Lord to take care of me. I hope He will soon return me to you again. Give my love to all the family. Isaac & Rufus are well, they were in town last night, and did not quite freeze. Be sure and write. As ever your loving Husban,

J. J. Hoyle
S. A. Hoyle

Petersburg, Va.
Nov. 9th, 1862

My Dear Wife:

I wrote you a letter yesterday, but as I have just received one from you, and have a chance of sending this by Mrs. White, I will drop you a few more lines. I read your kind letter with much satisfaction; for I am always glad to hear from you. I was on guard duty yesturday and last night in Petersburg. I was Sergeant of the guard at the jail. I had a warm house to lie in, but I did not get to sleep any, as I had to change the reliefs every two hours. I met up with a friend P. J. Johnson this morning. He belongs to Longstreets Corps and they have fallen back on this side of Culpeper Court house. He says Lee's entire army will fall back in order to obtain supplies. Reports say the yankees still keep advancing on Weldon. They seem determine to try it, and no doubt with a large force as this would be one of the most important places they could take. Our men are preparing to defend it. Troops are passing through Petersburg every day. We may look for an important battle in this vicinity before long, if the yankees come on.

Dear Sarah, I have almost forgotten all about that little slip I wrote you. So I cannot now write it so you would understand it. I hope I will get home some day and then I will explain it to you. If I cannot get off entirely, I hope I will get a furlough to come home after a while. Sarah, I would be so glad to see you, and how my heart leaps for joy when I think of seeing you again. This is the greatest earthly bliss I ever expect to enjoy. O will not the good Lord grant me this one desire. Sarah, let us pray that he will speedily privilege us to join in presence again. The Lord has said that he will withhold no good thing from them that love him. Sarah, you said you would write more if you could spell right. This is no excuse for I can read your letters very well so you need not make short letters on this account. Sarah, you think I can not read your letters but this is a mistake. I can read them very well. I have seen a great deal worse writing than yours. Remember your loving husban; though, he be far away, yet you are ever near his heart, and dear Sarah, you know I have a true heart. As ever, your loving husban,

J. J. Hoyle
Mrs. S. A. Hoyle

Petersburg, Va.
Friday, Nov. 21st, 1862

My Dear Wife:

I take the pleasure of writing you a few lines informing you that I am well at present. I came back to the company day before yesturday, after being gone nine days. I was one of the guard in taking some prisoners to fort caswell below Wilmington, N.C.[15] I wrote you a few lines when I was in Wilmington last week.[16] We staid in Wilmington from Wednesday evening till Saturday evening. We then took the steam boat and went down to fort caswell. We arrived at the fort a little after dark, and delivered up our prisoners. No boat went up on Sunday so we staid at the fort till Monday morning. We spent the time on Sunday looking at the curiosities around here. The ocean is in a short distance of the fort, and it is a matter of much interest to view it. I always have desired to see the Sea, and now I have seen it. I sent you some shells by Procter which I picked up on the beach. I can not now tell you of the many interesting things I saw, but I hope I may get home to tell you of them. I saw Robert Lacky in Wilmington. He is shoe making for the government at Greensboro. I found Capt. Mull and Dr. Osborne here when I got back, and I was very glad to see them; but I was somewhat disappointed at not getting any letter from you. I got two apples. Capt. Mull talked very short to our appointed lieutenant, and says he will get short of him if there is any chance. Conley has also appointed a third lieut. in our company. His name is Williams.[17] He is also a perfect stranger. Capt. will also get rid of him, if he can. They still keep fighting some below here and our men keep getting a few prisoners. We have 12 or 15 now in jail here. Every thing seems to favor a continuance of the war! Yet, let us still hope and pray for peace. When the Lord's good time comes then we will have peace, and no man knows the mind of the Lord. It is our duty to trust in Him and bear up patiently. I know you will not forget to pray with all your heart for me to be returned to you again. I do not know whether I can get off on account of being miller or not. But if you send me the petition I will try. I sent you the form of a petition, which I suppose you received.

Sarah, I lost your likeness while I was gone last week. I hate it very much, but I could not help it. But I have no use of a likeness to keep you in mind, for you are ever in my memory any how. Yet I am very sorry that I lost your likeness. Write whether you get the Spirit of the Age or not. I read a letter from Mary Self a few minutes ago.[18] Wm. & Berry's regiment is near Culpepper Court house. A battle is expected in that quarter. Dear Sarah, I must bring this hurried letter to a close. I hope you will not forget to write. Dear Sarah, I can not have any worldly happiness till I get back home with you again. And I hope the good Lord will grant me this privilege. As ever, yours in hope.

J. J. Hoyle

Mrs. S. A. Hoyle

Isaac & Rufus are well. Give my best wishes to all the family. Tell your father & mother I have not forgotten their kindness and I trust they will not consider my not writing any a mark of neglect.

Petersburg, Va.
Nov. 27th 1862

My Dear Wife:

I take the pleasure of dropping you a few lines informing you that I am just tolerably well, but I hope I will be better in a few days. I received your letter last Monday and was very glad to hear from you. You just done right with the money you got for your hog. There is a talk that we will get some money in a few days, but it is very uncertain. You stated in your letter that you had sent me a petition, but I can inform you that I never received it. I had been expecting one some time, but I have not received any yet. I want you to write whether you sent it by mail or not. You need not send any other till I write to you to so, because uncle Peter Mull is trying to get off in the same way, and if he does not get off, it is not my while to try. He will send his petition on in a few days. Dear Sarah I do not want you to be so anxious about me, but bear it all patiently. Trust in god's good grace to restore us to each other again and all will be well. You know, dear Sarah that my heart is as true as life to you. Tell Rooker that Capt Mull has seen Dr. Green (our Sergeon now)[19] The Dr. says he cannot discharge him without seeing him. Dr. says he will extend his furlough till the 1st of Jan, and probably he will be able till that time to come to camp when he can be discharged. I will have to close for the present. I remain as ever your loving husban.

J. J. Hoyle
S. A. H.

Petersburg, Va.
Thursday, Dec. 4th, 1862

My Dear Wife:

Your kind letter was received this morning, and I hasten you a reply. Your letter gave me much satisfaction; and I was especially glad that you stated by whom you sent my petition. Capt Mull has never given me any letter, nor said any thing about it. I think he has done rong in not giving it to me. He may have forgotten it, but I suspect he has kept it back on purpose: for I know he would be unwilling for me to leave the company: for I have to help do all the business that is done. He is trying to have me appointed 1st Lieutenant and will probably succeed, as Col Connally has promised him to remove Lillington.[20] Capt Mull is now gone to town, when he comes back I will ask him about that letter you sent by him and get it. I will get him to sign it, if he will, and send it over to Richmond.

Dear Sarah, nothing on earth would do me more good than to come home and stay with you again, yet I am as willing as any body to serve my country, and dear Sarah, this is the reason I can be content to endure the hardships of camp life. I would not be worthy the blessings of liberty, were I not willing to pour out my life's blood in defence of those glorious principles of freemen.

Dear Sarah, I have another object in view, if I should get off, that I have not told you of, but no doubt you know it. You know I had concluded to join the ministry, but was hindered from doing so by volunteering. If I get home, I will certainly join the Conference as soon as I can. And Dear Sarah, this is one of my strongest reasons for wanting to get off. Dear Sarah, I want you to keep these things somewhat of a secret, at least, keep them in the family. Dear Sarah, I should be very glad if you would come and see me, as it seems I cannot get to come and see you. You can go up to uncle Peter Mull's and see Emaline and she will come with you. If you come or can send them, I want a pair of gloves, and a pair of boots which I wrote to Rooker to get for me. Also some dried fruit and butter. In the mean time I will come home if I can get the chance.

Dear Sarah, I do hope this cruel war will soon terminate, yet, we can only hope and pray for peace, but we know God will answer prayer, and on this we may base our hope. But while it lasts I will have confidence in God for protection and trust his good grace for deliverence, and a happy union with my dear wife. I hope dear Sarah, you will do so too. Let us have the happy assurance that we shall meet again either on this earth or on Cainan's happy shores. How happy the thought that we will meet again. Dear Sarah, this leaves me well. Isaac has been very bad, though he is some better now. Day before yesterday, I did not think he could live; but he has undergone a great change since that time, and I think is in a fair way to recover now. Give my respects to all the family and especially to your father and mother. I remain, as ever, your loving husban.

J. J. Hoyle

Mrs. S. A. Hoyle　　　　　THINE FOREVER

Petersburg, Va.
Dec. 12th 1862

My Dear Wife:

I have just gotten out of the bed, and for the first thing, I take the pleasure of writing you a few lines, informing you that I am well at present and I hope this may find you well. I received your kind letter last week, and was glad to hear from you as I always am, but Dear Sarah, I would be more glad to see you. Yes for that is the very reason I got up so soon this morning because I could not sleep for thinking about you. Sarah, I know of but one way for us to get to see each other and that is for you to come out here. I know you will think it a hard undertaking but I want you to come. I have got a little chimney to my tent, and no body stays with me but Rufus, so we can have the tent to ourselves, and be very comfortable. Sarah, I do not know why you should not come and stay with me all this winter, if we stay here, which I expect we will. You have nothing to hinder you and why should we not be together, for we can not have any pleasure without being together. It will cost near $40 for you to come and go back; but what need we care for money if we can have no enjoyment. You need bring only money enough to bring you here. Dr. Osborne, and Uncle Peter have wrote for their wives to come and you can come with them. Or if Rook is able you can get him to come with you, as he will have to come here before he can be discharged. If you come, I want you to come immediately the quicker the better. I want you to bring me a shirt, not woollen and a jacket, my velvet jacket will do, and a pair of gloves if you can get them, and whatever else you think I will need. I had capt. Mull to search his trunk, and he found that letter you sent by him. He said he had forgotten it. I have not sent the petition on yet. Uncle Peter sent his and he has got no answer yet, and I expect never will. Though if I am not appointed an officer I will send mine too. It would do no good for me to take it myself even if I could get to. Capt. Mull has been doing every thing he could to have me appointed Lieut. and he now thinks he can have it done, so it would be using him rong for me to try to get off since he has been so kind as to do so much foe me, so I told him I would wait till I saw if he could have me appointed. He says he would rather loose any other man in the company than me. Besides, Sarah, it is doubtful whether I could get off any how. Sarah, you see I am in a close place. If I should try to get off I might loose the appointment and then not get off. So I thought it best to wait till I see further. I received a letter from L.S. Self yesterday. He says they are all about to freeze and perish to death out there. They are now at Guineas Station, Va. Isaac is mending as fast as could be expected. He is just able to walk a little. He is out of danger if he has good luck. Dear Sarah, I must close with the hope of seeing you before long. I remain as ever your loving husban.

J.J. Hoyle
Mrs. S. A. Hoyle

Petersburg, Va.
Thursday, Dec. 18th 1862

My Dear Wife:

I take the pleasure of writing you a few lines this evening informing you that I am well at present and I hope this will find you well. There is a great deal of fighting going on now, but I guess you will have heard as much about it as I could tell you. There are a great many troops going to N. C. now to drive back the enemy from Kinston. I do not think our regiment will be ordered, as we are guard in the city, though it may be. I wrote in my last for you to be sure and come out here. Dear Sarah, I want to see you very much, and I hope you and Rooker will come. If we have to move, I will write you immediately. I want a fine shirt and my collar, and a pair of pants, and my velvet jacket. If my wollen shirt is like Isaac's and Rufus' you need not send it. I also want a pair of gloves. I want these things as soon as you can get them to me. I think I will get the appointment of 1st Lieutenant if I get justice. I will have to be examined in a short time. To give you an idea how things are selling here I will tell you I paid $10 for a hat the other day. Dear Sarah, I don't forget to pray for you, and I hope you will pray for me, and for peace. I hope the good Lord will restore me to you again, but above all, let us prepare for a meeting in heaven where parting is no more Dear Sarah, think that we will be united never to part. Dear Sarah, remember your loving husban and know that he remembers you.

J. J. Hoyle

The following letter was printed in the January 5, 1863, issue of the *Spirit of the Age*.

Petersburg, Va., December 22, 1862.

Mr. Editor: While our army has again stood the shock of battle in Virginia, and our no less patriotic soldiers braved the storm of battle in Eastern N. C., all has been quiet here except that eagerness for news and particulars of the battles which might be expected.

The defeat of the Yankees at Fredericksburg, seems to be the most complete one which they have yet sustained. For such a resolute and determined army as Burnside's was boasted to have, to silently draw off and hastily retreat after a repulse without the least pursuit on our side, shows a defeat disastrous in the highest degree. The latest intelligence places Burnside's forces on Bull Run, and at Dumfries, "evidently moving slowly towards Washington."[21] Thus the army of the Potomac has been hurled back the third time upon the Federal capital, and the high expectations for Gen. Burnside woefully disappointed.[22]

Truly the God of hosts gives us the victory, and when will our brutal foe learn to recognize right and justice, and give over the hellish design of subjugating a free and innocent people.

But more particular to my subject.— This will inform the friends of the 55th N. C., that we are still on Provost guard in Petersburg. Nothing has transpired recently to alleviate the monotony of our regular routine of duties, except it may be a little undue excitement produced by camp rumors. But you must know that by this time, we have learned, by experience, what credit to give these idle rumors. So we avoid crossing the river before we come to it by passing the rumor by and await the transpiring of the event.

Frequent accessions to the guard house are of daily occurrence; and it seems strange that so many of our soldiers so far disgrace all claims to patriotism, as to act in so ignoble a manner.

We would hope that a noble spirit of freedom worthy of the just cause in which we are engaged should animate our brave defenders.

The health of our Regiment seems on the decline for the few last weeks, which is no doubt attributably to the exposure we have had to endure. For while we have comfortable quarters, it will be remembered that we are on duty at least half our time.

I scarcely know what to say about the religious condition of our regiment. Our Chaplain has not been with us for the last two months, and what little effort has been put forth in the cause of Christ, has been done by members of the regiment. And I am happy to tell you that we have a few praying men in our regiment; would to God they were all such. Were you to steal into our encampment after the last note of *tattoo* has died away, you would often hear the voice of prayer and praise ascending from the private quarters of some humble soldier. But this is far from being a general thing all over the encampment, for our regiment is not exempt from the prevailing wickedness of the army.

Thus you will see that we are deprived of the principal, and it might be true to say almost every means of grace; and as consequence you could not expect much advance in morals.

Let me, in conclusion, earnestly urge all our christian brethren, and more especially sisters at home, to give us the influence of their constant prayers. And at the same time, pray fervently for the restoration of peace.

J. J. H****

Sergt. Co F., 55th Reg. N. C. T.

Petersburg, Va.,
Thursday, Dec. 25th. 1862.

Dear Wife:

I have only time to write you a few lines, as Emaline will start in a few hours.[23] Osborne has got scared about the small-pox, and is hurrying them off. It is said the small-pox is about here, and one man of our regiment it is thought has got them. He has been carried off. The Drs. do not know for certain but they think it is the small-pox. But if you are ready to come I do not think you need to stop on this account, for if you wait for every thing to get out of the way, you will never come. Now would be a good time for you to come if it was not for this, as every thing is quiet about here now. I want the following things as soon as I can get them. My boots, a fine shirt and collar, a pair of pants, my velvet jacket, a pair of gloves, a _____ of slips, and any thing else you may think I need. If you have not all these things ready, you need not delay to get them ready. Also bring me a quire of paper, as you can get it cheaper there than I can here. Dear Sarah, this is Christmas morning, but I expect it will be a dry Christmas to me; without I could be with my dear Sarah. Isaac is about well again. Rufus is well. He is on guard in town today. I must close for the present. I hope I will get to see you before long. I remain as ever, your loving husban till death.

J. J. Hoyle
S. A. Hoyle

Petersburg, Va.
Dec. 26th 1862

My Dear Wife:

I take the pleasure of dropping you a few more lines. I sent you a letter yesterday by Mrs. Osborne. Doc. hurried them off on account of the small-pox, but some think Doc. Just wanted to go home himself. It seems plain he was not afraid of them getting the small-pox, or he would not of went home with his wife; for he was with the man that was said to have them. Sarah, I do not think you need stop coming out here on account of the small-pox. So I hope you and Rooker will come as soon as possible, if you have not already started, as I said before, the sooner you come, the better. I wrote what I wanted you to bring me in my other letter. You had not better try to bring a box as you will be troubled in getting it along on the cars. You would better bring my trunk, as they are bound to carry ones trunk. Dear Sarah, I did not enjoy much worldly Christmas yesturday. The most of our field & staff officers had what they would call a lively time, but I would call it a <u>drunken</u> time. Dear Sarah, I cannot help but look for you, and I hope I will see you before long. I have no news to communicate. I will close be saying, I hope to see you befor I write again. I remain, as ever, your loving husban till death.

J. J. Hoyle
Mrs. S. A. Hoyle

Petersburg, Va. Dec. 31st 62

Dear Sarah:

I have only time to write you a few lines; for it is now bed time, but I would rob myself of a little sleep any time, to write to my dear Sarah. I have received no letter from you since Carpenter came.[24] We have received no letters from Knob Creek for the last two weeks. I am getting very eager to hear from you, but I know it is not your falt. You wrote you would come out here this week, and I am anxiously looking for you, and I hope you will be here ere this reaches you. There is said to be some cases of small-pox in the hospital at Petersburg, but narry other case has occurred in the regiment. All remains quiet about here. Some hard fighting has been going on in the West, but I guess you know as much about it as I do. If you get this befor you come, I want you to send me the things I wrote for as soon as you can. Robt Hick is come home to get clothing for the company.[25] I would have come if it had not been for being examined. I have to go befor the military board to-morrow. If I pass the board, I will get the appointment of 1st Lieut. in our company. If I get justice, I have no fear but what I will pass the board. I will have to quit for this time. Dear Sarah, it seems like I want to see you more every day. I will feel so happy when I can get to grasp your dear little hand again. Good night. I hope we will come near together in some sweet dream tonight. As ever, your loving husban,

J. J. Hoyle

Camp French
Friday, Jan. 23rd 1863.

My Dear Wife: [Mrs. J. J. Hoyle, Knob Creek, N. C.]

I take pleasure of writing you a few lines this morning informing you that I am well at present, and I hope this will find you well. We have [*several sentences of this letter were unreadable*] ... Tuesday, and came to Camp French about 4 miles north east of the city. This is the same place we camped when we first came to Va. We have good quarters here made of pine poles. We are still doing guard duty in the city; and we now have to walk about 5 miles to get there, and through muddy roads. Dear Sarah, I have not heard from you since you left, though I expect to get a letter this evening or tomorrow evening. It seems like a long time since you left. I hope the time is near when this wicked war will close, and we be permitted to live together again. Let us hope for the best, and at the same time, be prepared for the worst, for God only knows how things are to turn up. Dear Sarah, let us make sure of meeting in heaven. This we can be sure of, while all earthly things are uncertain. Dear wife let us pray with faith. Your loving husban,

J. J. Hoyle

The following letter was printed in the January 26, 1863, issue of the *Spirit of the Age.*

Petersburg, Va, Jan 24th, 1863.

Mr. Editor: — Another year has dawned upon us; and although cruel war yet rages, we should be truly thankful for the favorable prospect of which the new year finds us possessed. We may not be as near the end of the war as we imagine, but we now have full assurance of our ability to maintain our independence. Some bloody battles may yet be fought, and many of our noble soldiers pour out their life-blood on the field of carnage, yet sooner or later, Southern independence will perch upon our banners. May we not hope that the happy time is near at hand? I know that many a sad heart would leap for joy, if they possessed sufficient evidences for an answer in the affirmative.

But every body would not be glad at the prospect of an early peace! WHAT! *every body would not be glad to hail the return of peace!* This looks strange, yet on a little reflection, you will agree with me. We have a class of *beings* (not men) who by taking advantage of our peculiar condition, are glutting themselves with earth's filthy lucre, at the expense of our country's good. Such persons are enemies to the South, enemies at home; — the worst of enemies. These heartless wretches would not be glad to see the restoration of peace, because their craft of speculation and extortion would then be at an end. I think this war will develop principles which will give rise to a new page in moral philosophy. Its heading will be *Men without Souls.* I hope some abler pen will undertake its investigation.

Mr. Editor, if the devil is not wise, he certainly possesses considerable tact, as displayed through his *agents.* I learn that distillers in the up country of the Old North State are making persimmons a cloak for the distillation of whiskey. Men that will make such shifts to evade the laws of the country, I ask, what will they not do? I leave the reader to answer.

"Every thing works together for good," and this war has shown us who is the patriot and who is the coward; who are the true benevolent countrymen and who are the greedy, selfish rogues; who are the christians and who are the hypocrites. Let all read and judge to which of the above classes they respectively belong.

J. J. H****
Sergt. Co. F, 55th, N. C. T.

Camp French, Va.
Sunday, Jan. 25th, 1863.

My Dear Wife:

I received your letter of the 21st last night, and you may be sure I was glad to get it; for this was the first I had heard from you since you left. I did not get the letter which you said you wrote on the 12th, and I was sorry of it, as I suppose you wrote more fully in it about your trip home, as you say little about it in this one. I wish you to write me how much it cost you to get home and all about it. I will not do any thing about tryin to get off till I see how Congress alters the Exemption bill. They are considering it now, and no doubt will make very important changes in it.[26] I hope you will not be discouraged at this. I have write you two letters since you left, and was sorry to hear that you had received none yet, but I hope you will get them both. I directed them to Dicksons, and will continue to direct there till you give me <u>further orders</u>. I have very good quarters here. I and Rook, and Rufus, and Isaac, stay in the Captains cook house. I have gone back to Christopher Buffes mess, because I cannot cook as long as there is any other chance.[27] Dear Sarah I would be so glad if I could be with you this Sabbath morning. My own heart feels so lonesom when <u>its mate</u> (your heart) is far away. Like the melancholy dove, fain would it steal away into some silent place and call moanfully for its image mate. But that <u>mate</u> (your heart) is so far away that it cannot hear mines lonesom calls. I know your blessed little heart is lonesom too, and I would to God they could be joined on earth again, as I have full hope they will be joined in heaven.

None other earthly bliss I crave;
But the united presence of my dear wife,
Blessed Lord denie me not
But give me my dear Sarah back.

Dear Sarah, I hope you will forgive me for writing such love letters; for you know what sort of a heart I have got. I sometimes think it is made out of love. I remain as ever, your loving husban,
S. A. Hoyle   J. J. Hoyle

<u>All are well</u>   If any body administers on Berry's estate, I want you to write to me immediately.

Camp French Va.,
Friday night, Jan. 30th, 1863.
My Dear Wife: [Mrs. J. J. Hoyle, Lincolnton, N.C.]

This will inform you that I am well at present and I hope this may find you well. I received a letter from you a few days ago, and read it with much pleasure; for you may be sure I am always glad to hear from you. You wrote to me to make a trial to get off at once, but as I wrote you in a former letter, I think I had better wait till I see what Congress does with the exemption bill. There is no doubt but what they will change it in some way. I know I ought to come home, but you will have to get along the best way you can, and I will come if I can. We all expect peace will be made till spring, and then I hope we all will get home. Let us pray that it may be so.

Dear Sarah I pray continually that we may be permitted to join each other in presence again on earth, while I have I have steadfast hope of meeting you in heaven. Dear Sarah if I cannot be with you, yet it does me good to think that I have such a confiding and devoted wife. I thank God for giving me such a good wife, and you may be sure, dear Sarah, you possess equal claims upon my heart. Another of our company died today James Willis.[28] This is the 17th one whom we have lost. I have no war news, except a large number of yankee prisoners have passed through here recently. They were parolled and being carried down to City Point to be sent home.[29] You must excuse bad writing, as I have to write by a very sorry fine light. I have been so busy all day that I had no chance to write. I am acting Orderly Sergeant since P. P. Mull Left. He is gone home after recruits. We received a full supply of clothing to-day so I reckon the Petersburg boys will not call us the Ragged Assed 55th now. Isaac & Rufus are well. Rook is getting along tolerably well. He has none but the capt. to cook for now.

Dear Sarah I will have to bring this letter to a close. I hope you will write regularly and as much as you can. I remain as ever, yours in hope.
S. A. Hoyle   J. J. Hoyle

I love to think of thee, dear wife. Thus our hearts are linked together, never to be separated.

The following letter was printed in the February 9, 1863, issue of the *Spirit of the Age*.

Camp French, Va., Feb. 2d, '63.

Mr. Editor:— The reader will observe that we have changed positions since my last letter. Our present encampment is about four miles east of Petersburg, thou we are still doing guard duty in the city. We have very comfortable quarters, made of pine poles and earth, and our boys are living as handsomely as if they inhabited palaces. Although the soldier endures many hardships and privations, yet he enjoys many agreeable hours, which none but the soldier can appreciate. Human nature covets enjoyment; in fact man cannot live without it. Place him in any condition, whatever, and he will invent some mode to gratify this craving principle of his nature. Sociality forms the great principle of enjoyment in camp, and as this is a rich medium of information, you would naturally conclude that soldiers ought to become wise men; but unfortunately conversation is generally conducted to excite the ludicrous propensities, rather than to any instructive end. But I would be doing injustice, were I not to tell you that some of our men apply their unoccupied time in reading and other useful pursuits.

Our Regiment has just received their winter clothing. It came late though in a very good time, for we are having some very cold weather just now. We had a considerable snow storm this morning, and old Boreas is sweeping moaningly around our huts this evening, which makes us draw close to our little fires, and think of comfortable homes far away. And in these reflections we have the consolation of knowing that we have loving friends there who sympathize in all our hardships.

I would say one thing more in regard to our clothing. I see that a portion of it, at least, was donated by the noble women of our beloved old State; all honor to their patriotic generosity. But how is it that the government then charges the poor soldier $9 a pair for pants, $6 for shoes, and $1 a pair for socks, for this same clothing? Surely there is something wrong in this. Is not this a base imposition on the noble generosity of our Southern ladies, as well as a base fraud upon our brave defenders? I pause for a reply.

J. J. Hoyle,
Sergt. Co. F, 55th Reg. N. C. T.

Camp French, Va,
Feb. 6th, 1863

My Dear Wife:

Your kind letter was received a few days since; and I now proceed to answer it. I am sorry to say I never received the first letter you wrote me after you got home, and hence I failed to receive the account of your trip. I have no news of interest except it is the bad condition of the weather, though it looks like clearing off this evening. Sometimes we have some prospect of peace, and I hope it may speedily come. Let us continue to pray for it. Sarah, I think may be I will get to come home shortly for a few days. I have a furlough writ and sent up to head qrs. and I expect it back every day. So I hope I will get. Berry has a part in three packs. One stands down the creek at the end of Wm. Hunts, over half this pack is his. Another stands behind S. Youngs, half this pack is his. [*The reset of this letter is missing.*]

Camp Green. Va.,
Friday, Feb. 27th 1863

Dear Wife: [Mrs. J. J. Hoyle, Lincolnton, N. C.]

This will inform you that I reached the regiment yesterday evening. I had a hard time in getting along. I had to lie over a day and night in Charlotte and also a day and night in Weldon. I found out that the regiment had left Petersburg before I arrived at Weldon. I found them about six miles from Franklin. I got off the train at Franklin where I had to leave my trunk and box until I can get them hauled. I found all the boys well and in good spirits, and better fixed than I expected, though our shelter leaked a puddle of water in my boot last night. We are in close proximity to the enemy here and have to do picket duty, and are subject to have a fight any day. But Dear Sarah, put your trust in the Lord, and pray that he may shield us all. I will try and write more satisfactory next time. Rook says he is fattening up, and indeed he looks much better than he did. Give my love to all. I remain as ever, your loving husban,

J. J. Hoyle

Direct your letters to Franklin Depot, Va. This is written badly, as I have a poor chance to write. I will try and do better when I write again.

Camp Green,
6 miles from Franklin, Va.,
Wednesday, March 4th, 1863,

My Dear Wife: [Mrs. J. J. Hoyle, Lincolnton, N.C.]

I am happy to inform you that I am well at present. I wrote to you last week, which I hope you received. Our time here is taken up in drilling and doing picket duty. We are guarding a pass on the Black water river about two miles from our camp. It takes about 100 men every day to form our picket guard. We have seen no yankees yet, but they may come any day. The yankees made a dash on Franklin to day and captured two of our pickets below there.

Thursday Morning, March 5. Sarah, I stopped to eat supper last night, and befor I got through, Sergeant Mull and his recruits came in, and so I did not get to write any more last night. I have to go on picket to day, so I must finish my letter this morning. This morning is very cold. We had a little snow yesturday morning. This is a very low marshy country, and much resembles Eastern N.C. We can get water any where by digging 2 or 3 feet deep. We have no tents here. We have shanties made by setting up poles and then throwing earth upon them. It is the general opinion that we will not stay here long, but this we do not know. When we leave here, we will have to carry all we take with us. Dear Sarah I do earnestly pray that this cruel war may stop for I want to come home and live with you again, for this is the only earthly bliss I expect to enjoy. Dear Sarah it seems like I will get to come back to you again, and I know you pray for it and I hope the good Lord will answer your prayers. Let us put our trust in him, and look to him for all that we expect to enjoy. Our hearts are knit together in fondest union, and time and absence only serves to strengthen the ties of union and fidelity. But I am getting so cold, that I must close. I remain, as ever, your loving husban

S. A. Hoyle   J. J. Hoyle

The following letter was printed in the March 9, 1863, issue of the *Spirit of the Age*.

Camp Green, Southampton Co., Va., March 2.

Mr. Editor: Since my last, I have had the good fortune to enjoy the privileges of General Order No. 5. But when a soldier obtains a furlough to visit his home a few days, most his time is consumed in traveling thence and back, owing to the irregularity (*mismanagement*, I might justly say) of the train connection on the N. C. road has become obsolete, and, if by chance the train makes time, every body is inquiring what has happened. The public good, as well as convenience, demands a remedy for this evil. The proper authorities should give it their serious attention. I returned to camp a few days since, and found our Regiment on the Blackwater, in the region of Franklin depot. We have on tents here, but the experienced soldier can soon construct a substitute, and hence, we have temporary *shanties* which serve every purpose; and the pits from which we get earth to cover these shanties, from wells which give ample supplies of water. Thus, you see we practice economy.

Our business here is to guard a pass on the river. Hence, we are being initiated into the principles of *picket duty*. All has been quiet since we have been here, though the enemy is not far off, and may advance any day. Our boys are in good spirits, and will show the yankees Southern valor should they come.

J. J. H****,

Sergt. Co. F, 55th Reg. N. C. T.

Camp Green Va.

March 6th., 1863,

My Dear Wife: [Mrs. Sarah A. Hoyle, Knob Creek, N. C.]

I snatch a few moments to drop you a few lines. We are under orders to leave here, we are going 10 or 12 miles below here. We have to carry all that we take with us so I send my trunk home. I send you, by E. Mull, $115 and Rook sends $100 in the same roll.[30] You can borrow enough more and pay that note Uncle Peter Mull holds aganst me, or have it done. I expect we will see hard times while we stay in this country, but I hope in God and abide his all wise will. Be not discouraged, but pray to God. Our address will still be Franklin, if we go where we expect we are going. Remember your loving husban,

Joe

Saturday morn, March 7th

Dear Sarah, We are not gone yet but will start soon. Ezra Mull will leave my trunk at Lincolnton. Isaac, Rook, & Rufus have some clothing in it. You will have to get it from Lincolnton some how. Ezra will leave the key and my money at mothers. Yours in haste,

J. J. Hoyle

On Black water

Below Franklin, Va.

March 8th 1863

Dear Sarah:

I proceed this Sabbath morning to drop you a few more lines for I cannot be more agreeably employed than in writing my dearest one on earth; for although we are far apart I know we are near in heart, and let us hope that the time is near at hand when we will be permitted to join in presence again. We left our camp yesterday in the forenoon and arrived here late yesterday evening. We have made camp on the bank of the river, and have to do picket duty. I cannot tell how long we will stay here. Of course we will not know when when we may be moved again. This is a low marshy country, and we have very bad water. We have no tents yet, and it would amuse you to see our little shanties dotted through the woods this morning. You would properly infer that are boys would be cut down in spirits at these kind times, but I tell you the opposite spirits forbade our men. All is life and glee among us, and every body seems satisfied the best in the world. I have not received any letters from you yet. We have not got any male for last week yet. Dear Sarah live in hope and believe that you have a faithful and confiding husban, and one that loves you passionately. As ever, yours in hope,

J. J. Hoyle

Sarah, after this I will give you my letter in regular diary form, and thus you will have my every day life. I think this will interest you more, and I will do anything to please you.

Camp Kirkland, Va.,
Saturday, March 14th., 1863.

My Dear Wife:

I take the pleasure this morning of dropping you a few more lines. I want you to send my trunk back to me by Ezra Mull if you can. May be you could get Carpenter to take it to Mull for you. I and uncle Peter want it between us If you send my thing in it, I would be glad if you would send me a little card. I wrote you in yesturday's letter to send my fine shirt, and collar, and jacket. If you can get any nuw checked or colored stuff, I wish you would make me a shirt or two and send them the first chance you have. I have bought me a uniform coat, it cost me $50. We had an alarm yesturday in our camp, caused by the yankees driving in our pickets two or three miles from here. Our Regt. was quickly on the march to meet the expected attack, but the yankees never came up so after staying an hour or two, we returned to camp again. All is quiet now. This is a bitter cold morning, and so was yesturday all day.

Dear Sarah, I pray the good Lord will let me join you in presence again. Let us hope for the best, and at the same time be prepared for the worst. Isaac, Rooker, and Rufus are well. You may know Rooker is getting better, for yesturday when the long roll beat, he gathered his gun and was for going any how, and even cried when I would not let him go.[31] (I was commanding the company)[32] It is not often that men cry because they cannot go when a fight is on hand.[33] I remain as ever, your loving husban,

J. J. Hoyle

My dear wife S. A. Hoyle, If you cannot send my trunk by E. Mull, send it as soon as you can.

Camp 55th Regt, N.C. T-
On the Blackwater, Va.
March, 1863- (No. 2 New Series)

My Dear Wife:

I now have the opportunity of penning you my second number of this kind of writing; and this number will embrace two weeks, as I had no chance to write for last week. So you see whether I write every week or not, you will have an account of all that transpired any how. But you may be sure I will write every week if it is possible for me to do so. I want you to tell me in your next how you like these kind of letters.

Saturday, 14 — This is general wash day, and hence there is no drill. We received marching orders this evening, and are preparing to go.

Sunday, 15 — We are still not gone but have orders to march at 8 in the morning. This Sabbath has been spent irregularly, and I have read but little.

Monday, 16 — We are on the march to day, and as usual, a great deal of jolity is prevalent. Our march is up the river. We pitched camp this evening 6 miles above Franklin, near our old camp (Green)

Tuesday, 17 — This is a beautiful bright morning, but the loud roar of cannon tells us that deadly strife is going on near by. The firing is in the direction of Franklin. The alarm was beat in our camp, and we were quickly on the march for the scene of action, but we did not proceed far till we countermarched and came back. The firing ceased after an hour or two. The engagement was near Franklin, against some yankee cavalry. The enemy lost several, our side one.

Wednesday, 18 — We are on the march again to day. We pitched camp this evening 3 or 4 miles this side Brodwater Bridge, where I expect we will stay some time. We have to guard two passes on the river here.

Thursday, 19 — I am on picket duty to day, and for this reason I had no chance to write to you. The snow and sleet is falling thick and fast. We were relieved and returned to camp this evening. You can tell aunt Sarah Mull that I saw her brother Jo. to-day, and had a long chat with him. He is camped a few miles above Franklin. He looks well.

Friday, 20 — It sleeted all night and, it is still falling fast this morning. The ground is covered 3 or 4 inches now. This is decidedly the roughest day I have seen since I have been in camp. Some are making fires, some are shivering round the fire, and some are rolled up in their blankets under their shanties. I tell you tis a hard time among us to-day.

Saturday, 21st — It has ceased snowing, though still cloudy. The ground is covered about 6 inches. We received 4 tents for our company to-day.

Sunday, 22nd — The sun is visible again this morning; and the snow is melting fast. I have endeavored to spend this Sabbath in a proper manner; though I have been disturbed a great deal; but I could expect little else here in camp. May God help me to live a better Christian every day of my life.

Monday, 23 — This is a beautiful bright day. I have been busy to-day in putting a chimney to our tent. We (officers) have a comfortable place to stay in now. We have just put us up a table out of pine puncheons. Sarah, I know you would laugh, if you could see all our curious arrangements, but we have to make out as best we can.

Tuesday, 24 — Regular drill has been resumed to-day. And as Capt Mull is gone, I have to drill the company. Yours in hope and love,

J. J. Hoyle
Lieut- Co F 55th Regt, N. C. T.

Camp Holms, Va.
Wednesday, March 25th 1863

My Dear Wife: [Mrs. J. J. Hoyle, Knob Creek, N. C.]

I start you this letter early in the week so you may be sure to get it. I have received no letter from you for last week, but I expect it has come to Franklin and is being there. Dear Sarah, hope still keeps me up; for if I had no hope of seeing you any more, I dont believe I could live. I would give every thing in the world, were it mine, to stop this cruel war, and I pray continually for it to stop. O! would God hear our prayers, and return us to each others sweet embrace again. Will not the good Lord be pleased to give me back to my dear Sarah again? God has said in his holy word that he would withhold nothing good from those who love him- Then dear Sarah, let us love him with our whole hearts, and trust all to his good will. We know he will do what is best. If you cannot send my trunk and things by E. Mull, you will send them the first opportunity you have. This leaves me in common health, and I hope it may find you well. Give my love to all. Tell Lemuel & Alice I send them howdy. Isaac & Rufus are well. Rooker is complaining a little, I remain as ever your loving husban,

Joe

I AM THINE IN HOPE AND LOVE, DEAR SARAH

Hd. Quarters 55th N. C. T.
March, 1863

Dear Wife:

I have wrote several letters since I received any from you. It seems like a long time since I heard from you, and I am getting over anxious to hear. But I know it is not your fault for I know you write regularly.

Wednesday, 25th — The weather is warm to-day. I am engaged in drilling our company.

Thursday, 26th — This day has passed as usual.

Friday, 27 — This is fast and prayer day, appointed by the President, hence, we have no drill.[34] I held prayer in our company this morning; and may the good Lord hear our prayers and give us a speedy peace. I have endeavored to spend this day in a solemn manner, and have not failed to pray heartily for peace.

Saturday, 28 — Rainy to-day. We are under marching orders again.

Sunday, 29th — I have been reading the prophecy of Daniel (Bible) to-day. Its contrast with ancient history is very remarkable and interesting. Sarah, I hope you often read the bible, and, indeed make it your constant companion; for it is able to give you comfort, and resignation.

Monday, 30 — We are on the march again to-day. Our course is down the river. We pitched camp this evening 4 miles above Franklin. So you will have to direct your letters to Franklin Depot again.

Tuesday, 31st — This has been a rainy day, but we have cabins to stay in, so we are faring very well. Another little fight occurred at Franklin yesterday, with a loss of 2 or 3 to the enemy. None to us. I do hope all our people have prayed this day as they never prayed befor, and if such has been the case I have hope that the good Lord will cause an early peace to come. Sarah, I do believe if every Christian in the land would pray in faith that peace would come; because God has promise to hear our requests. Read from the 5 to 14 verse of the 11th chapter of St. Luke. It is hardly necessary for me to repeat that I pray constantly for peace etc, and I hope yes I know you do too, dear Sarah. Dear Sarah, no doubt we are frequently both praying at the same time, and I believe God will answer our prayers, for he has said that he would withhold no good thing from those who love him, and is not this a sweet promise. Then let us love God with all our hearts, and all will be well.

Wednesday, April, 1st — My dear Sarah, this morning finds me well, and I hope it may find you enjoying the same blessing. I sent you some money by E Mull and I want you to let me know whether you received it or not, and how you have disposed of it. Also write how Linsey is getting along at the mills. I never forget my dear little wife, because you are always nearest my heart. The fond recollection of thy love and devotion, always fills my heart with gladness, and I frequently exclaim in my thoughts, "Thank God for giving me such a good wife" I remain as ever, Dear Sarah, yours in love, and hope,

Mrs. S. A. Hoyle   Lieut. J. J. Hoyle

Camp near Franklin, Va
April 3rd 1863

Dear Sarah: [Mrs. J. J. Hoyle, Prerceville, Cleveland Co., N. C.]

I started you a letter yesturday, but as I received a letter from you yesturday by Wm Craige, I will drop you a few more lines this morning. I was very glad indeed to hear from you as I always am for how could your letters fail to gladden my heart when they breath such true love and devotion. That little fringed slip was duly valued, and you may be sure I was glad to hear of you spending that day so proper. I hope you will make a regular habit of reading — and I wish you would make your letters a regular dairy like I am writing mine now so I would have a daily history of your life, and you may be sure this would be very interesting to me.

Dear Sarah let us give each other all the comfort we can in writing for this is all the pleasure we can have. Sarah, I want you to have me a box made for us officers a mess box — get Jo Linsey to make it as follows — have it about 2½ feet long, 1½ feet wide, and 1½ feet deep — make it out of light quarter popular plank, and have thin sheet iron bound round the corners, have small hinges and a lock put to it, but if you cannot get a lock, have every thing fixed to it for one, and we can get one here. We want it as light as possible. Send it to us as soon as you can. May be you could send it by Thomas Willis you can show this to your father and get him to have Linsey to make it.[35] If you have not already started my trunk: I want you to send it as soon as you can. I am needing it very much. I have wrote to you about sending my best collar and shirt so you know what to do. Direct your letters to Franklin Depot, Va, again. As ever, yours in love and hope, To my wife,

Lieut. J. J. Hoyle

Hd. Qrs. 55th N. C. T.
Near Franklin Va
April, 1863

[Mrs. J. J. Hoyle, Knob Creek, N. C.]

Thursday, 2 — We are engaged in clearing off a new camp to-day. Wm. Craige came in, and I received a letter from you — you may be sure I was glad to get it; for I had received no letter for two weeks before. It breathed that spirit of pure love and confidence which your letters allways contain. Sarah I do not mean to flatter you when I say, if any man has cause to be proud of a wife I have; for truly you are to me as my own heart.

Friday, 3 — The day is cold. I am drilling the company. Accord to general orders — We (officers) assembled at the Col's quarters this evening for recitation in tactics etc. We have to take a lesson every day in tactics and Army Regulations.

Saturday, 4 — We are engaged in working at our new camp to-day. Our tents have come and we are clearing off a place to put them up. It is bitter cold, and the snow is falling fast this evening.

Sunday, 5 — I am on picket duty to-day. It is Ester Sunday, and plenty snow is on the ground. I cannot help letting my mind run back, and think where I was last Ester — Then I was enjoying the sweet smiles of a dear wife, and of a truth I did not know how happy I was — But now I am far away from my dearest one on earth, and may be never to see her any more on earth. Yet one hope revives my breast — I know we are joined in Christ, and have hope of meeting each other in heaven — May God be merciful toward us!

Monday, 6 — The sun is shining beautifully this morning, and the merry birds are singing as if sweet spring was here indeed. I returned to camp this morning. We put up our tents and moved to our new camp to-day.

Tuesday, 7 — We are fixing up generally to-day.

Wednesday, 8 — I received three letters from you this evening by B. Garner. I was very glad to get them, and I read them with usual interest. I also got my trunk and all was right in it — my pen is so bad I must quit for to night.

Thursday morning, 9 — Dear Sarah, I am very glad of what you sent me and especially of the meat for we will have to pay one dollar a pound for our meat from this time on. I wrote you in my last to have us a mess box. You will have it made as light as possible; for we have to have every thing weighed that we have hauled and every officer is only allowed 60 pounds. You will make me a homade shirt — make it small checked, and of some dark colors. I think the stripe you sent me of your dress is very nice, and I wish I could be there to see how your dress fits you. Dear Sarah, we have orders to march to-day at 11 O'clock. We are going to make an expedition against the yankees, and no doubt will have a fight before we get back. Sarah do not be uneasy, but trust in God. If it should be his good will for me to die, I submit, and you must do the same. Sarah I know this will make you uneasy, but I would be doing rong not to tell you of it. I will write again the first opportunity. The boys are well. I remain as ever, dear Sarah, your loving husban

S. A. Hoyle   Lieut J. J. Hoyle

The following letter was printed in the April 13, 1863, issue of the *Spirit of the Age*.

Deteriorating Influences of War. No. I

This important topic justly claims the attention of all good men and women; for it has a direct bearing upon the cause of virtue, and furnishes a wide field of labor for the philanthropist.

Any one who has had any experience in camp life will readily testify to the success of the evil influences which pervade the camp in every conceivable form. Many who practiced strict morality at home, and some who even professed christianity, are daily being drawn into the maelstrom of sin and corruption; whose turbid waters are continually agitated by the increasing excitement of its hellish material. Could the Godly mother, who has trained up her son in the way of right; hear the bitter oath and corrupt conversation which fall from his lips, would her heart not be wrung with torturing sorrow? Could the fond sister behold that brother, who formerly seemed so steady and so richly merited a kind sister's precious love, join the game of cards, and all the incidental scenes of depravity, would not that kind sister's heart, which once he was so careful not to wound, be struck deep with grief? Could the devoted and confiding wife, whose very destiny is wrapped up in the being of her husband, behold his reckless disregard of virtue, and his many acts of wickedness, and moral corruption, would she not wring her hands in unconsolable grief, and dampen her pillow with tears of sorrow.

O, Soldier, think! Think when you are thus running into sin and depravity, of those loved ones at home — think with what arrows of grief and despair you are piercing their hearts. Husband, think how unworthy you are making yourself of a confiding and praying wife. Will you thus cast away yourself, and pierce with torturing sorrow that being whom you promised to love and honor.

There must be a cause for this deterioration of morals in the army. Of many which might be adduced. I would suggest a prominent one, viz: *The want of female influence.* Women of the South, here you have a negative demonstration of the power of your influence. Let me entreat you to consider it, and then persevere in your great mission of love to the lords of creation. While the army is deprived of your influence and of this greater part of your influence, endeavor to render a compensation through the medium of letters and the press.

1st Lieut. Co. F, 55th N. C. T.

Camp near Suffolk, Va.
Thursday, April 16th 1863

My Dear wife:

I take an opportunity of dropping you a few lines informing you that I am well at present. We are now in about 4 miles of Suffolk. We came here last Saturday; and we expected a fight before now. Our pickets have been fighting ever since we have been here. The yankees shell our pickets every day from their breast works. We have a heavy force here. General Longstreet is in command. I believe the object is to take Suffolk, and I believe we can do it. Though it is strongly fortified. A general engagement may take place any day. Our Regt. was on picket yesterday. I did not have to go out to our out posts, but those who did were shot at all day. Rufus was out and had many balls shot at him. One man of Company "A" had his arm broke. No body else in our Regt. was hit. From our picket lines, the town is plainly seen. In fact our picket stand within a few hundred yards of the yankee breast works. So you see we are pushing in very close upon them. Dear Sarah, be not too uneasy, if it is the good Lord's will that I should die, I will die at my post doing my duty to my country and my God. Isaac & Rook were left at camp. We are down here without any thing except a blanket. I and Capt have two blankets a piece. We are faring <u>like soldiers now</u>, you may be sure. Yet our men are all cheerful and in good spirits. We have got so used to shooting that we pay little attention to it any more. There is less firing going on this morning than there has any day since we have been here. Dear Sarah, let us trust in the Lord; for we know he will do all things for the best. I have wrote this short letter without knowing whether I will have a chance to send it or not. As ever, your loving husban,

J. J. Hoyle

Hd. Quarters 55th N. C. T.
April, 1863 — No. 1. (N.S.)

My Dear Wife. [Mrs. J. J. Hoyle, Knob Creek, N. C.]

I have been hindered from writing you my regular series, but as I keep a regular diary I just copy from that, so you will have an unbroken narrative any how. This letter will have to reach back to the time we first left camp.

Thursday, 9 — We took up the line of march this morning going down the road. We proceeded 3 or 4 miles (2 miles from Franklin) and camped for the night. Our men are all cheerful, and seem eager for a fight. We had a noble roast of potatoes to night.

Friday, 10 — We did not resume our march till 11 this morning. The road has been crowded all morning with troops and artilery passing down. Our regt joined the Brigade (Genl Davis), and we (brigade) filed left and passed down by Murfey in order to cross the river at South Quay. (South Quay is some 5 miles below Franklin). We pitched camp near South Quay.[36]

Saturday, 11 — We resumed our march this morning, crossing the river

(Blackwater) at South Quay. We marched cautiously all day and pitched camp 4 miles from Suffolk. A large force is concentrating here. Some of the enemy pickets were captured this evening and the rest drove in — we expect bloody work to-morrow. Our company is on picket to night.

Sunday, 12 — We joined the Regt. this morning again. All was quiet with us during the night. At 8 this morning, our brigade moved and formed into line of battle and thus we have lain all day. The disposition of the forces are as follows: General Picket commands the right; General Jenkins, the center; and General Hood the left; the whole under General Longstreet.[37] Picket firing has been going on in front. We camped for the night a few paces in rear of our position in line.

Monday, 13 — We took our position in line this morning. Picket firing with some cannonading has been going on all day.

Tuesday, 14 — Slow firing has continued all day. Our regt went on picket this evening.

Wednesday, 15 — We returned to our original position this evening. One man of Co "A" had his arm broken by a ball no other harm done us.

Thursday, 16 — An alarm was made this evening, which caused us to march one mile down the road, but nothing occurred and we soon returned.

Friday, 17 — The day is pleasant. We remained our camp (original position) all day.

Saturday, 18 — We (our Regt.) moved this morning over to the left, on the river below Suffolk, and pitched camp in shelling distance of the enemies gun-boats. We came here to support a battery which is being planted on the river bank to night — We dare not have any fires, and have to keep still.

Sunday, 19 — The gun-boats engaged our batteries between 11 and 12 A M. and firing more or less frequent has continued ever since. The enemy landed this evening and captured one of our batteries, and our Regt was ordered down to support it. A part of our company (including myself & capt) was stationed above to prevent the enemy from coming in on the rear: A perfect storm of shells have been bursting around us this evening, and continued all night. The scene is awfully sublime.

Monday, 20— We have held our position all day, and the enemy have continued to shell us — No one has been harmed in our company yet — 8 or 10 are wounded in the regt 2 only bad. I feel thankful to the God of host for preserving us amidst danger. May I be enabled to serve him better every day of my life.

Wednesday, 22 — We are still at this place. Dear Sarah, this leaves me well. We have been down here near two weeks and I expect we will remain here and may be take Suffolk. Direct your letters still to Franklin depot. I have got no letter from you since B. Garner came back. I remain as ever your loving husban till death.

Sarah   Joe

Let your father see this.

Camp near Suffolk
Wednesday evening, April 22nd 1863

My Dear Sarah:

I have just received a letter from you dating up to the 15th inst, so I will drop you a few more lines. I am well pleased with this last letter, and I hope you will write all after the same manner. I concur in your plan of numbering our letters. You wanted me to inquire of P. P. Mull of that note. He is not with us now. He is back at the camp sick. But I ask him about it some time ago and he told me it was at his home. So it must be there if his wife would look it up. I do not know when I will get to see him but if you do not get it arranged till I see him. I will know about it and let you know. David Cline, and his substitute Goodson arrived here to-day. Cline will not get him in our company. He is trying to get him in some other company though I think the chance is bad. I need say nothing more about it as you know I am bitterly opposed to the substitute business.[38] Dear Sarah, let us have hope in God. He alone deserves our love & he rightly claims us all. I do hope peace will soon come, but we must leave it all to God. Yours in love and hope.

My Sarah   Joe

Dr. Osborn put a little slip in this letter which he requests you to hand to his wife.

Hd. Qrs-55th N. C. T.
April, 1863........No. 2 (N. Series)

My Dear Wife:

Your kind letter No. one, was received and I read it with much interest. You may be sure that I highly appreciate such letters, for by this means I have an every day history of your life. As you say we will number our letters. You can take a form for heading your letters from mine, making the necessary change as to place.

Thursday, 23 — Our Regt. is on picket to-day; and it is very rainy. All has been quiet except the usual picket firing, and that is so common that we take little notice of it — We returned to camp again this evening.

Friday, 24 — Still rainy — an alarm was beat this evening; and we formed line but did not move off.

Saturday, 25 — To-day is remarkably warm, as if summer was here. We have remained quiet all day.

Sunday, 26 — This is a calm and beautiful Sabbath; and it brings to my mind those happy days when we could go to St. Peters to-gether. Sarah I love to think of those happy times, and sometimes my mind becomes so imbued with those happy days that I can scarcely believe that we are in the midst of war, and I am so far from my dearest friend, my second self. May the time soon come when I may realize these happy dreams.

Monday, 27 — Our regt. is on picket to-day. All has been quiet except picket firing, and a few stray shell which whized rather close to be agree-able. Though our pickets and the yankees are firing at each other almost constantly, yet they rarely hit each other.

Tuesday, 28 — We returned to camp last evening, and have remained quiet all day to day. Our camp is about 4 miles from Suffolk, near the Seaboard Railroad. We had prayer in our company to-night, which we expect to continue every favorable night.

Wednesday, 29 — We are working on breast works to-day. Extensive fortifications are being put up around here, and we will soon be prepared, should the yankees come out and give us a fight, But I do not believe they will come out from their breast works, and I think it doubtful whether we will attack them. Though I believe we will stay down here, and hold these lines. We have obtained a large amount of corn, bacon, and forage in this country since we crossed the Blackwater.

Thursday, 30 — We had drenching rain last evening, and it is still cloudy this morning.

Dear Sarah, this leaves me well and I hope it will find you well. I expected to receive a letter from you yesturday evening, but the mail did not get in. It will be here this morning. I received a letter from Wm. Hoyle day before yesterday. He was well, and had joined his company again. I wrote you last week about that note. It is certainly at Uncle Peter's though I have not seen him yet. When you pay it off I want you to let me know what amount you paid. My Dear Sarah, I hope, and pray too, that the happy day may soon come when we will be united to each other in presence again. As I have before said, let us hope for the best, and at the same time be prepared for the worst. Rufus is well, Isaac & Rooker were the last I heard from them a few days since. Give my love to all. Tell Lemey and Alice I have not forgot them. I remain, as ever, your loving husban,

Mrs. S. A. Hoyle   Joe

Forever Thine I Am.

The following letter was printed in the May 4, 1863, issue of the *Spirit of the Age*.

Camp Near Suffolk. Va., April 27th, 1863.

Mr. Editor:—As you are aware the forces on the Blackwater moved down upon Suffolk two weeks since. The enemy's outposts were captured or driven in as we advanced, and finally our forces took position four miles in front of the town. Our lines form a semicircle around the place, the right resting against a swamp, and the left on the Nausemond river below. The disposition of the forces is as follows: Gen. Picket commanding the right, Gen Jenkins the centre, and Gen. Hood the left. Gen. Longstreet commanding the whole. It is not my purpose to say what number of troops are here, but I think the number is adquate to the object in view.

Our picket lines extend within rifle range of the enemy's fortifications, and picket fire is a daily business, but little damage is done thereby. The yankess also expend a great deal of ammunition in shelling our picket lines, but they rarely hurt any body.

One week ago an attack was made to secure the river below the town from the passage of gunboats, by planting batteries on the shore. But the enterprise proved a failure for the present, and after a day's engagement the guns were withdrawn. We lost one battery of five guns by the experiment—damage to the Yankees, if any, unknown. Our regiment (55th N. C.) was detailed to defend the batteries, but unfortunately for the one lost we were not ordered forward till it was taken. The enemy then poured shot and shell among us terribly, and our boys will long remember that memorable Sunday night; 8 or 10 were wounded in our regiment—only 2 badly—none killed.

Of course, we know nothing of the plans and intentions of our Generals, but you may be prepared to hear of bloody work here at any time. Our men are in good spirits and I believe will do their duty whenever called upon. May the God of battles be with us and give us such victory as will lead to an early peace, and the independence of our Confederacy.

J. J. H.,
Lieut. Co. F, 55th N. C. Reg.

Camp near Suffolk, Va.
Sunday, May 3, 1863.

My Dear Wife:

I hasten to drop you a few lines this morning informing you that I am well at present. I will not say any thing about our fight day before yesterday in this short letter as I will give you a full account of it in my regular letter for this week. It is thought we will fall back from here, and we may move at any time. The yankees are pressing on Fredericksburg again, and no doubt this is the reason of us falling back.[39] Dear Sarah, this is a beautiful Sabbath morning, and O how happy I would be if I could be at home to enjoy its lovliness with you. You know I love to enjoy nature, lovely nature, in sweet spring time; and I know you have not forgot how I used to gather flowers, and enjoy their lovliness, I love flowers because they are pure, and; lovely because they are natures beauties, and made by natures God — Sweet beauties of spring — how they all conspire to raise emotions of love and praise in my heart.

Dear Sarah, I want you to gather a bunch of flowers for me, and put it on my desk; for I cannot be there to do it myself and I know you will love to do any thing that I love. I want you to love the flowers and natural beauties of gentle spring because I love them. Dear Sarah let us be joined in love and in Christ, and we will be happy whether we meet any more on earth or not.

Dear Sarah, I feel happy and full of hope this morning, though I am far from my dearest earthly friend, and I do not know what makes me feel so, yet I hope it is an omen for good to us. I remain, as ever, dear wife, your loving husban,
Mrs. S. A.   Hoyle Joe
My loveliest flower.

Hd. Qurs. 55th N. C. T.
May, 1863. (New Series) No. 3.

My Dear Wife:

Your very kind letter bearing date up to the 22nd April is to hand; and I have read it and reread it with much pleasure. Sure enough I had forgot about giving you the bible for your husban till I returned, but I am glad you have not forgot it, and more glad that you are useing it, as I directed you. I want you to love it more than you love me; for it will make you a better husban than I can be to you. Dear Sarah, you do not know how much good it does me to know you are striving to serve God with all your heart, and I do pray he may enable you to live a better Christian every day of your life; for thus we know we shall see each other again whether we live or die. Dear Sarah, you may be sure it gives me much pleasure to know you are making the bible your regular companion. I am also glad to see that you are improving writing. I can read your letters very well, and I am sure they are written much better than the first ones you wrote.

Friday, 1st — This has been a lovely May-day, but a very memorable one to us; for we have been in the heat of battle this evening. We were on picket to-day. The picket lines are close down to the yankee breast works. We have pits dug on this line to stay in. We put 4 companies in these pits, while the balance stays about one half mile back behind the rail road, as a reserve. Our company was back in the reserve this evening. About an hour by sun this evening the yankees sent out two regts. to charge our pits, and when they advanced, our company, and others, were sent down to reinforce our pickets in the pits, and now came the trying time with us. We had to go about one half mile in open view of the yankee batteries and they rained shot and shell upon us all the while, but no one was hurt except Noah Cook who had his leg broke — since cut off.[40] It is marvelous how we escaped so well; for I reckon shot and shell never fell much faster. God be thanked for our preservation. But the yankees had been driven back before we reached the pits — we staid here till after dark, when we were relieved and returned to camp. Six or seven were wounded in the Regt. none killed.

Saturday, 2 — This is a bright and lovely day. We have remained quite all day.

Sunday, 3 — We have been under marching orders all day but did not move till night. Our forces are leaving here.

Monday, 4 — We marched all night, and landed in the banks of the Blackwater this morning, here we rested till evening and then crossed the river.

Tuesday, 5 — We marched near all night last night, and reached our camp this morning at 3. We have to leave again at 5 so you see we get little rest. We are on the march up the Blackwater to-day, we are all nearly give out, having been on the march two days and nights.

Wednesday, 6 — We have marched part of to-day, going up the river apiece and then turning back the same road. It seems we cannot get a place to stop at.

Thursday, 7 — We had rain last night but we have a fly with us this time.

Dear Sarah, this leaves me in good health. Your last letter was received and read with pleasure. You may be sure I was glad to hear of the revival at St. Peters for I often pray for you all there. I sent a check for $25 with J. E. Osborn to get the money for me. I told him to take enough out of it to pay his trouble and pay the rest to you. I want you to write if you get the money and how much. I want you to pay Jo. Willis or whoever is Steward at St. Peters $5 for my quarterage, and let me know it. Dear wife I am under obligation to give to the Lord as I am prospered.

The following letter was printed in the May 28, 1863, issue of the *Spirit of the Age.*

Joiner's Church, *near Franklin, Va.,*May 15th, 1863.

Mr. Editor:— For the satisfaction of our friends at home, I give you a few lines. We are still on the Blackwater. Our permanent camp (only nominally permanent, for we are very little in it) is about 12 miles above Franklin. The greater part of our time is consumed in marching up and down the river, conforming to the expected movements of the enemy. We have been out from camp three days and nights, and have now halted here to await further orders.

The yankees are in force at Carrsville, 5 miles or 6 miles below here. Day before yesterday Gen. Jenkins moved down upon them, but finding them already fortified and too strongly posted to be dislodged with his present forces, he fell back and we are now quietly awaiting their advance. They seem slow in advancing any further, and I think it doubtful whether they will do so at all or not. I learn they have been guilty of more than their usual depredations on the citizens I the track of their march, being incensed at the late pressing Gen. Longstreet gave them.

Our scouts in their rear continue to capture a prisoner occasionally. Yesterday they succeeded in capturing a Major, Captain and two men near Suffolk. Tis a pity that we have not more of these daring scouts on this line. Yours in haste.

J. J. H.,
Lt. Co. F, 55th N. C. T.
Our address is still at Franklin, Va.

5. The Gettysburg Campaign, June–July 1863

"In the very jaws of death"

When the Federals, under the command of Major General John J. Peck, ventured into the Confederate trenches and rifle pits on the morning of May 4, they discovered that the Rebels had abandoned their siege of Suffolk. Lieutenant General James Longstreet had received orders on April 30 to return to General Lee's army, which was positioned near Fredericksburg. Concurrently, Lee had realized Major General Joseph Hooker intended to attack him, and so he sent word to the Confederate War Department requesting reinforcements. Longstreet gathered his forces the best he could but was unable to disengage immediately. However, by the evening of May 3, he managed to send out orders to all of his division commanders to withdraw from Suffolk. Although Longstreet's troops never arrived in time to support Lee, the Army of Northern Virginia was successful in repulsing Hooker's forces at Chancellorsville.[1]

Brigadier General Joseph R. Davis was ordered to have his men guard the fords and crossings of the Blackwater River. The 55th North Carolina spent most of May performing picket duty, building earthworks, and skirmishing with Federal pickets. On May 10, the regiment was camped about twelve miles above Franklin Depot and by the end of the month, the 55th had become an official member of the Army of Northern Virginia, under Henry Heth's division of the newly formed Third Corps.

On June 2, the regiment received orders to cook three days' rations and be prepared to march. Under incessant rain, the men of the 55th North Carolina struck their tents and gathered what they could carry. At 3:00 A.M. on June 3, Davis's brigade prepared to march away from southeastern Virginia, and by 5:00 A.M. the troops were on the move toward Ivor Station. The brigade reached Ivor Station around three in the afternoon and, after several hours of rest, boarded railcars headed to Petersburg. After arriving at Petersburg, Davis's men marched twenty-three miles to the outskirts of Richmond. By June 6, the majority of the brigade had arrived at Hanover Junction, having ridden railcars from Richmond. The 55th North Carolina, however, had to march from Richmond to Hanover Junction, having been assigned the task of guarding the supply wagons.[2]

By June 7, the regiment was positioned near Fredericksburg. Lee had ordered Lieutenant General A. P. Hill to use his force to resist any attempts by the Federals to cross the Rappahannock River in strength. Using sporadic demonstrations to deceive the Federals into believing the Army of Northern Virginia was still encamped around Fredericksburg, Hill stood alone against the Federals while Longstreet and Ewell's corps began moving north.[3]

Believing the Federals would surely attack Hill's position, the men of the 55th North Carolina braced daily for the assault. Although the men received better care and more rations at this location, the overall health of the regiment declined, a fact Lieutenant Hoyle attributed to the poor quality of water in the area.

During the evening of June 13 the men of the 55th heard the sounds of an army on the move. Believing the noise indicated a Federal attack, the men of the regiment prepared for the ensuing melee. The next morning the Confederates were surprised to see that the Federals had withdrawn from their defenses. That evening, Davis's brigade moved west on the south side of the Rappahannock to Falmouth. Over the next several days, the men of the 55th marched northwest through Culpeper, across the Rapidan, and toward the Shenandoah Valley. By June 20, the brigade and most of Hill's corps had reached the vicinity of Winchester, and finally crossed the Potomac River on June 25, settling near Cashtown, Pennsylvania, at the end of June.[4]

On July 1, 1863, Heth ordered brigadier generals James J. Archer and Joseph R. Davis to reconnoiter the area around Gettysburg. The goal of the Confederates was to occupy the town, and they marched on, unaware that the Federals were waiting for them. The 55th North Carolina had about 640 men ready for combat but did not expect to see much, if any, action that morning.[5] Brigadier General Joseph R. Davis's official report outlines the action his brigade participated in during the three days of battle at Gettysburg.

> Major: I have the honor to submit the following report of the operations of Major-General Heth's division in the battle of July 3, at Gettysburg: On the evening of the 2d, this division, under command of Brigadier General J. J. Pettigrew (Major-General Heth having been wounded in the engagement of the 1st), moved to the front, and was formed in line of battle, with Archer's brigade on the right, commanded by Colonel B. D. Fry (Brigadier-General Archer having been wounded and captured on July 1); Colonel Brockenbrough's brigade on the left; Pettigrew's, commanded by Colonel James K.

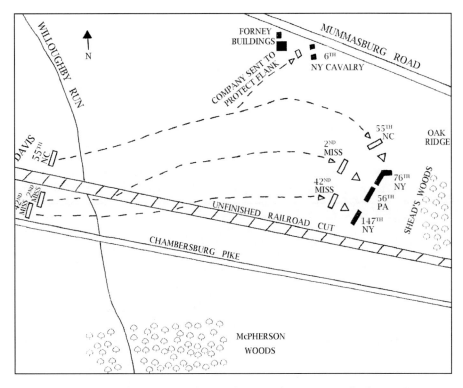

Davis's brigade advances toward Gettysburg on the morning of July 1, 1863.

Marshall, of the Fifty-second North Carolina, on the right center, and Davis'
on the left center immediately in the rear of our artillery, which was in position on the crest of a high ridge running nearly parallel to the enemy's line,
which was on a similar elevation and nearly 1 mile distant, the intervening
space, excepting the crests of the hills, being fields, intersected by strong post
and rail fences. In this position we bivouacked for the night. Early on the
morning of the 3d, the enemy threw some shells at the artillery in our front,
from which a few casualties occurred in on of the brigades. About 9 A.M. the
division was moved to the left about a quarter of a mile, and in the same
order of battle was formed in the rear of Major Pegram's battalion of artillery,
which was posted on the crest of a high hill, the ground between us and the
enemy being like that of our first position. About 1 p.m. the artillery along
our entire line opened on the enemy, and was promptly replied to. For two
hours the fire was heavy and incessant. Being immediately in the rear of our
batteries, and having had no time to prepare means for protection, we suffered some losses. In Davis' brigade 2 men were killed and 21 wounded. The
order had been given that, when the artillery in our front ceased firing, the
division would attack the enemy's batteries, keeping dressed to the right, and
moving in line with Major-General Pickett's division, which was on our

right, and march obliquely to the left. The artillery ceased firing at 3 o'clock, and the order to move forward was given and promptly obeyed. The division moved off in line, and, passing the wooded crest of the hill, descended to the open fields that lay between us and the enemy. Not a gun was fired at us until we reached a strong post and rail fence about three-quarters of a mile from the enemy's position, when we were met by a heavy fire of grape, canister, and shell, which told sadly upon our ranks. Under this destructive fire, which commanded our front and left with fatal effect, the troops displayed great coolness, were well in hand, and moved steadily forward, regularly closing up the gaps made in their ranks. Our advance across the fields was interrupted by other fences of a similar character, in crossing which the alignment became more or less deranged. This was in each case promptly rectified, and though its ranks were growing thinner at every step, this division moved steadily on in line with the troops on the right. When within musket-range, we encountered a heavy fire of small-arms, from which we suffered severely; but this did not for moment check the advance. The right of the division, owing to the conformation of the ridge on which the enemy was posted, having a shorter distance to pass over to reach his first line of defense, encountered him first in close conflict; but the whole division dashed up to his first line of defense — a stone wall — behind which the opposing infantry was strongly posted. Here we were subjected to a most galling fire of musketry and artillery, that so reduced the already thinned ranks that any further effort to carry the position was hopeless, and there was nothing left but to retire to the position originally held, which was done in more or less confusion. About 4 p.m. the division reached the line held in the morning, and remained there thirty hours, excepting an attack from the enemy. No demonstration was made on any part of our line during that or the following day, on the night of which we began our retreat to Hagerstown. In the assault upon the enemy's position, the coolness and courage of officers and men are worthy of high commendation, and I regret that the names of the gallant men who fell distinguished on that bloody field have not been more fully reported. In this assault, we are called upon to mourn the loss of many brave officers and men. Colonel B. D. Fry, Thirteenth Alabama, commanding Archer's brigade, and Colonel James K. Marshall, of the Fifty-second North Carolina, commanding Pettigrew's, were wounded and taken prisoners while gallantly leading their brigades. The number killed and wounded was very great, and in officers unusually so, as may be seen from the fact that in Archer's brigade but two field officers escaped, in Pettigrew's but one, and in Davis' all were killed or wounded. Brigadier-General Pettigrew had his horse killed, and received a slight wound in the hand. Not having commanded the division in this engagement, and having been exclusively occupied by the operations of my own brigade, this report is necessarily imperfect, and I regret that I am unable to do full justice to the division.[6]

With roughly 50 men fit for duty, Company F marched into Pennsylvania, under the command of 1st Lieutenant Joseph J. Hoyle. They would return to Virginia with fewer than twenty. Among the casualties were Sarah Hoyle's brothers, Isaac and Rufus Self. Isaac was captured on July 1, and Rufus was wounded in the hand. The 55th, along with the rest of Davis's brigade, fought bravely on July 1, 1863, and then participated in the Confederate attack on July 3. Joseph Hoyle led his company during these horrific days, and although his letters express a deep feeling of sorrow, his words could not describe the sense of despair and fear he must have felt after the guns fell silent on the battlefield.

* * *

Camp on Blackwater , Va.
May, 1863 ...No. 4 (New Series)

My Dear Wife:

Once more we have a prospect of enjoying a short rest, at least. We have now been in camp at one place near a week, and I hope we will remain here some while. We are now guarding a ford on the river, known as Joiner's Ford. The enemy has made no move on this line, that I am aware of since we left around Suffolk. I learn they followed us when we left down there, but they took care to keep a respectable distance behind. They took some of our worn out men, who stopped behind prisoners.

Friday, 8 — This is a cold damp day. We have a tent to stay in again, and are faring very well.

Saturday, 9 — We are just staying here doing nothing except keeping up our picket post. We have constructed us a bed to day.

Sunday, 10 — It is one year to day since I enlisted, and at that time I had no idea I would be in service a year, surely another year will not roll around till peace will come. I pray it may not be another month. We have had preaching to-day, which is a rarity with us, but we have prayer meeting in our company every favorable night.

Monday, 11 — Our company is on picket to-day, and we have had a pleasant time in the cool recesses along the bank of the river. All has been quiet.

Tuesday, 12 — We returned to camp this morning and I have been engaged in making out our pay rolls nearly all day. Sarah I know you recollect this day one year ago. It was a very solem day to us. It was the day I first left home, and I did not think then that I would be parted from my dear wife one long year, but who knows the decrees of fate? Yet I pray the time of our separation may not be much longer. I received your kind letter to-day bearing date up to the 6th. I am sorry you cannot get my letters regular, but I can not help it.

Wednesday, 13 — We are preparing to move again this morning. We are going a few miles further up the river. I have no news yet of the killed and wounded in the late battle at Fredericksburg. I am very anxious to hear. I hope God has shielded our friends. I learn General Jackson has died since the battle, a great loss to our cause.[7] Sarah, I want you to send me a pair of slips the first opportunity you have. I have some nice cloth for a pair of pants if I could have an opportunity of sending it home for you to make up. We have reached our new camp this evening and have been engaged in putting up our tents. The sun is just sitting far in the west, and I cannot help thinking of my dear wife far away in that direction too. Dear Sarah, I wonder what you are doing this beautiful evening. Me thinks I see you sitting near the kitchen door looking out with your head lent upon your hand, in deep study, no doubt thinking of me and wondering where I am and what I am doing. Why Sarah, it seems like I can almost lay my hand upon your dear head and smooth back your gentle hair. O might it be so indeed. I remain yours in hope and love.

S. A. Hoyle   Joe

On Blackwater, Va.
May, 1863, No. 5 (New Series)

Dear Wife:

Friday, 15 — This evening we were ordered down to Franklin. The enemy is advancing on that place.

Saturday, 16 — We marched all night last night, arriving at Franklin about day. Here we rested a few hours and then crossed the river, when our company was ordered on picket. All has been quiet during the day with us, but the S Carolinians had a skirmish with the enemy.

Sunday, 17 — We recrossed this morning before day, and rested till day, when we marched up the road to Blackwater church. Joseph Mull visited us this evening, and took supper with us.

Monday, 18 — We were aroused this morning before day, and marched down the road to Joiner's Church, where we have remained all day.

Tuesday, 19 — Late this evening we were ordered back to camp, the yankees having gone back, where we arrived about midnight. I am unwell to-day, and had a hard task to reach the camp.

Wednesday, 20 — I am still unwell I have dysenterry — I received a letter from Wm. R. Self, he came through the battle safe. Lemuel also came through safe. Thomas Shuford is killed.[8] Dear Sarah, I have made this letter as short as possible, as I do not feel well enough to write much. Your kind letter was received a few days since, and was read with much pleasure, as they always are. I pray the good Lord will keep my dear wife from harm, and grant us the happy privilege of a union again on earth, and above all a union in heaven.

Thursday, 21—I am some better this morning. I remain yours in love and hope.

S. A. Hoyle   Joe

On Blackwater, Va.

May, 1863... No. 6 (New Series)

Hope is the balm of life! How it sooths the sorrow-stricken hearts!

Dear Wife:

Friday, 22 — Our company is on picket to-day at Joiner's Ford, about one half miles from camp. All has passed off quiet with us though the yankees are within a few miles beyond the river. They are doing all kind of mischief upon the people over there, burning houses, and turning good women and children out of homes. They burnt two houses this evening worth $15000 a piece and I am informed they actualy locked two women up, and then burned down the houses over them. Is not this horrible! I hope the villains will get their deserts some day.

Saturday, 23 — We returned to camp this morning. Early this evening we (Regt.) were paraded and marched off down the road. We came to Blackwater bridge and laid off our blankets before crossing the river, and we all made sure we were a going to have a fight this time. Several other Regts. and some artillery also crossed over. We went about three miles beyond the river, and drove back a company or two of yankee pickets, when the yankees treated us to a few shells, but no damage was done. We remained till after dark, when we fell back across the river, and returned to camp.

Sunday, 24 — I have spent this holy day principally in reading. We had inspection this evening.

Monday, 25 — I am in charge of a working party at Blackwater bridge to day. We are building extensive fortifications here. I received a letter from you to-day, and as usual I read it with gladness. I found a nice little bunch of flowers in it, which gladdened my heart. I pressed them to my lips and thought of the dear little hand that gathered them. O could I grasp that dear little hand itself how happy I would be. That money you paid is all right. I cant see how you get so much money of your own.

Tuesday, 26 — I am still on duty at Blackwater bridge, and expect to be all this week, and I do not know whether we will get done our work this week or not. We generally go back to camp of a night. The distance is about 3 miles.

Wednesday, 27 — Still at Blackwater bridge.

Thursday, 28 — We staid down here last night. Wm. Craige caught some fish last night and I helped him eat them this morning. The yankees beyond river have fallen back nearer Suffolk. We are building fortifications for two batterys of artillery now. Far away is my wife to me most dear, but love's charm measures the distance, and I feel thy precious love most near.

                                                                    Joe

---

On Blackwater, Va.
May, 1863....No. & (New Series)

My Dear Wife:

Friday, 29 — I am still on duty at Blackwater Bridge. I am reading Baxter's Saints Rest. It is a good book, and I find instruction and comfort in reading it.[9]

Saturday, 30 — We staid down here (at bridge) last night. Returned to camp this evening.

Sunday, 31 — The Chaplain of the 42 Miss Regt. came over and preached for us to-day.[10] His subject was the <u>Reasonableness of Religion</u>; and he did it justice. By the By, I am glad to tell you that myself, J. A. Kennedy, and a few others hold prayer meetings in our company every favorable night, and I am happy to say that some seeming interest at least, is manifested in it by our men.[11]

<u>June,</u>

Monday, 1 — I am again on duty at Blackwater bridge. I returned to camp this evening and found a letter from you awaiting me. Dear Sarah, you do not know how my heart was filled with joy to hear that my dear mother had joined the church. I stopped reading and thanked God from the bottom of my heart for it, and for answering my prayers; for long have I prayed the good Lord to reclaim her, and now I feel that he has heard and answered my prayer. Dear Sarah, God will hear faithful prayer. Blessed be the name of the Lord! Dear Sarah, I often pray for you all at St. Peter's and I hope God will hear my feeble prayer and bless you all.

Tuesday, 2 — We are under marching orders, and will start in the morning for Richmond, and I expect we will go on to Fredericksburg. May God's protection go with us.

Wednesday, 3 — We marched to Ivor this morning, and took the train for Petersburg, where we arrived this evening. We camped near the city. It rained upon us, but I lay down in the water and slept tolerably well.

Thursday, 4 — We took up the line of march this morning for Richmond. The distance is 23 miles. After a hard days march, we camped near Richmond to-night.

Friday, 5 — We will go into Richmond this morning and I do not

know where we will go to from there. I will write you again as soon as I
can. I remain yours in love and hope.

Mrs. S. A.   Hoyle Joe

Near Fredericksburg, Va.
Monday, June 8th 1863

My Dear wife:

My last letter will inform you that we had left Blackwater, and this
will tell you that we are on that memorable and sacred spot of ground in
the vicinity of Fredericksburg. We marched from Petersburg to Hanover
Junction, 25 miles above Richmond, and took the train there yesterday
morning, and came up to Hamiltons Crossing; which is 2 or 3 miles from
Fredericksburg. We moved down on the lines below, and in sight of Fredericksburg late yesterday evening, and have been in line of battle ever
since. The yankees are across the river in our front but they have made no
advance upon us yet, and some think they will not, though they are fortifying on this side. There is nothing but an open bottom between us and
the yankees. We have a plain view of their camps and batteries beyond the
river, and we can plainly see them marching up and down the river on this
side. Our pickets and the yankee pickets stand in about 300 yards of each
other; but they do not fire at each other. It is a grand sight indeed to view
every thing about here. The 34 Regt. is close by here, some of our boys
have been to it. Lemuel is not with the Regt. he is sick in the hospital at
Richmond. I have not heard any thing of the 57 Regt. yet. We are in General Heath's division now.[12] I will close for the present, for I do not know
whether I will have a chance to send this to you or not. I remain as ever,
yours in love and hope.

Joe
Direct your letters thus.
Lt. J. J. Hoyle
Co. F. 55th N.C.T.
Davis Brigade
Richmond, Virginia

June 10th 1863

Dear Wife:

I have wrote you a letter this week, but as I have a chance to send this
I will drop you a few more lines, simply to let you know that I am still
well, and we are still being here in sight of the yankees. They have made
no further advance yet, and it is uncertain whether we will have a fight or

not. I hope we may not. Dear Sarah be not over anxious but put your trust in God, and all will be well. As ever, yours in hope & love.

Joe

No. 8 [New Series]
June, 1863

My Dear wife:

I received your kind letter bearing date up to 2nd inst- and I read it with interest for it allways makes my heart glad to get letters from my dearest one on earth. I am sorry to hear that you get my letters so irregular; for I assure you I write every week, and last week I sent you two. The fault must be in the mail.

Friday, 5 — We passed through Richmond to-day. The ladies showed us many acts of kindness and sympathy, giving us water, milk, blackberry wine etc. The city is magnificent and extensive beyond any thing I have yet seen — We camped 3 miles above Richmond.

Saturday, 6 — After a hard days march, we camped at Hanover Junction to night. We had another severe rain to night, but we made out better than you would expect.

Sunday, 7 — We took the train this morning, and after a few hours arrived at Hamilton's Crossing, near Fredericksburg. We were moved down on the lines this evening, and formed in line of battle. The yankees are across the river about one mile in our front. They are fortifying.

Monday, 8 — This morning we have a grand view of the yankee camps etc. and as nothing separates us but an open valey, we can see all their maneuvers.

Tuesday, 9 — We are still in our position, in line of battle along our breastworks. Our batteries and the yankees exchanged a few shells this evening; but no damage.

Wednesday, 10— Still in our position, all quiet. The yankees are working away.

Thursday, 11— Nothing new.

Friday, 12 — Some fears of an attack were had last night, but all passed off quietly.

Saturday, 13 — Our company was on picket to-day all has been quiet except some shelling between our batteries and the enemies.

Sunday, 14 — We apprehended an attack last night and lay on our arms, but behold when day light came this morning, they yankees had all left this side of the river.[13] Our men captured several prisoners this morning who did not get over the river quite soon enough. They left some plunder on this side and some guns, showing that their retreat was somewhat confused. Where they are gone or what are their intentions, of course, we know not. We had to send our trunks, and nearly all our bagage back to Richmond. We cannot get them hauled out here. I will send my trunk home if I can. The Capt is at the hospital in Richmond with a sore arm. I expect he will go home, and maybe he will take my trunk. So you see we will have to fare like soldiers up here. Of course we will all get lousy when we have so little chance to change our clothing.

Monday, 15 — We moved a few miles further up the river last evening. Dear Sarah, we are liable to have a fight here at any time, but do not be too uneasy, let us trust in the Lord, knowing he will do whatever is best. Let us continue to pray for peace, and that we may be united in presence again, and God will hear us, if we pray right. Hope, sweet hope cheers my breast and blesses me up. Sarah, we could not live without hope. I remain as ever, yours in hope and love.

Joe

My Sarah, Direct your letters to Richmond, Davis Brigade.

The following letter was printed in the June 29, 1863, issue of the *Spirit of the Age.*

Near Fredericksburg, Va., June 15th.

Mr. Editor: This will inform you that we are now in the memorable vicinity of Fredericksburg. We came here nine days ago, and took up our position on the lines immediately below the village. The enemy were across the river in our front fortifying with all might. We lay thus for eight days, our pickets and those of the enemy confronting each other at a distance of not more than four hundred yards. I should here remark that the ground to our front was an open valley to the Stafford hills beyond the river; and the yankee camps and fortifications were open to our view.

Night before last, a continual crossing was heard over their pontoons, and we lay in readiness all night, expecting an attack in the morning. But, behold, when the morning's light dawned, they had all left this side, except a few stragglers who were captured by our men. They left a number of articles behind and, among them, some guns, which showed that their retreat was hurried. They had constructed formidable breast-works, and had mounted ten pieces of artillery upon them. Whether the whole affair was a feint, or some exigency caused them to withdraw, is not known. Their balloons were up frequently all day yesterday. I suppose they were anxious to know how their withdrawal affected our forces. Of course some change was made along our line. — We moved a short distance last evening.

Although this is a hilly country, yet we have sorry water here, and the health of our Regiment is declining since we came here, though I hope we will fare better when we become used to the water and climate. The portion of the army that I have seen here are in fine order and spirits.

J. J. H.,
Lieut. Co. F, 55th N. C. T.

In hope, my heart is joined in thine.   Near Culpeper, Va.
Wednesday, June 17th 1863.

My Dear wife:

As we are resting a little while this morning, I will drop you a few lines. We have been on the march since Sunday 12 O' clock. As I wrote you in my last the main body, if not all, the yankee army has left Fredericksburg, and hence we were not needed there any longer. Our troops have already penetrated into the valey of Va., and a few days ago, General Ewell's corps captured Winchester including 12,000 prisoners.[14] This may not be the correct number. We are going up in that direction and it may be you will hear of us going into Maryland before we stope. I do not know where Hooker's yankee army is but I expect we will have plenty fighting to do before we reach the Potomac River. It is very warm and hard marching, but we all stand it as well as could be expected thus far. I blistered my feet the first day we left Fredericksburg, but since then they have done very well.

Dear Sarah, we are beginning to see hard times now, but I am very willing to endure them, for we are no better than the poor soldiers who have to endure such hardships. I am willing to do my part for my country, and if it is Gods will that my life should be sacrificed in the service of my country, I will die contented. So Dear wife, let us trust all to the Lord, but at the same time, let us not forget to pray constantly and vehemently for what we want, for God has promised to hear prayer. What a blessed promise is that which says; "Ask and ye shall receive, seek and ye shall find, knock and it shall be opened unto you" Dear wife, let us believe this when we pray; for the Lord himself has spoken it.

Dear Sarah, it will be a happy time with us if we are so fortunate as to get to live to-gether again, and if we are never privileged to meet again on earth, O let us have a lively hope of a permanent union in heaven, that better land. Dear Sarah, I expect we will have few chances of sending letters after we leave this place, but I assure you I will write every chance. And you must continue to write regular. I will enclose you an envelope, for a copy how to direct your letters. I have heard nothing of Wm. R. Self yet, but I suppose he is up about Winchester. Isaac and Rufus are well. I remain, as ever, your loving husban,

Joe

Thou art my first love, My dearest little dove, Sarah.

No. 9 [New Series]
June, 1863

My dear wife:

As I have a little time this evening (24th) I will bring up my every day notes to this date. As you know, I keep a daily note of every day. I can copy from this at any time. To keep up the connexion I will have to begin back at the time we left Fredericksburg.

Monday, 15 — We left our position below the vilage last evening, and are on the march again to-day. We passed through the late battle field this evening.[15] The timber and every thing else is torn up suppprisingly.

Tuesday, 16 — We are still on the march, going up the river toward Culpeper, Court House.

Wednesday, 17 — We passed through Culpeper to-day and camped for the night.

Thursday, 18 — We have marched very hard to-day, and the heat has been very burdensom. I am told, several men in the division died on the road with excessive heat. We had a fine shower this evening, which makes the air more pleasant.

Friday, 19 — The march has been more agreeable to-day, not so warm. We camped at the foot of the Blue ridge.

Saturday, 20 — We crossed the mountain this morning. Passed through the town of Front Royal to-day. The ladies showed us their usual kindness in giving us water. We crossed the Shenandoah River to-day; we had to foard it, and to this end had to pull off all our clothes but our shirts. The scene was nover and peculiar another pelting rain fell on us this evening.

Sunday, 21— This holy Sabbath finds us still on the march. We left the Winchester road this morning turning to the right toward the Potomac river. We camped near a little place known as Berryville this evening.

Monday, 22 — We have remained in bivouac (camp) all day to-day. I am reading the Bible some. I have a little pouch in which I carry my bible and writing utensils, and your likeness, and I carry this with me continually. So you see what things I esteem most highly.

Tuesday, 23 — We are on the march again to-day, going toward Harper's Ferry. I received your letter to-day, dating up to the 9th inst. I was glad to get it.

Wednesday, 24 — We passed through Charlestown this morning, amid the cheering demonstration of a thousand hats and handkerchiefs. The ladies not only showed us sympathy by waving hats and handkerchiefs, but were very generous in giving us bread, milk, butter, honey, etc. I have never seen a more unanimous show of kindness.[16] We passed in sight of Harper's Ferry, going above, and camped in a mile or two of the Potomac, near Shepperds Town. I suppose we will cross the river in the morning. A great many of our forces have already crossed. I suppose we are going as far as we can get, and I expect we will have to fight before we go far. May God be with us and lead us aright. This part of Va. is the finest country I have ever seen. There is abundance of wheat here and plenty old wheat which has not yet been thrashed. I see the finest cattle here I ever saw. Dear Sarah, this evening finds me well, and I hope it may find you well. My dear Sarah, I hope you will not be too anxious, but put your trust and hope in the Lord, as I have often said, let us hope for the best and at the same time prepare for the worst. My letters will necessarily be irregular now, and I do not expect to get yours any thing like regular if at all, but I will write every chance. Direct your letters as I formerly instructed you, to Richmond. I remain as ever, yours in love and hope.

Mrs. S. A. Hoyle   Joe

Hagerstown, Md.
July 9th 1863

My Dear wife:

After a long silence I take the pleasure of dropping you a few lines, not knowing, however whether I will have a chance to send them or not. After crossing the Potomac, we proceed through Maryland into Pensylvania, and went quietly on till we came to a town by the name of Gettysburg; here the yankees were concentrating their forces to fight us. On the 1st day of July, our forces attacked them, and after a hard fight we drove them back out of town. Our brigade was foremost in the fight and suffered severely. I might say truly that I was in the very Jaws of death, yet the good Lord saved me. I will now give you a list of the killed, wounded, and missing of our company: The killed are Wm. J. Self, W. F. Bracket, Thomas Willis, and William Craige — making 4.[17] The wounded are, Eli Newton, Jno. Smith, Robt Swofford, Daniel Canipe, J. A. Canipe, Samuel McNeily, Jonathan McNeily, Aron Cook, and Henry Norman — making 9.[18]

The missing are, John Cline, I. R. Self, A. P. Iveston, D. A. B Garner, Wesley Brendel, P.M. Bivens, Wm. Elmore, Sol Hoyle, Joel Hoyle, Robt. Norman, Peter Lael, Wm. S. Seagle, Wm. Swink, Jno. Swink, David Turner, Robert Willis, Samuel Willis, Noah Canipe, Noah Warlick, and

Jackson White — making 20.[19] These missing I think are prisoners. A man who was a prisoner and got away told me he seen Isaac a prisoner — You will see by this how severely we suffered, and the balance of the Regt. suffered equally as severe. All our field officers were wounded, and our Lieut Col. has since died, and our Col has been taken prisoner.[20] But this is not all, the fight lasted three days and on the 3rd we were into it again, and this was a hotter time than the first day, though it did not last so long. We charged the yankees posted behind a stone fence and heavily supported by artillery. We had to advance near a mile through an open field, and their batteries rained shot and shell upon us, but we went on till we got within about 100 yards of them when they so thinned our ranks that we had to fall back. The ground was almost covered with our dead and wounded. In this fight our loss in our co. is as follows: None was killed that I know of. The following were wounded: Alfred Newton, Rufus Self in the hand; Wm. M. Boiles, and Harrison Cook.[21] The missing are Lieut. Mull, C. Goodson, and Anderson Self[22] — These missing may be killed, as the yankees held the battle field and we could not tell whether they were killed or not. — The next evening we fell back and are now at this place, and suppose we will recross the river as soon as it gets low enough. The rain having raised it. I do not think any of my company are dangerously wounded. Our troops are badly cut up. Brigades now are not larger than Regts were befor the fight. I have 14 in my co. now. Our Regt has about 100. We also damaged the yankees a great dear, but I cannot say who was hurt the worst. If we get back across the river I will write you again.[23] I remain yours in love and hope,

Joe

Bivouac 55th N. C. T.
Wednesday evening, July 15th 1863.

My Dear wife:

I take the opportunity this evening of dropping you a few lines, although I am so tired and broken down that I do not feel like doing any thing. I can inform you that we recrossed the Potomac yesturday and are now in Va. below Martinsburg. We had another fight yesturday just before we crossed the river with the yankee cavalry. They dashed upon us while we were lieing resting, and completely supprised us, but we formed and held them in check till we got across the river. By Gods good will I came through safe again, but I had my hat brim torn with a bullet. Levi Wise of our co. was killed and James Stamy, and Franklin Shuford are missing.[24] We are falling back toward Culpeper and I learned we are ordered there. Our men are nearly worn out, and marching goes mighty hard. I will give you a regular account of our trip over the Potomac whenever I can. I do pray that this cruel war will end and we all get home again, O happy day. I wrote you a few days ago about our other two battles in Pennsylvania, but for fear you do not get it, I will give you another list of our killed, wounded and missing in our company. — First Fight Killed — William J. Self, Wm Craige, W. F. Bracket, and Thomas Willis — 4. Wounded — Jno. Smith, Eli Newton, Robt. Swofford, Sam McNeily, Jonathan McNeily, Dan Canipe, J. A. Canipe, Aaron Cook, and Henry Norman — 9. Missing — John Cline, I. R. Self, A. P. Iverster, David B. garner, Monroe Bivens, N. J. Canipe, Wm. Elmore, Sol Hoyle, Joel Hoyle, Peter Lael, Robt. Norman, Wm. Seagle, David Turner, Robt Willis, Samuel Willis, Jack White, Wesley Brendel, Wm. Swink, Jno. Swink, and Noah Warlick — 20. Second Fight — Killed — none known of. Wounded — Rufus Self in hand, Alfred Newton, in thigh, Harrison Cook in wrist and Wm. Boiler in foot. Missing — Lieut Mull, Anderson Self, and L. Goodson.[25] These missing may be killed or wounded, as the yankees held the battle field. I received a letter from you the other day though it is an old one. I remain as ever, your loving husband,

Sarah   Joe

June, 1863 — No. 10

My Dear wife:

I will now proceed to continue my regular series of letters, and as you see I will have to go back to the time we crossed the Potomac, as that is the time I left off.

Thursday, 25 — We waded the Potomac this morning below Shepardstown, going into Maryland. We passed through Sharpsburg, and went on to Hagerstown, where we bivouaced* for the night. Considerable regard has been displayed by the Maryland ladies toward us.

Friday, 26 — We are passing on toward Pensylvania, and crossed the line into it (Pa.) this evening. The day has been rainy, and marching is very disagreeable. I am unwell, but have kept up with the Regiment.

Saturday, 27 — Still on the march northward. We passed through Fayetville this evening, and bivouacked.

Sunday, 28 — We remained in bivouac all day. Although it is Sunday, yet necessity compels us to wash our clothes, etc. Indeed this looks like there is no Sunday in war.

Monday, 29 — Took up the line of march again this morning. We are traveling through the mountains again. We bivouaced near Cash Town on the mountain side.

Tuesday, 30 — We have remained in bivouac all day — Raining. I saw brother Benick this evening. He is looking well.

July, 1863

Wednesday, 1—We moved forward this morning to attack the enemy who is in our front. Our brigade is in front and opened the fight. We found the enemy in position immediately in front of Gettysburg, Pa. We (our brigade) attacked him and after a sharp struggle broke two of his lines and drove him back. But the yankees soon brought up reinforcements on our right, and we, having no forces to cooperate with us on the flanks, after a hard contest, had to fall back.[26] We fell back slowly some distance and awaited reinforcements. Our loss was heavy in this onset, a great many being captured. Ewells forces now came up on our left, and the balance of our Corps on our right, and the battle raged furiously along the whole line. Our forces moved steadily on, though the enemy gave back very stubbornly, but against sunset we had drove them back at all points and held the town. The yankee loss was heavy in killed wounded and prisoners, evidently heavier than ours. This days fight was a decided victory for us. But alas! it has been bought with the life-blood of many of our brave boys. Our division was permitted to pass back to the rear to night and rest. Our Regt went into the fight this morning with about 525 men, and we came out this evening with 123, and our division generally has suffered equally as much. So you can form some idea of our loss. I carried 48 into the fight and came out with 11. A ball struck me on the rump as we were falling back, but did not enter. I would give the blessed Lord all thanks for preserving me, while death reigned so near around.

Thursday, 2—We rested till late this evening when we were moved round to the right, and took position on our lines, bloody work is before us again. Hard fighting has been going on to-day, but, as you see, our division was not in it. The enemy has a very strong position, and our men have failed to route them to-day.

Friday, 3—We have been shelled nearly all day, and this evening the most terrific cannonading occurred that I ever heard. We had over 100 pieces of cannon engaged and the yankees, I suppose, had equally as many. The cannonading continued one hour. Our line was then ordered to move forward and charge the enemy, who were posted behind a stone fence, with their artillery on rising ground in their rear. An open field lay to their front through which we had to advance. We moved forward, exposed to a hot fire of grape shot and shells, yet we moved on. When we came in range of their small arms their fire became destructive in the extreme yet we moved on till within about 100 yards of their line, when our ranks were so thinned that we could proceed no further. So our line broke in confusion and every man got out the best he could.[27] It must be remembered that while we were going back, we were equally exposed as when we were advancing.

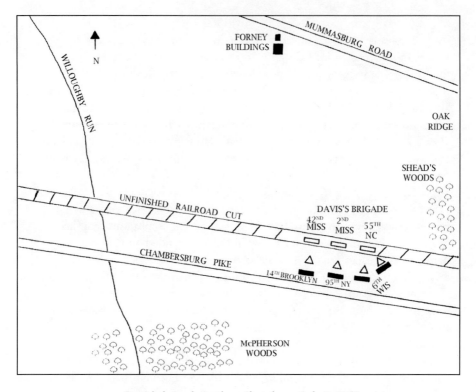

Davis's brigade in the railroad cut, July 1, 1863.

God's good grace again shielded me, and I came out unhurt. Rufus was wounded in the charge, and Lieut Mull never came out I do not know whether he was killed or not. A great many, in fact most of our wounded and dead could not be gotten out. Our Regt went in this time with about 120 and came out with 40.[28] The rest suffered equally as much. We now formed on our original line and rested for the night.

Saturday, 4 — Lay in our position till dark this evening, when we commenced falling back. A heavy rain fell this evening, and the roads are extremely muddy. Added to this the darkness of the night makes the most difficult and laborious marching I ever experienced. We marched al night.

Sunday, 5 — We halted a little while this morning, after passing through Fairfield. Then took up our march again and have been going all day. The roads are desperately bad. We are falling back toward the Potomac. Bivouaced near Waynesboro, Pa.

Monday, 6 — Continueing our retreat. We traveled late to night, and bivouaced near Hagerstown, Md. The march is setting very severely upon us.

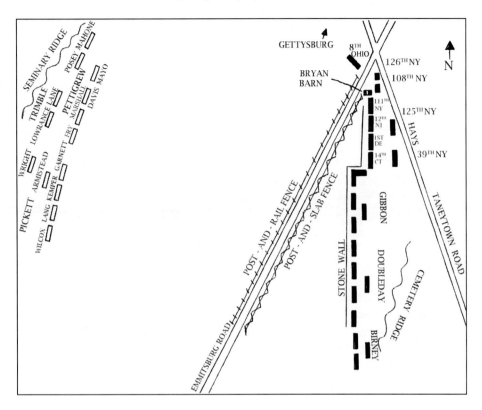

Location of Pettigrew and Pickett's divisions on the afternoon of July 3, 1863.

Tuesday, 7 — We passed through Hagerstown this morning, when we filed out and took up camp. Here we have remained all day and night, and we are very glad to get to rest, for we need it very much.

Wednesday, 8 — We have not moved to-day. The Potomac is so full we can not cross it and hence our staying here.

Thursday, 9 — Remained in our place all day.

Friday, 10 — Still in our place, fighting has been going on to the south this morning. We filed out in that direction this evening and formed in line in rear of where the fighting has been to-day. WE remained here till dark when we drew off toward the river, 1 or 3 miles.

Saturday, 11 — We filed out to the left and formed line this morning, and are fortifying. The yankees are in our front. Skirmishing is going on. A battle is imminent. May God be with us.

Sunday, 12 — Still being in line, expecting the yankees. They drove back our skirmishers this evening, advancing theirs in sight of our line.

Monday, 13 — Skirmishing continues. Our forces drew off this evening at dark toward the Potomac. It is raining and the roads are desperately muddy. This night has been the worst marching I have done yet.

Tuesday, 14 — Our Division halted and formed in line faced to the rear this morning, about 1½ miles from the river, to protect the rear while crossing (We are crossing on a pontoon bridge) We stacked arms and lay down to rest but we did not lie long till the yankee cavalry dashed in among us befor we knew it, completely supprising us. We had to get our arms and form as best we could while the bullets were whizzing among us. We formed after a little, and held them in check till we could cross the river. We lost a good many men in this affair. Mostly prisoners, I think. After crossing, we passed on a few miles and bivouaced.

Wednesday, 15 — We have been marching all day to-day, passing through Martinsburg, going toward Winchester. Took up camp to night on Bunker's Hill, 12 miles from Winchester.

Thursday, 16 — We have not moved to-day.

Friday, 17 — Still in our place.

Saturday, 18 — We are still staying here. It looks like we are going to stay some while.

Sunday, 19 — This blessed Sabbath finds us still in camp I wish I could be at home to go with you to preaching.

The following letter was found in the Peter Mull Collection, North Carolina Department of Archives and History, Raleigh, North Carolina.

Bunker's Hill, Va.
July 17th, 1863.

Mrs. Wise:

It becomes my painful duty to inform you of the death of your husband Levi Wise. He was killed on the 14th inst, while bravely fighting the enemy. He died a patriots death, and I hope is gone to rest. You have my heart-felt sympathy in your grief for that loss which cannot be returned. Nothing he had was secured. Yours with respect[29]

Lieut J. J. Hoyle
Comdg. Co. F 55th N. C.
Bunker's Hill, Va.
July 17th 1863.

Bunker's Hill,
Monday, July 20th 1863.

My Dear wife:

This morning still finds us in camp here. I am just tolerably well, though I think I will be stout again in a few days. I have received letters from you bearing date up to the 6th inst. Dear Sarah, I pray continually that we may have a speedy peace, and I hope God will hear my prayers, and soon permit us all to come home. But we must be willing to await God's own good time. "His will be done." We have 14 men in our company now. Rufus I reckon, is gone on to Richmond. I heard of him being at Stanton. I know nothing further of Isaac.

Joe

Near Culpeper,
July, 25th 1863.

My Dear wife:

I have the opportunity of dropping you a few lines this evening, informing you that I am not very well. I have been unwell since we left Winchester, and the march has set very hard upon me, but I have held up to come through. We arrived in the vicinity of Culpeper this morning, and pitched camp. I cannot tell how long we will stay here, though I hope we will get to rest awhile, for we all need it very much. We have been now nearly two months since we left Blackwater, and we have been marching or fighting nearly all the time. We have seen a hard time of it, if any body ever did. Every body is sicker of the war than they ever was before, and I fear many will run away. I do pray the war will close before long for why should we continue to kill up each other. If Capt. Mull gets home, he will bring my cloth and I want you to make me a pair of pants and a jacket out of it. You will have to guess at the fit as best you can. I do not want the jacket collar mad to turn back. I want it military fashion. Dr. Osborn, I guess can tell you how that fashion is. Capt has buttons for it. I have 2 yards of the cloth. May be you will have a chance to see Capt. Mull's jacket, and then you will know how to make it. I have received no late letter from you but I know it is not your fault. Dear Sarah I will close for the present, as I do not feel like writing. I will write you again in a few days. I remain, as ever, yours in hope & love.

Joe

Mrs. S. A. Hoyle   Give my love to all.
I have no stamps nor change, so you will have to pay the postage.

Near Culpeper, Va.
July 28th 1863.

My Dear wife:

I take the pleasure this morning of dropping you a few lines informing you that I am still unwell, though I think I am a little better this morning. And if I could have the gentle hand of a dear wife to wait upon me, and speak kind and sympathizing words to me I know I should feel better. But alas! my dearest earthly friend is far away, and I have to be alone in my sick hours. But I have a heavenly friend that will always be near me, and I lean on him for support. The religion of Jesus supports me.

Dear Sarah be not too uneasy, for I hope I will get well after a while. I have no news to give you. Every thing seems quiet with us now. I do not know where the yankees are or what they are doing. But there is no sign of no fighting, for we never know of a fight till we are almost into it. I can not give you any further news of Isaac or Rufus. You can tell mother's folks how I am, for I am so feeble that I do not feel like writing to them too now. If I do not begin to mend in a few days I am a going to try to get to go to the hospital in Richmond, and if I get a chance of course I will come home. As ever, yours in hope & love.

Joe

I have received no letter from you for some time, but I am looking every day.

6. The Calm Before the Storm, August 1863–April 1864

"When all is silent in the night"

Morale was low in the Army of Northern Virginia after the defeat at Gettysburg. Desertions increased as men lost the desire to fight for a cause many felt would never be achieved. After all their sacrifices and triumphs they were no closer to winning the war than they had been in July 1861. And now, with the loss in Pennsylvania, they were on the retreat.

President Davis and General Lee did what they could to stem the tide of desertions, offering pardons and furloughs to help keep men in the army. By October, with the addition of new conscripts and the success of governmental interventions, the ranks slowly began to swell.[1] Although defeat and lack of supplies had reduced morale, most Confederate soldiers continued to support the war.

Some citizens in the Old North State, however, began to speak out openly against the conflict. William Woods Holden, owner of the newspaper the *Raleigh Standard*, began a rhetorical crusade urging the Confederacy to seek peace with the North, and wrote numerous articles beseeching officials of all Southern states to convene a conference to negotiate an end to the war. When President Davis and other Southern political leaders refused to even hear his request, Holden focused his attention on his own state and hoped he could push for North Carolina to secede from the Confederacy.[2]

Conscription and the recent military defeats had swayed many North Carolinians into believing that the South should sue for an immediate end to the war. The opposition to this movement was led by former Confederate officer and current governor Zebulon B. Vance. Vance, and his followers, believed there could be no peace with the North without honor. The soldiers in most North Carolina regiments agreed with Governor Vance, and those in Lee's army held a convention in August 1863 to support the war effort. Lieutenant Thomas J. Hadley and Lieutenant Charles R. Jones represented the

55th North Carolina. To express their contempt for those in their home state that wished to seek peace with the Federals, the convention voted on and then ratified several resolutions including an assertion that the fighting men from the Old North State would accept only an honorable end to the war. The following summer, North Carolina allowed its soldiers to vote by proxy, and Vance, with the soldier vote, won the election. With his victory the state continued to support the Confederacy, although not always agreeing with the course the nation was following.[3]

Company F and the rest of the 55th North Carolina were conscious of the feelings of those living in their home state, but the war left little time to contemplate politics. The 55th spent most of August and September near Orange Court House, Virginia, drilling and picketing the fords of the Rapidan River. The Federals, under the command of Major General George Meade, were positioned just north of the Army of Northern Virginia. Pickets on both sides, which probably included Joseph Hoyle, fraternized with each other, even though their commanders forbade them to do so. The fighting men of the Union and the Confederacy felt a common bond and understood the difficulties and deprivations soldiers experience in times of war.[4]

In October, Lee received intelligence that troops from the Army of the Potomac had been transferred to the Western Theater, and he therefore made plans to attack Meade's right flank near the Rapidan. Davis's brigade, with the rest of Hill's corps, moved toward Culpeper, which forced the Federals to make a rapid retreat toward Centreville, Virginia. Hill's troops caught up with the Federals near Bristoe Station, and without waiting for support or even reconnoitering the field the lieutenant general ordered his men to attack. Although the Third Corps held the ground the battle proved costly and futile.[5]

Davis's brigade had been held in reserve during the battle but had been ordered to support Brigadier General John Cooke's brigade and thus came under fire. Three men from the 55th North Carolina were killed and two were captured during the battle. Joseph Hoyle, like the rest of his company, spent the night of October 14, 1863, lying on the battlefield forced to listen to the cries and groans of the wounded and dying.[6]

Company F, along with their fellow comrades serving in the 55th North Carolina, remained near Culpeper and Orange Court House throughout the remaining days of 1863. Though they were ordered to march out and meet the Federals in battle several times during the last months of the year, they never engaged in combat. The 55th North Carolina settled into their winter quarters and their rations, consisting of mainly flour and beef, began decreasing the men's health, causing another depletion in morale. Joseph Hoyle spent his second Christmas away from home and wrote of how he missed his wife and life before the war.

As the New Year began, Alfred H. Belo returned to the 55th North Carolina and assumed command. The soldiers spent their time writing letters home, drilling and challenging other regiments to snowball battles, one of which was viewed by General Lee astride his faithful horse Traveler. Desertion, however, continued to plague the Army of Northern Virginia throughout the winter months. Joseph Hoyle had to witness a man from his regiment being shot for desertion, an event he freely admitted was one of the "most affecting sights" he ever saw.[7]

Religious fervor pervaded Lee's army during the winter months, much as it had during the previous year. Joseph Hoyle spent time in camp organizing prayer groups and supporting the spread of Christian fellowship throughout Davis's brigade. Historians have long debated the notion that religion can affect how motivated men are to participate in mortal combat. Undoubtedly, the sight of soldiers suffering and dying on the battlefield encouraged many fighting men to practice their devotion to their god more reverently. As the winter snow melted and the roads began to dry, the thoughts of every soldier unquestionably focused on the coming campaign season. The notion that the last days of April 1864 could be the last they would spend among the living, many soldiers continued to pray and repent. As April approached, the religious revivalism that had spread throughout the army remained strong as the men awaited the order to prepare for battle. With the rise of Ulysses S. Grant to the level of commander of all Union forces, the Confederates would face their most ardent opponent, and a man who understood that the key to victory for the Federals was the complete destruction of the Army of Northern Virginia.[8]

* * *

Near Culpepper, Va.
Aug 1st 1863

My Dear wife:

I again take the pleasure of writing you a few lines informing you that I am still very bad off. Although I think I am improving a little. I have the yellow janders and they are the worst thing that I ever had. I have been over a week now that I am just able to walk about. Dear Sarah I hope you will not be too uneasy about me. I hope the Lord will take care of me. Nothing of interest has transpired since we have been here, though we now have marching orders, and may move at any time. I have received your letter wrote 21st July, and I was sorry to hear that you had received none from me since the battle, for I have written several times. I want you to send me some pants and slips as soon as you can, for I am getting nearly naked, though I will buy if I can. I hope you will excuse this short letter, as I have nothing of interest to write, and also do not feel like writing. You can tell mothers folks how I am. Give my love to all. Tell Lemuel & Alice howdy for me. I remain as ever, yours in love and hope.

Joe

Officers Hospital No. 4,
Richmond, Va.
Aug, 7th 1863.

My dear wife:

I drop you a few lines to let you know that I am now staying at the above named hospital. I came here from Gordonsville last Monday. I am not very sick any more, but I am too weak and feeble to do duty yet. I also have a very sore mouth which troubles me a great deal. I made application yesturday to get to come home, but I could not get off. So I will remain here till I get able to return to my regiment. We have very good fare here. Indeed I think it a very good place to stay at. It costs me $2 per day to stay here. I think if I keep improving that I will be able for duty in ten or twelve days more. Dear Sarah, I would be the gladdest in the world to see you, but it seem I cannot have the blessed opportunity now. We must trust in God, and patiently await his good pleasure. I have not received a letter from you in a long time, but I know one has come to the Regt. for me before now, but I will not get them. If you write to me here, direct your letter thus.

Lieut J. J. Hoyle
Officer's Hospital No 4
Ward "D"
Richmond, Va

I have some money I want to send to you, if I had the chance. I received my pay to-day up to the 1st of Aug. Making $420.00. I had to buy a pair of pants and shirt here which cost very high. I paid $30 for the pants, and they are very common at that. I do hope this wicked war will soon close, for I am getting very tired of it. I want to come home and turn my attention my purposed: and cherrished object. May God soon grant me the privilege. I remain as ever, yours in hope and love.

Joe

Mrs. S. A. Hoyle
Knob Creek, N. C.

Near Orange C. H.
Aug. 20th 1863.

My Dear wife:

I take the pleasure this morning of dropping you a few lines, informing you that I am well as usual and I hope this will find you well. We are still staying in the same place yet and I think it probable that we will stay here some time. The yankees are lieing still also, and there seems to be no prospect of an immediate battle. General Lee has instituted the furloughing system again in this army.[9] One mane can be furloughed for every 50 present for duty. We are sending 4 out of our Regt. Our company does not get to send any one this time. We drew lots what companies should send. We are so scarce of officers that there seems little chance for me to get a furlough, but if it continues I will try after a while. Dear Sarah, I want to see you very much, and nothing on earth would gladden my heart more than to get to return home to stay with you again. How happy we would be: Yet God only knows whether we will be privileged to enjoy this earthly blessing or not, as I have often said, let us hope for the best and at the same time be prepared for the worst. Let us put our whole trust in the Lord; for He will do whatever is best.

Dear Sarah, if it had not been for my trust and hope in God, I reckon I should have gone crazy or done something else bad before now, but with this reliance, and trust in the Lord, I am very well content to stay here till his own good time comes. I will tell you what clothing I want. It may be you have already started some of it to me. I want my pants & jacket you are making out of the cloth I sent, and two pair of slips, and 2 pair of socks. I want you to write whether Capt. Mull brought my trunk home when he came or not. I have not received any letter from you this week, but I hope I shall soon. I remain as ever, yours in hope and love. Give my love to all.

Joe

Near Orange C. H. Va.
Aug. 28th, 1863

My Dear wife:

Your kind letter of the 18th inst came to hand yesturday, and I read it with usual interest. It was forwarded from the hospital at Richmond. I get about all your letters, though some are behind time. We have been getting mail very irregularly for several weeks now, and it is causing a good deal of complaint among the soldiers.[10] Some go so far as to say if they do not get letters from home, they will not stay in the army. And indeed it is very hard when we cannot even hear from home, and our loved ones.

Dear Sarah, you seem very much out of heart in your letter in regard to the prospects of peace and the success of our cause. But I do not think we have any cause for despondency. The darkest cloud will soon pass away and leave us in the enjoyment of sun–shine again. We should recollect that our country is sinful, and wicked, and for these things God will punish us; yet if we will return into the Lord, He will return unto us, and with His blessings upon us we will finally gain our independence. As for those sneaking wretches who are being at home, willfully dead alike to the good of that country which gives them protection, and to all moral obligations; they should, and, I trust do, receive the scorn and contempt of every good man and woman. A just retribution is in store for them when the brave soldier returns home after our independence is achieved.[11] But I will stop on this subject. I have nothing in the way of war news. We are quietly enjoying camp, and there seems no prospect of an early fight. I was glad to hear that Rufus & Rooker had got home. And you may be sure I was glad to know that Wm. Craige was a prisoner instead of being killed. Although Henry Willis yet thinks that he buryed him, though of course he is mis-taken. I have heard nothing of Isaac since Cline came through. I wrote you in my last what I wanted in the way of clothing, etc. But I will state it again. I want my pants and vest, a pair of socks, 2 pair of slips, and if my trunk is at home, send my uniform coat, I also want Isaac's sachel sent back again. If you can do so send me a small box of provisions when Rufus comes. Send some fruit, butter, and whatever else you can. A small box, or even a bag that he could carry in the car with him would not be much trouble. Tell Rooker I wish he would get me another pair of boots made after a while, if he can. Give my love to all. I would write to Wm, but he may be gone ere this reaches you. I can say that we have had two cool nights up here. I am well at present, and very hearty. I am fatening up again and it looks like I ought to fatten on butter at $3. per pound, and Irish potatoes at $10.00 per bushel, and every thing else equally high. I am as ever yours in hope and love.

Joe

My own dear Sarah, may the Lord let us meet and enjoy each others presence and society again on earth.

Near Orange,
Sept. 1st 1863.

My Dear wife:

Your kind letter of the 25th inst came to hand and I read it with much pleasure. I have received all your letters up to this time, and I hope I shall get them more regular now than I have been doing. Every thing continues quiet here, and we are calmly enjoying camp life. I wrote you a few days ago, stating what I wanted from home and you will send them the first opportunity. It seems that the men of my company who are now at home, and whose furloughs are out are not coming back. I have wrote to Capt. Mull to attend to them, and I trust he will do so.

Dear Sarah, all that we can do is to pray and hope for peace and for our meeting again on earth, and await patiently God's own good time. No body wishes peace and independence more ardently than I do; yet while the good Lord sees fit to scourge us with war, we must patiently endure the judgment. Dear Sarah, I delight to think about the happy times we have spent to-gether, and although we may never enjoy such privileges again, yet I cannot help but look forward, with hope, and by God's good favor expect to meet thee again in the flesh, may it be so. As I have nothing important to write I will cut this letter short for I have been writing all day on the company pay rolls. I can tell you I have taken up a regular course of <u>study</u>. The subjects are as follows;— The Bible; Hymn book, Mental Philosophy, and (reading) Baxters Saints Rest. So you see I can not lay aside my books even in camp. Ah. I think I hear you say "that is just what I expected." Sarah, I long to get rid of this war that I may apply my mind more ardently to <u>study</u>. This is the craving of my soul and, if God is willing, I intend to gratify its desires. I can say that we have some cold nights up here, almost cold enough for frost. And our men are poorly provided with blankets for cold weather. I have plenty of blankets. This leaves me well. Write how my mills are doing. As ever yours in hope and love.

Joe

Near Orange C. H. Va.
Monday, Sept. 8th 1863.

My Dear wife:

Your kind letter of the 1st inst is to hand and I read it with usual pleasure. I can inform you that I am as well as usual. We are still at this place, quietly enjoying camp. Every thing in the way of army movements continues remarkably quiet. Dear Sarah, you may be sure I would be as glad to see you as you would to see me, and whenever I can get an opportunity I will come home. Though there seems to be no chance just now, for we have so few officers in the Regt. There is only one captain an 7 Lieuts. now with the Regt. O how happy I would be to join the company of my dearest one on earth again. May God grant us the sweet privilege! I am glad to tell you we have some preaching in our Brigade now. Chaplains from other Brigades occasionally preach for us. We had a very excellent sermon yesturday. Aided by J. R. Willis, I hold prayer in my tent every night, and I am happy to say the most of our boys attend it. May God bless our labors. You can take that money Capt. Mull left at Carpenter's for you and pay my debts. John Mull also has a note on me of near $100. If you do not get to pay that one which Wm. R. holds you can pay this one. These two notes and what I owe your father and Rooker, and mother, I believe is all I owe. I have to pay so high for what little I get to eat that I cannot save much of my wages. My board costs me not less than $40 forty dollars per month. I get $90.00 per month.[12] Give my respects to all. Commending you to the care of our good Lord. I close. As ever. Yours in hope and love.

Joe
My own dear Sarah.

Near Orange C. H.
Sept 14th 1863.

My Dear wife:

Your kind letter up to the 8th came to hand yesturday, and was read with pleasure and satisfaction. You may be sure I was glad to read your nice little love letter. It was short, it is true, but it was sweet. I hope you will often write such.

Dear Sarah, I am sorry to tell you that our quietude is at last disturbed. Yesturday the booming of the cannon again met our ears in the distance, and we learn that the enemy is advancing. This morning we were marched up near Rappidan Station, where we are now being waiting for the enemy to come on. The cannon is roaring in our front and we may become engaged any moment.[13] May God be with us as he has been in the past. This leaves me well I will write you again if the good Lord permits. I have not time to answer Rookers letter. Tell Rufus, if he is not able to come back, he must report here promptly by a Dr. I have to act very strict in this matter. Rufus furlough is now out. As ever yours in hope and love.

Joe

Tuesday 15. We are still being here this morning. The yankees came in sight last evening, and our artillery played on them all evening. I have no news from the front this morning, all is still thus far. None of our infantry has yet been engaged yet here. We have not been ordered up in line yet, but I do not know how soon we may be.   Joe

---

Rappidan Station, Va.
Sept 17th 1863.

My Dear wife:

We are still at this place as I wrote you a few days ago. We have moved our camp up here. This is about one mile from our previous camp. All has been compartively still for the last two days here, but the enemy is still in our front beyond the river, and some reports say in heavy force. If this be the case, which is doubtful, they may advance and a fight ensue any day. If we have to enter the field of blood and carnage again, I hope God's good grace will keep us as it has in times past. Dear Sarah, my own bosom friend, be comforted then, and put your hope and trust in the Lord, who only can reconciles us to our lot, and turn our sorrow and grief into praise and rejoicing.

Dear Sarah, I am glad to tell you that I think I am growing some in love toward God, though my evil heart and nature doth grieve me a great deal for I want to be holy and pure and separated unto the Lord, entirely. And my dear one, may the good Lord enable you to grow in grace and love toward him. And Oh, let us be a holy couple, then shall we have comfort here, and eternal bliss when we are united in Heaven. Dear Sarah, there will be no chance for me to get a furlough, till Capt. Mull comes back. Then if the furloughing system continues, I think I can get off. It makes my heart glad to think of seeing you again, yet I know it is wrong to be anticipating when things are so uncertain. <u>May the good grace of our Lord keep us in security and love</u>. I remain, as ever, yours in hope and love.

Joe

When all is silent in the night,
And my eyes in sleep are closed,
Then comes flushing, pure and bright,
Thy image lovely as an angel robed.
Your dearest one.

Near Rapidan Station Va.
Sept 21st, 1863

My Dear wife:

Your kind letter of the 15th came to hand yesturday, and was read with usual interest. I must say that I am not well at this time. I have been suffering with the Dysentery for two or three days, though I hope I shall get better in a day or two. Every thing continues still here yet, though the yankees are close in our front, but there is no telling when they will advance upon us, if at all. Their force is represented to be strong. I can inform you that I saw Wm B. Hoyle, the other day.[14] He came up here, on business, and gave us a call. He is looking well. As I formerly wrote you I do not think there will be any chance for me to get a furlough till Capt

Mull comes back then I think may be I can get off. At any rate I will live in hope. And you may be sure I will seize the first opportunity. I should be glad that you could get my clothes to me for I begin to need them, but I know you will do the best you can. Dear Sarah, I will cut this letter short as I have nothing important to write, and my bowels are also troubling me. Give my love and respect to all. As ever I remain yours in hope and love.

Joe
My own dear Sarah.

Near Rapidan Station Va.
Sept. 28th 1863.

My Dear wife:

This will inform you that I am about well again, and I hope it may find you well. The weather is cold up here now, and we have frost plenty, and some of our men are poorly provided for cold weather. Some have no blankets at all, and I fear we will not get any from the government soon. I have two of Capt. Mull's blankets, and one of my own and a bed tick, so I fare very well in this line. There was some cavalry fighting up here last week. We were ordered out, and expected the general fight was coming on, but the yankees soon went back, and all is now quiet again. It is hard telling what the enemy aims to do here. It is quite sure they have a heavy force in our front, and yet they do not advance. Though they may come when we least expect it. I think our army is now in a great deal better spirits than they have ever been since we came out of Pa., and if the deserters know how cheerful our brave soldier's now are, I think some, at lest, would come back. And I would here say that deserters are faring but midling here now. 10 or 12 have been shot lately. One was shot in sight of our camp last week, but we being on picket at the time, I did not see it. I believe that hundreds of the deserters will now be shot. It seems very hard, but the cause demands it.[15]

Dear Sarah, I cannot help some times, but think about getting home to join your sweet company again after the war ends. I know this is wrong, for we may never see that happy time, but a great many times I am thinking about it before I know it. Dear Sarah, I would to God that we might realize it in truth. Then would our hearts be happy indeed. Let us hope and pray that the happy day may soon come. But while it is God's will that we should be apart, let us be content. With my hope in God I can bear afflictions contentedly. Can you not, too, dear Sarah? I can tell you of one happy thing we may think of which is not wrong, and that is that our meeting in heaven. Sarah, let us think more about this and no doubt it will do us good. We should be more heavenly minded. I can tell you we had preaching this morning, and will have again this evening. Tell Rufus and Rooker I send them my best wishes, I would be glad to see them again. I expect Rufus and Sue will make up the match, tell them to go it, if they feel like it. You know I believe in marrying <u>with</u> <u>all</u> <u>my</u> <u>heart</u>. I remain yours in hope & love.

Joe

<u>My</u> <u>own</u> <u>dear</u> <u>Sarah</u> I received a letter from you last evening, containing the nice little bunch of flowers. How they remind me of your love and devotions. May the good Lord keep my dearest one.

Rapidan Station, Va.,
Oct. 4th, 1863.

I REMEMBER THEE.

My Dear wife:

Your kind letter of the 28th inst came to hand yesturday, and was read with usual pleasure. This leaves me well, and I hope it may find you enjoying the same. We are having some fine days here now, just about cool enough to be agreeable. All is still quiet here, though the enemy is near by, and may make an attack any day, but appearances for a fight are less now than they were two weeks ago, and as you say, I pray we may never have another fight. Oh that the Lord's good time might be near at hand, when peace will come. The weary soldier looks forward to that happy time, with joyous aspirations. I would here say that our soldiers are getting in good heart and spirits again, and every body calculates that we will give the yankees a sound whipping whenever they come against us. We feel that the god of battles is with our armies again, and if God is for us, who can be against us? Therefore let us put our trust in God, and rely on his strong arm for the issue. Dear Sarah, this is a bright Sabbath day, and my mind runs back, when I used to enjoy the sweet privilege of being with you, and going to church with you on such bright Sabbaths. These were happy days to us. But alas! how soon were they gone. Only about one year and a half, and we must be parted, sad indeed has been our fate. But I will not indulge longer in these sad thoughts. Let us look to charming hope for better days. We are now drinking the bitter cup of life; and may we not hope that the sweet is yet in store for us. But dear Sarah, let us not dote too much upon these prospects of earthly happiness, for nothing earthly is sure. Uncertainty and disappointment is written on all things earthly. But blessed be our kind Redeemer for a union and home were disappointment and sorrow and uncertainty can not come, and where we shall live in sweet communion for ever. Let us rather hope and strive for this heavenly home and meeting.

Oct 5th — This morning finds me well. Give my love and respects to your father and mother and all the rest. Tell Lemuel & Alice I send them howdy. I remain as ever, yours in hope & love,

Joe

My own dear Sarah, as ever.

Army Northern Va.

Oct, 1863

My Dear wife:

As we are again on the march I will again give you a brief daily narrative as we go along, hoping to thus make my letters more interesting to you.

Thursday, 8 — According to previous order, we took up the line of march at day break this morning, passing through Orange, and then bearing up the river. After going 1 1/2 miles from Orange we stopped to cook up 3 days rations, and ready to move at 5 in the morning. We know not where we are going, but the sequel will tell.

Friday, 9 — Moved off this morning. Crossed the river (Rapidan) and took the road toward Madison C. H. After marching slowly all day, we pitched camp a few miles before reaching Madison. The indications seem to be that the object of our move is a secret one, probably to get in the enemies rear, as we have cautiously shunned all places that might expose our march to the enemy. All Hills Corps, except 2 brigades are along.[16]

Saturday, 10 — Took up the line of march early this morning, passing through Madison, and after a few miles made a short turn to the right crossed the Robison river, and going toward Culpeper. Our object is to get in the rear of the enemy at Culpeper. Bivouaced 12 miles from Culpeper. Cooks Brigade came up to day and has been attached to our division.[17] I saw W. B. Hoyle this evening, and we will all be near to gether now at least while we are on the march.

Sunday, 11 — This bright Sabbath still finds us on the march, and although on the weary march, I have been trying to raise my heart to heaven to-day and I am thankful to say I experienced some comfort. We have gotten in the rear of Culpeper this evening, and camped in 5 miles of it. We are expecting the fight tomorrow. All are in good spirits. I pray the god of battles will be with us.

Monday, 12 — Behold! the enemy left Culpeper passing out below us, last night. Consequently we canged the direction of our course as if to flank them again. Bivouaced on the pike this evening, running up the river. The idea seems to be to pass to their rear again before or at Manasses Junction.

Tuesday, 13 — Crossed the Rappahannock this morning, and took the road to Warrenton, but when we arrived there, the yankees had again left. Bivouaced here for the night.

Wednesday, 14 — Firing was heard nearly all night last night. It is Ewell, pressing the enemies rear. We took up the march very early this morning, taking a round about road for Manasses. Our division came up with the yankees this evening at Bristol Station, 5 miles from Manasses, and a fight ensued. We opened the fight by shelling their camp and wagons. Then we advanced upon them, our Brigade being held in reserve, they were strongly posted behind the Rail Road, and after a fierce charge, our men were compelled to fall back, but we soon formed and advanced again for enough to hold the field, and here we lay (on the battlefield) all night. The yankees shelled us furiously after this last advance for a short time, but dark soon came on, when the noise of battle sunk into silent repose. Nothing broke the stillness of night, but the cries and groans of the wounded. Sad, indeed, it is to lie upon a battle field. Our brigade was not engaged though we suffered some loss, being exposed. Eli Hoyle of my company had his foot slightly hurt, and two or 3 others in the Regt were wounded.[18] Our loss was considerable.

Thursday, 15 — The yankees retreated last night, and we all feel relieved, for we expected bloody work to-day. We are burying our dead and caring for our wounded this morning. The yankees, we learn have fallen back to Centerville. We took up the march this evening, also falling back, going along the Rail Road we can do the yankees no more harm.

Rappahannock River, Va.
Wednesday, Oct 21st, 1863.

My Dear wife. [Mrs. J. J. Hoyle, Knob Creek, N. C.]

I take the opportunity of dropping you a few more lines. Nothing of interest has occurred among us since I last wrote you. We crossed the Rappahannock last monday, and have been in camp a few miles on this side (west) since then. I do not think we will stay here long, it is thought we will fall back across the Rapidan where we started from. I had thought that Capt Mull would have been here till now, but I received a letter from him yesterday, stating that he would not be here till the first of next month, and we all are thinking that he is not coming back at all. He has now been absent from the company near five months. The men have lost confidence in him. Tell Rufus I want to see him come back very much, and I hope he will come as soon as his hand will admit. I want you to send me another pair of pants beside my uniform ones, for I am just about out of pants. Also I want you to send my over coat if it is worth sending. I forget whether it is worn out or not. There is no chance for me to get a furlough till Capt Mull comes back, if then. Dear Sarah, with the help of God's grace, let us bear up under these trying scenes, and hope for a better day in the future. I see Wm. B. Hoyle almost every day, he is well. As ever, yours in hope and love.

Joe

My own dear Sarah, Though many miles separate us, our hearts are bound together for life and eternity. True, I have sworn ever to be Thine.

Camp on the Rappahannock
Oct 27th, 1863

My Dear wife:

    I take the pleasure of dropping you a few lines this evening, informing you that I am as well as usual, and I hope this may find you well. I received your kind letter of the 20th day before yesturday and was glad to hear from you as I always am, though I was sorry to hear that you had not had a letter from me in so long a time. I assure you I write every week when it is possible. I get your letters very regular, even more so than I could expect up here. Nothing new in the way of army movements has occurred since I last wrote you. We are camped on the west side of the Rappahannock near Brandy Station, and about 9 miles from Culpeper. The yankees are on the other side. We frequently see them and our pickets some times shoot at them. But I do not think they have sufficient force to advance upon us. The weather is getting cold up here and I hardly think there will be any more general engagements between the two armies this fall any more. There is opinions among us that our Corps (Hills) is going to the west to help Brag out, But this is only opinion, and hence very uncertain. Tell Rufus he need not come back till he is able, but be sure and come as soon as he is able, and while him and Rooker stays away they must continue to send me certificates. Their last certificates were received. I would write them a letter but I have been writing all day and feel tired.

    Dear Sarah, it makes me think of you to be weary, for I used to come home weary of an evening, and allways find enough love and goodness in thy kind words and looks to make me forget all my weariness. Alas! will those happy days never return to us any more? Let us rest in hope. And be submissive to the will of our Lord.

    Wednesday 28th — This morning finds me well. As ever yours in hope & love.

Joe

Camp on Rappahannock,
Nov. 4th, 1863

Dear wife:

I have the pleasure of dropping you a few lines this morning informing you that I am well at present, and I hope this may find you well. Every
thing continues quiet up here, and there seems no prospect of an early
fight. We moved camp yesturday a few miles up the river, and I expect we
will go into winter quarters here. I sent up an application for leave of
absence to come home the other day, but it was not approved, General Lee
having ordered that no more leaves of absence be granted till late in the
season. So you see I will have to wait awhile longer before I get to come
home. You may be sure I was very sorry of it, for I want to see you very
much. How happy I should be to see you once more, and you may be sure
I will come as soon as I can. I have received no letter from you this week,
but I am anxiously looking. I saw Wm. B. Hoyle yesturday evening. He is
well. Their Brigade is camped very near us now.

Dear Sarah as I have nothing interesting to write, this letter will be
short. Also I will be busy to-day, fixing up my quarters. Tell Rufus &
Rooker they must keep me posted with certificates while they stay at home.
I am now reporting 9 of the company absent without leave. Some of the
men who have had the good fortune to get home are acting very mean in
not coming back. I am as ever, yours in hope and love.

Joe
My own dear Sarah

Camp on the Rappahannock,
Nov. 7th, 1863

My Dear wife:

I have the pleasure this morning of dropping you a few lines, informing you that I am well and I hope this will find you well. I have received
no letter from you for near two weeks now, though I know it is not your
fault. We are still enjoying quietude here, and all are busy in putting up
huts to protect us from the approaching cold of winter. We have a very
pretty site for our present camp — plenty of wood, and good water. I only
wish we may get to remain here during the winter, if we must remain in
this army. Dear Sarah, you do not know how glad I would be to see you
again. And how happy would I be to return home from this cruel war to
remain with my dear Sarah as long as life shall last. I pray the happy time
may not be far off. Yet I will be content to await the Lord's own good time.
His righteous will be done. Though if I cannot come home to stay with
you, I think I can get to come and see you for a few days some time this

winter. I can not come now but will as soon as I can. I have some more
money I would like to send home, but I have no chance. Every thing is so
high here that it takes the greater part of my wages to pay my board &
other necessary expenses. My expenses now are between $50 and $60 per
month. In addition to the clothing you are sending me, I want a pair of
gallowses. Also send me, by Rufus, my Greek grammar and Greek Reader
that I sent home in my trunk last Spring. I might say we are having some
fine weather now. The days are almost as warm as summer. As ever, yours
in hope & love,

                                                                      Joe

To Rufus I want you to go and get our Company Book from Capt Mull
and bring me when you come. I suppose you will come soon. We have
given Capt Mull finally out. Yours

                                                            J. J. Hoyle

Please hand the enclosed bundle of advertisments to J. A. Mull

---

                                               Rapidan Station, Va.
                                                  Nov. 10th, 1863

My Dear wife:
    Again I have the pleasure of dropping you a few lines, informing you
that I am well, except bad cold. I wrote you in my last, that all was quiet,
but even while I was writing fighting was going on down the river, and
that same night we had orders to be ready to march at day break next
morning. And accordingly early on the morning of the eighth we commenced falling back. After marching 6 or 7 miles and 2 miles before we
reached Culpeper, we formed line of battle and all day awaited the
approach of the enemy, but none came except a force of cavalry on our left
and they were repulsed by our skirmishers. Night coming on, we resumed
our retrograde movement passing through Culpeper at dark. We continued
our march at night and suffered considerably both from cold and fatigue.
On the morning of the 9th we halted and got something to eat. We then
resumed of march, and crossed the Rapidan in the evening and took up
camp in our old position at Rapidan Station. It was just one month yesterday since we left the place. We have cold weather now, and yesterday, we
had a considerable snow storm — enough to cover the ground, but it did
not lie. Two of our deserters were brought in the other day. Jno Smith and
John Ledford. They are now under guard and will have to stand a court
marshal.[19]
    Wednesday 11 — I received your letter of the 4th last evening and read
it with pleasure. Also John Cline came in yesturday evening, and we were

all glad to see him. He had the misfortune to loss his box in coming from Richmond, but it may come on yet. I am as ever, yours in hope & love,

Joe

Camp near Orange C. H. Va.,
Nov. 17th, 1863.

My Dear wife: [Mrs. J. J. Hoyle, Knob Creek, N. C.]

Your kind letter of the 10th inst came to hand yesturday, and was read with usual interest. This leaves me well and I hope it will find you in good health. I have no interesting news to give. All has been quiet with us since we crossed the Rapidan, though some cavalry fighting has occurred in the front. The yankees are following us up. We are now holding our old lines along the Rapidan, and if the yankees come on we will have another fight, but I think it doubtful whether they will advance upon us or not. I cannot tell you how my pants and jacket fits as I have not tried them on yet. You must excuse me for this as you know I never try on any thing till I go to wear it. You may be sure I appreciate them very much, and the more so because they were made by you. They are neatly made and I prise them as the work of those dear little hands that I am proud to call <u>my wife</u>. Reuben Hoyle staid with me the other night. He is on a visit to the army. I sent one hundred dollars to you be him. He will send it to Noah Hoyle and you can get it from there. You can pay the note J. A. Mull has against me with it, or any other debt you please of course. I intend you to make use of as much of it as you want. I do not know when whether I can get a furlough when Capt Mull comes back, now or not. But I will try. You may be sure I will come the first chance I can get, for I know I want to see you equally as much as you want to see me. May God's protection and goodness be with you! I remain as ever, yours in hope and love,

My own dear Sarah,

Joe

I sent some advertisments to J. A. Mull in my last letter to you, but for fear they did not reach you, I send a couple more in this which you will hand over to J. A. Mull if the others did not reach you. All the absentees had better take warning, and come in for I cannot indulge them any longer. Tell Rooker if he is not able to come back yet he will have to go to Charlotte and report to me through the hospital there.

J. J. Hoyle

Dec. 1st 1863
In line of Battle.

My Dear wife:

I have the opportunity this morning of dropping you a few lines. I am well as usual, and I hope this may find you well. We are again facing the enemy, and expecting a battle every hour. The yankees crossed the river last Thursday, a few miles above Chancelorsville, and we moved down on them next morning. (Friday) A skirmish took place on Friday evening. Our Brigade was not under fire, except our skirmishers. On Saturday morning we fell back a little piece and took a position, and we have been expecting the yankees to attack us ever since. We are now in sight of them, and constantly expect the fight to commence. We have good breast works, and are confident with, Gods blessings, of whipping them. Dear Sarah, be not uneasy about me. I hope the good Lord will shield me. I will write you again soon if God wills. I have only time to write a few lines this morning. Rufus & S. S. Self got to us yesturday. Capt Mull turned back at Gordonsville. Rufus had the misfortune to loose his sachel and all the clothing & blankets in it at Raleigh. He had to sell out his box at Gordonsville, though he bought me some butter and apples. I received your letter and the nice little — hair plat thanks to you for it! Dear Sarah, let not this letter trouble you. Let us trust in God and all will be well. As ever, yours in hope and love.

Joe

My own dear Sarah. We have stinging cold weather now. You can tell mother how I am getting along. I have not time to write her now, and we only have a chance now and then of sending out letters in such times as these.

Near Orange C. H. Va.,
Dec. 4th, 1863.

My Dear wife:

I have the pleasure of writing you a few lines this morning, informing you that we are back at our old camp near Orange. The yankees have all gone back across the river, and we returned to our old camp yesturday. I will give you a narration of our expedition. On the morning of Friday the 27th inst, we left camp, directing our march on the plank road toward Fredericksburg. The yankees had crossed the river the day before 5 or 6 miles above Chancellorsville, and now had possession of the plank road, opposite the place at which they crossed. Giving to the hard frozen conditions of the ground our march was attended with some difficulty in the morning. Many a fellow caught a fall over the slick frozen ground. We continued our march till about 2 in the evening when we came up with the enemies advance. Our division was in front. We were formed in line of battle on each side of the road, and some artilery and skirmishers were thrown out to the front, and a considerable skirmish ensued. The yankees gave way after a brisk fire, and we pushed forward after them. Having driven them some half a mile till dark, we halted and lay in line all night. We lost 2 men killed (that I have heard of) and several wounded in this affair. The dead yankees were left on the field and fell into our hands. On the next morning (28th) we fell back about 2 miles to get a position. Our division was placed in the reserve now, and we were engaged all day in maneuvering and fortifying. This was a very rainy day, yet we worked nearly all the time, if you would call gouging with our bayonets and scraping dirt with our hands work.

Sunday, 29 — We also spent in maneuvering and fortifying. In the evening, we were moved up on the front lines. The yankee lines were in sight to-day, and a general engagement seemed on the point of occurring.

Monday the 30th, opened clear and cold. Early this morning cannonading commenced on the left, and quickly ran up the lines to the point occupied by our brigade. We all expected this the signal for the general engagement, but after a few rounds the cannonading ceased, and all remained quiet during the balance of the day.

Tuesday the 1st Dec, every thing remained remarkably quiet with us. Late in the evening some picket fighting occurred on the right, and things indicated that the enemy was moving to the right. At 4 O'clock on the morning of Wednesday, the 2nd, we (our division) were moved to the right to a point which the yankees had pressed the evening before. Here it was expected they would attack our lines at daylight. But when day-light came behold not a yankee was to be seen. Our pickets were advanced and it was soon discovered that they had finally withdrawn from their position in the direction of the river. Andersons & Wilcoxs divisions were now sent in persuit of them; but the flying yankees had too much the start. They recrossed the river before our men got up with them. On the morning of Thursday, the 3rd, we took up the line of march for our old position near Orange, and arrived there and went into camp this evening — having been gone seven days. The weather was severly cold most of the time. Thus again has Mead been offered battle, and he declined. Our men were in good heart and counted on giving them a sound thrashing if they had been presumptious enough to attacked us.

Dear Sarah this leaves me well, and I hope it will find you likewise. I wrote you in my letter the other day that Rufus lost all his things. He says for you to send him the blanket that he sent home last winter. I remain, as ever, yours in hope and love.

Joe
My own dear Sarah.

Camp near Orange C. H. Va.
Dec. 8th, 1863.

My Dear wife:

I have the pleasure this morning of dropping you a few lines informing you that I am well, and I hope this will find you well. All has been quiet here since the yankees fell back across the river. We have very cold weather here now, but we are getting along as comfortable as could be expected. Capt Mull was out to see us but he staid only 2 days. His arm is not well yet. I do not know when I can get a furlough, though you may be sure I will come the first chance I can get. Though you need not look for me, as I do not expect I will get to come till Capt Mull comes back to stay. You need not send me any more clothing at present. I bought a very nice pair of pants the other day.

Dear Sarah you must excuse this short letter, and I promise you a better one next time. Yes, I will promise you a love-letter next time, if circumstances permit. Yours as ever.

Joe

To J. R. Self—You will have to go before the medical board at Charlotte or Raleigh to have your furlough extended.

J. J. Hoyle

To Lemeul Self—Those men who have gotten guns from deserters may be reported to Governor Vance, through the Adjt. General of the State. Two or more responsible with refses should be given in the report.

J. J. Hoyle

Camp near Orange C.H. Va.,
Dec. 13th, 1863

My Dear wife:

Your kind letter of the 6th inst came to hand yesturday, and was read with pleasure, and especially did I read that little poem with emotions of most agreeable satisfaction. Why, I did not think my little Sarah would turn poet, and I must confess that I am very agreeably supprised at your nice loving verses. I hope you will often give me such loving and confiding lines of your own make; for they do my heart good. I promised you in my last that I would write you a love letter this time. You know I used to be good at writing love letters, but then I was <u>seeking to win you</u>; and it was necessary for me to tell you of my love to you. But now I know you are fully sensible of my devotion to you. I know you can testify from your own heart that I love you dearly, yes, devotedly, and fully as my heart is capable. And I also have the testimony in my own heart that you love me devotedly.

Yes dear Sarah, you are all to me that I could desire. And what more can I say. Ah! me thinks could I lay my hand upon your bosom, and look lovingly into those charming eyes and upon those sweet lips which I have so often kissed, I should then be happy. God grant that we may again enjoy such sweet and satisfying privileges. Dear Sarah, I must tell you that I dreamt of kissing you the other night — I thought that you were standing close by me, when I turned and looked lovingly toward you, and opened my arms (as I often used to do) and you ran into them and pressed your sweet lips to mine. O I was as happy as an earthly mortal could be, and I was sorry when I awoke and found it only a dream.

Dear Sarah, I feel thankful to God even for this sweet pleasure of dreaming about you, though it is of short duration. I would say in conclusion, that we had rain and hard wind last night. Our tent (fly) proved inefficient for such a storm, and we got tolerably wet. This morning is clear and fine.

Monday, 14th — This morning finds me well. We had more rain last night. I remain as ever, yours in hope and love,

Joe
My own Dear Sarah.

Camp near Orange C. H. Va.,
Dec. 29th, 1863.

My Dear wife:

I again have the pleasure of writing you a few lines, informing you that I am well at present, hoping these lines may find you enjoying good health. Your last letter was received and read with pleasure, as they always are. I was glad to know that you had heard from Isaac, and that he was well. We are all busy here now in building winter quarters. Our camp now is about 2 miles on the south side of Orange. We are getting up very comfortable cabins. I have a very good warm cabin, and almost feel like I was at home, no, I will take that back. It would not seem like home unless I could see my dear little Sarah by me. O happy day, when I could be with my dearest one on earth again! We are having rough weather up here now, both rain and cold. There can be no army movements while the weather continues so bad, and we are all glad of it. Think we will get to rest awhile at least. I hope we will get to stay here all winter. We have wood plenty, and water tolerably handy.

Dear Sarah, I still hope I will get to come home sometime this winter. If I find I will not get to come at all, you must come and see me. If we both live we must surely see each other before Spring somehow. Let us ask the good Lord to permit us to meet and enjoy each others company again on earth, and thereby may we be enabled to live more holy, and prepare for the enjoyment of heaven. While I know we love each other to the fullest extent, let us learn to love God more. Sarah, often do I ask God to take care of you and comfort you with his holy love, and I know you ask the same for me. Sarah, I must tell you that I have enjoyed more of the comforts of religion since I have been in the army than I ever did before, and no doubt your prayers have been a principle cause of it. O Sarah, I would not take every thing else for your prayers. I know they come from a true and full heart and God will answer such prayers. Above every thing else, don't neglect to pray for me, that I may be kept in the arms of almighty love. I remain, as ever, yours in hope and love,

Joe

Camp near Orange C. H. Va.,
Jan. 2nd, 1864

My Dear wife:

Your kind letter of the 23rd is to hand, and was read with usual pleasure. This will inform you that I am well, and I hope it may find you well. Army matters are all quiet here now, and it is not likely that there will be any movements during the winter. We have very cold freezing weather here now, and our cabins are passing us very well. It might interest you to know how I spend my idle hours here these times. Well, I am employ most of my spare time in studying greek, and reading History. By this means my time passes off very agreeable. Besides, we have just organized a Bible class of which I am teacher, and this is proving to be a very interesting thing. The class recites a lesson every night in my cabin; concluding with prayer. All these things tend to make my present life agreeable. But, alas! One emotion of my heart still lacks an object of enjoyment. I have no loving wife here to speak kind words to me. My hearts is absent. Thy presence only can make up the sweet of life to me. But while the good Lord sees proper to give me the bitter cup, I will submit without a murmur, and if he sees fit never to give me back this dearest object of my heart, I know He will give me its enjoyment in heaven. O the happy thought of meeting, and forever be with my dearest one in heaven Gods righteous will be done.

When I think, Dear Sarah, of thee,
And lonesome feel because absent I must be,
Then I will cast a thought to heaven so fair,
And pray God to unite us there.

I remain as ever, yours in hope and love.
My own dear Sarah   Joe.

Richmond Va.,
Jan 28th 1864

Dear wife:

This will inform you that we are thus far on our road. We got here last night but cannot get off till to morrow morning. We got along very well till we came here last night, and then we met with a severe misfortune to me. I lost my valice and every thing in it, and I will tell you how I came to loose it. We put our boxes and my valice in a negroes wagon to have them hauled to the Central depo, and I put Rooker in the wagon to go with them, while I went by the transportation office. When Rooker got to the depo he had all the boxes taken out, but forgot to take my valice out of the wagon. So the negro hauled it off. We have been looking out for the negro to-day, but as we did not know his name we have failed to find him. I dont think I ever was worse mortified about any thing in my life. I had cautioned Rooker about taking it out when he got in the wagon, but of course he could not help it. I am not as much pertered about my books, and company papers. I do not know how I will get along without my company papers. But I will have to take it easy and do the best I can. Sarah I know this will perter you too but it cannot be helped now, so we need not grieve about it. I hunted up my trunk to-day and will take it with me so I will have clothes to do me till you can get me some more. You may send me another shirt, pair of pants, pair of draws, pair of socks, pair of gallows that is all I think of now. I will write you again when I get to camp. Yours in hope and love.

Joe.

Near Orange, Va.
January, 30th, 1864.

My Dear wife:

I have the pleasure of dropping you a few lines, informing you that I arrived at the company yesturday evening. I got all my boxes here safe, but lost my valice and every thing in it. But I wrote you from Richmond about this. I found the men tolerably well though there is a good deal of sickness in the Regt. at this time.[20] Dear Sarah, I had to witness one of the most affecting sights to day, I believe I ever did in my life before. That was the shooting a man in our regiment for desertion. The whole brigade was marched out in a square to see it. Although I was out I could not look at him when they shot him, so I turned my eyes off him when they went to fire. I felt very solemn indeed, and all appeared very serious. I will agree with you now that it is not rite to shoot a man. Dear Sarah, I got your and Belindas letters all right. Rufus had broken them open, but I do not know whether any body else seen them or not. I wrote you from Richmond what clothing I wanted you to send me, but I will here put them down again. A pair pants, pair draws, pair gallows you need not send me any shirt, as I had two in my trunk. Also a pair socks, and any other little thing you may think I will need. I have nothing further to write, except the weather favors snow.

Jan — 31st — This morning finds me well. As ever yours in hope and love.

My own dear Sarah   Joe

Near Orange C. H. Va.,
Feb. 6th, 1864

My Dear wife:

I again have the pleasure of dropping you a few lines informing you that I am well at present and I hope this will find you well. Every thing continues quiet with us. We have some fine weather now, and have drill every day. We are living very comfortable now, and will think ourselves very fortunate if we just get to stay here till spring. I am afraid the yankees will make a move of this fine weather continues. Dear Sarah, as you may expect I feel lonesom sometimes, and oh how I wish I could be with my dear one again. But I know I am not as lonesom as you are, and I do pray the good lord to make your lot as easy as possible. I went out last night, and got down upon my knees and prayed to God for us both, and I felt relieved afterward. Dear Sarah I hope you will not fail to pray in secret every day. O how much comfort it gives me to know I have a praying wife. Dear Sarah, if we can not hear each others voice, yet one, God can hear both our voices. "Earth has no sorrow that heaven cannot heal." Dear Sarah I have received no letter from you yet, but I expect to in a few days. Tell my mother I will write to her before long. Give my love to all. I remain as ever, yours in hope and love,

My own Dear wife.   Joe.

Near Orange C. H., Va.
Feb 8th, 1864

My Dear wife:

This will inform you that I am well, and I hope it may find you well. We had an alarm here yesturday. The yankees made an advance day before yesturday, and early yesturday morning, we were moved out to meet them.[21] The roads were very muddy, and we started before day so it was very dark, and marching was very difficult. About 10 a.m. we reached the

river a short distance below the Rail Road Bridge, and here we remained all
day in quietude, no yankees making their appearance. Further up the river,
the yankees advanced upon Wilcox' division, and a considerable fight
occurred, which resulted in driving the yankees back.[22] About dusk, we
were ordered back to camp, and after another dark and muddy march, we
reached camp about 9 o'clock. I feel a little sore this morning from the
effects of the march. Dear Sarah, I have received no letter from you yet
though I expect to-morrow evening, but I will have to send this off to-
morrow morning. I am faring very well in the way of eating now, and will
while my box holds out. But living well in the way of eatables, does not
make up the agreeableness of life to me. I want to live with my dear wife
again, nothing else, dear Sarah, can make life happy to me. Let us continue
to pray the Good Lord to grant us this much coveted desire. God knows
we desire it from a pure motive, that we may learn to love Him more, and
serve him better. My whole desire is to love and serve God with all my
heart, yet I want a bosom friend to whom I may freely communicate all my
feelings and difficulties, just such a one as you are, dear Sarah. I remain as
ever, yours in hope and love,
My own dear Sarah   Joe.

Near Orange C. H., Va.
Monday, Feb, 15th, 1864.

My Dear wife:

Your kind letter by A. McClurd came to hand yesturday evening and
was read with pleasure as usual. I got all my things safe, and was glad to
receive them. You guessed right, I did not loose my bible. I had it in my
little pouch. I bought me other Greek books in Richmond. I hated the
worst the loosing of the book I procured from Brother Pell in Raleigh,
because I cannot get an other one like it. I can inform you that I am getting along with my Greek study about as usual. Though we have to drill a
great deal now, so I have not as much spare time as I did have. I am also
getting along tolerably well with my bible class. We had sacrament meeting
in the Brigade chapel yesterday. We also have preaching there nearly every
night. You asked me how I was getting along with my business. I do not
know whether I understood you or not, but I will answer by saying I have
not got an answer from Brother C yet. If you hear any thing on the subject
at any time, please write me about it. My Dear Sarah, I also wish, and pray
too that the war would end and let us all get home to our loved ones again.
If there is any earthly thing I desire it is to get home and live with you
again. Dear Sarah, we never knew how tenderly we loved each other till
since we have been parted. I pray the Good Lord to comfort and keep you

and prepare us both for reunion in heaven. I remain yours in hope and love,

My own dear Sarah   Joe.

Near Orange C. H. Va.,
Feb, 15th, 1864

Dear Sarah,

I must tell you about us all re-enlisting for the war last Saturday. The whole Brigade was ordered out and General Davis gave us a stirring speech upon the subject. Our Regt. seemed somewhat backward at first, but on a second speech by Genl Davis, nearly all the Regt came out. All my company re-enlisted but one, namely, Jesse Tallen. Re-enlisting is going on very extensively in this army. And surely this will have some effect upon many of our people at home who are whipped already. This patriotic move on the part of our soldiers speaks in the soundest terms that our soldiers are not whipped, and I think that much good will result from this patriotic movement. We soldiers want peace as much as any body, and if any people in the world know the value of peace we do, and our friends need not think that we desire the war continue be re-enlisting, but we know that the stronger position we can show, the sooner we will have peace. We know we will have to fight any how till the war ends. Then let us all rely upon the god of hosts and strive to do our duty and deliverence will come. I can say that all is quiet here now, and the snow is falling fast. We are drawing close round our fires, and enjoying our cabins finely.

Tuesday, 16th — This morning finds me well. The ground is covered with snow. Rooker is complaining. As ever, yours in hope and love,

My own dear Sarah   Joe.

Near Orange C. H. Va
Monday, Feb. 22nd, 1864

My Dear wife:

I again have the pleasing opportunity of dropping you a few lines, informing you that I am as well as usual. I have nothing new to write you, except the weather is more pleasant again. We have frequent preaching in our Brig chapel these times, and I am glad to say they are well attended. Dr. Lacy, our corps missionary gave us two very good sermons yesturday.[23] And to-day, he gave us a very excellent address on the life and character of General Jackson. The speaker dwelt with emphasis upon the Christian habits of Jackson, showing that he was a devout Christian as well as a brave soldier. I can tell you I saw L. S. Self to-day. He was over to see us. Dear

Sarah, I have just received your letter of the 17th and, as you say, it allways makes me feel glad to get a letter from you, and oh how I long for the time when I can hear from you through your own dear lips. How happy could I then live. Dear Sarah, I will close for this time. I hope you will excuse haste. Let me know whether your father is getting the Advocate, and if you are taking the Catawba Journal. As ever, yours in hope and love,
My own dear Sarah   Joe.

Near Orange C. H. Va
Monday, Feb 29th, 1864

My Dear wife:

I again have the pleasure of writing you a few lines, informing you that I am well and I hope this may find you well. I received your kind letter by Craige, and read it with usual interest. Dear Sarah it is sweet pleasure to get letters from those we love so dearly. I read them, and think of the true and trusting heart from which they come. It is a comfort indeed, and one which I am thankful for that I have on loving heart whose very happiness is wrapped up in my welfare. Dear Sarah I ask God every day to comfort and consol you, and be a husban to you o He can be a better husban to you than I could if I were with you, and I can safely and willingly resign you to his care.

Dear Sarah, I know it is distressing for us to live this way, and it goes as hard with me as it does with you, but I am glad to hear you say you can be satisfied if it is Gods will that we should be parted, this kind of language comes from the heart of the true Christian, and I am glad to hear such submissive language come from the heart of the one I love so dearly, and in which my earthly happiness is wrapped up. If it Gods good will, we shall be permitted to live to-gether again on earth, and it is my daily prayer that he will so permit us to live again, but then I must say "not my will, but thine be done."

Dear Sarah, I have no news to write you, except we have a very interesting meeting going on in our Brig now. We have preaching twice every day, and a great many are earnest about the interest of their souls. I believe God is working a great work in our midst, and I pray it may so turn out. I am sorry to tell you that there is another man to be shot for desertion in our Regt. in a few days. His name is Smith he belongs to Co. B. Chapman is sentenced to 4 years labor with ball and chain. Bracket and Hoyle will loose 2 years pay, and be at hard labor for that length of time, but not to be excused from marches and fight. Chapman will be sent to Richmond. Hoyle and Bracket will be kept here. I am glad they excaped shooting. I did all I could to get them off as light as possible. Dear Sarah, I expect W. B. Hoyle will be at home against this reaches you. If you send me any provisions by him, send me some butter, you can buy it if you have not any of your own though you need not put yourself to any trouble about it. I received a letter from Isaac a few days ago wrote the 22nd of Jan, he was well. He said he had wrote 5 letters home, but had got none from any of you. I remain, as ever, yours in hope and love,

My own Dear Sarah,   Joe.

Near Orange C. H. Va.
March 7th, 1864

My Dear wife:

Your kind letter of the 29th inst. came to hand yesterday evening and was read with usual interest. If you could mail all your letters through Box N0. 10 I would get them a day or two sooner. This will inform you that I am as well as usual, and I hope it may find you well. I have no news to give you, except 2 more men of our Regt. are to be shot this week. I also learn we will have to go on picket in about a week. I can say to you that we sent Rooker before the board, but they would not discharge him. They detailed him for ambulance driver, but of course he is not able to do this. So if he does not get able to stay with this, he will have to be sent to the hospital. He is a good deal better now than he has been. If he goes to the hospital I will give him a recommendation, and I think they will furlough him. Dear Sarah, as I am busy to-day, I will close for the present. I remain, as ever, your loving husban,

My own dear Sarah   Joe.

A. G. Peeler is starting home this evening so I send this by him.[24]

Picket post on the Rapidan
March 14th, 1864

My Dear wife:

This will inform you that I am on picket to-day. Our Brigade moved to the river this morning, and I am on duty on the picket line. The day is beautiful, and every thing is quiet. We have a very strong position along the bank of the river, and I have little idea the yankees will ever attempt to cross here. The country along the banks of the Rapidan is generally cleared, and from the hight which I occupy a beautiful view streches out over large and rich farms, and the blue mountains rise up in the distance. But alas! for this cruel war, very little life and agricultural persuits meet the eye. The red dirt heaped up marking the soldiers rifle pits, and the little spear of smoke curling up along the river's banks where the vigilant picket keeps his watch, is about all the signs of life or animation which meets the eye.

Dear Sarah, as I thus sit on the lone banks of the Rapidan, my heart feels lonesom. Yes, I am not happy. A kind of strange feeling steels over me, and my heart seems to be longing for something. Yes the whole secret is my heart longing for its counter part, and I feel lonesom void in my heart, and nothing can fill it but thy presence. O God give me back to my dear and loving wife again. Let my heart again unite with its love its only mate. Fill up this lonesom void in my heart with the sweet presence of a dear wife. Then may I be better prepared to love and serve Thee, and give glory and honor to thy name for all thy benefits. I remain as ever yours in hope and love.

My own Dear Sarah,   Joe.

Camp 55th N. C. T.
March 15th, 1864

Dear Sarah,

This morning finds me well. Being relieved on picket, I joined the Regt this morning. Our present camp is near Payton ford on the Rapidan. We have very bad wood here but plenty of good water. We have a tent to stay in. The men are fixing up huts to shelter them. Sarah, if you can, I want you to make me a couple of shirts of some kind of dark small checked cloth. White shirts do not suit to wear in camp and if you can make me these and send them to me. I will send my white shirts home. I received your kind letter of the 9th inst this morning, and was glad to hear from you as I always am. I cannot send you the "age" at present as I have not the money to pay for it. We are all waiting till the new issue of money comes out before we draw money. I must praise your writing in backing my letters. You back them very well indeed. It allways makes me glad when I trace your well-known hand on the envelop. I remain as ever yours in hope and love,

My own dear Sarah,   Joe.

Camp on Rapidan River, Va.
Sunday, March 20th, 1864.

My Dear wife:

Your kind letter by W. B. Hoyle has just reached me. Rufus came over to-day and brought it to me. I also received the one you sent by Gant, both were read with much pleasure as all your letters are.[25] The beautiful little plat of hair which you sent is thankfully received and highly valued by me. I have put it on my arm, and will wear it there. You must pardon me, for I must tell you that I could not keep from kissing it. O how happy I would be to kiss the gentle hand that made it. I have no news to write you. All continues quiet with us. We are having some windy <u>March</u> weather now. We had preaching to-day in the Brigade. I have already written you about the deep religious concern in our Brigade. I am now holding prayer meetings every night in the different companies of our Regt., and a great deal of interest seems to be manifested. There are now three prayer-meetings in our Regt, and I think I can organize two more. I also intend to try to hold a prayer meeting for the Regt. daily, at some hour in the day time. Pray the good Lord to be with us. I feel happy in working for my master, and I pray he will bless us all. Dear Sarah, I do not forget to pray for you all at home for you are the objects nearest my heart. I desire the sweet privilege of living with you again, but I am willing to leave it all to God. I have not yet received the provisions you sent by W. B. H., but I will to-morrow, or some day soon. Yours in hope and love.

My Sarah,   Joe.

March 20th, 1864.

Dear Sarah,

I am glad you wrote me what brother Cline said about my case. I have received no letter from him yet, and I began to think he had not received my letter, or something was wrong. If I should be fortunate enough to obtain licens, I will try for the chaplainey of some regiment. I have a strong desire to enter the ministry and work for my heavenly master, and I hope the good Lord will permit me so to do. Yours as ever,

Joe.

Monday, 21st — This morning leaves me well, and I am on picket guard again to-day.

Joe.

Camp on Rapidan, Va.
March 27th, 1864

My Dear wife:

I have only the time to write you a few lines this morning. I am well. The letter of cousin John Dellinger you sent me came safely to hand, and I was very glad to get it. We had a heavy snow the first of this week, it was from 10 to 12 inches deep, but it is about all melted away now, and the sun is shining beautifully this morning. All is quiet in the way of army movements. I got all my things right by W. B. Hoyle. Many thanks to you for all of them. I must tell you that Col Belo is going to try to have my name dropped as an inefficient officer.[26] Mark, he does not doubt my competency. He says I am sufficiently intelligent to make an officer, but I have not proven efficient as a disciplinarian. He says my fault is I am too lenient or easy on my men. Since he has commenced it I intend to see it through. Though unless my mind alters I do not intend to remain with the Regt. even if he is not able to have me dropped. But you will hear more as the case progresses. Say nothing about this to any body. As ever, yours in hope and love.

Joe.

Camp on the Rapidan, Va.
March 31st, 1864

My Dear wife:

Your kind letter by J. R. Willis came to hand yesturday evening, and was read with usual pleasure. This will inform you that I am well, and I hope it may find you well. We are still doing picket duty on the Rapidan, but all has been quiet since we came here. We have had a great deal of rain in the few past days, and the river is unusually full. We expect that the yankees will make a move upon us as soon as the weather becomes good, but we are all hopeful, and expect with Gods blessings to give them a whipping whenever they come. Dear Sarah, this seems to be a dark hour, every thing looks to hard fighting this summer, but I am not discouraged — God controls all things, and in his hands we are safe. If we are true to the Lord and ourselves, we will finally win our independence. The Lord pulleth down one and setteth up another. Then let us trust in the Lord and all shall be well with us. My Dear Sarah, it is the uppermost desire of my heart to return to your sweet companionship again, and I continually pray the good Lord to grant us this sweet privilege, but God knows what is best for us, and we must say "Thy will be done." O that this cruel war was over, and I could return to the sweet embrace of my wife, so dear.

April 1— This morning finds me well. As this is the first of April, I send you the following puzzle: An Enigma

I am composed of 15 letters

My 1, 2, 5 & 8 is a common work animal

My 3, 6, 2, 13 & 9 is a place where men settle disputes legally

My 4, 10 & 8 is a farmers tool

My 7, 6, 9 & 8 is what men do at elections

My 11, 12, 13, 14 & 15 is the object dearest my heart

My whole is what I give to my wife.

Find out what I am, and you will say tis true.

My own Dear Sarah,

Joe.

Camp on the Rapidan, Va.
April 4th, 1864

My Dear wife: [Mrs. J. J. Hoyle, Knob Creek, N. C.]

I have the pleasure of dropping you a few lines, informing you that I am well, and I hope this may find you well. I have no news to give except we are having rough weather. It snowed day before yesterday, and is snowing again to-day. We have now been down here on the river four weeks, and we have had three snows on us and an abundance of rain. The yankees are all being quiet, but we expect them to move whenever the weather gets good. Our term of picket duty down here is two days over half out. I received a letter from Rev. R. P. Franks, the presiding elder of your district, yesturday. He wrote me that Brother Cline presented my case at conference, but that it could not be acted upon because I was not present. He said there was nothing in the way but my absence. He informed me that the next quarterly meeting would be held at Dry Pond Camp ground on the 11th & 12 of June — If I can get off, I will come home then and attend to it. I have procured enough uniform cloth to make me a suit. It cost me $40. I will send it home the first opportunity.

Tuesday, 5 — Dear Sarah, this morning finds me well. It continues raining and hailing. I remain, as ever, yours in hope and love.

My own Dear Sarah,   Joe.

Though far away in presence, yet near in heart.

Camp on the Rapidan, Va.
April 17th, 1864

My Dear wife:

I have the pleasure again of dropping you a few lines, informing you that I am well, and I hope this will find you well. We are still having a great deal of rain, and, although it puts us to some inconvienice, yet we are not sorry to see it rain, as we know it keeps off the fight some longer. When it is raining, you will frequently hear some one say, "This rain has prolonged many a man's life" and it is a true saying, as we expect the yankees to move upon us whenever the roads get in condition. (or may be we will move upon them, I don't know). I am happy to say that a spirit of hopefulness and confidence prevade our army, and I believe it will do its whole duty when the time comes. May God be with us and shield and deliver us. We had preaching to-day in our Brigade. There is still a bright manifestation of religious feeling in our Brigade. While here on picket, we have poor opportunities for religious services, nevertheless I am glad to see that a hopeful religious feeling still exists among us.

Dear Sarah, I long for this cruel war to be over, and make it a subject of much prayer. I want to return to the sweet embrace of a dear wife, that we may go hand in hand toward the kingdom of heaven. Dear Sarah, I know it is not necessary for us to be united in order to love God with the whole heart, and it may be for our own good that He has caused us to be separated, yet it seems to me I could live a more devoted Christian, if I could be united again in life with you. If this is a rong desire of my heart, I pray the good Lord to forgive it. I am willing to abide His righteous will, yet I cannot help craving to be united again in life with you — with my dearest Sarah, and I also make this a subject of prayer — It is a principle of religion, that we should never wish, or engage in, any thing which we cant not pray for consistent with conscience. My Dear Sarah, let our trust be in God.

Monday 18 — This morning finds me well. The sun is shining bright this morning, and looks as though we might have some fair weather. The weather is smartly cold, and plenty of snow is yet visible on the mountains.

> Often when sleep closes mine eyes
> And forgetfulness takes all care away,
> Then come that dearest one, my wife
> And nestles near, near my side,
> Her gentle hand is laid in mine,
> Her dear lips to mine are pressed,
> O then I am happy in dream land.
> But I awake, alas my happiness is gone.
> My Dear one has flown away, and I
> Again am alone — Thus time
> Passes away in dreamy flight

I remain as ever, yours in hope and love,
My own Dear Sarah,   Joe.

Camp on Rapidan, Va.
April 20th, 1864

My Dear wife:

I have the pleasure again of dropping you a few lines, informing you that I am well and I hope this finds you well. I received your kind letter of the 12th inst, and read it with pleasure, I was sorry to hear that you get my letters so irregular, and if I could I would surely remedy it for you know I do not like to hear of you having the "mosses." You must have patience, and bear every thing with a mind of meekness and Christian fortitude. You say there will be a two days meeting at St. Peters before long, and I would that I could be at home to go with you to meeting, as I once did, what happy days were these for us, dear Sarah, when we could bow down in prayer to-gether, and worship in each others presence. These were happy days for us and my mind loves to dwell upon them, and if we are never permitted to talk them over in this world again, they will be sweet subjects of communion when we meet in heaven. No doubt Sarah, these things will be received with sweet meditation, when we get to a better world.

Dear Sarah, I would that we could draw more of our comfort and happiness from heaven, we are too earthly minded. Our hope is in heaven, and why is it, that our hearts are no more there? Surely our hearts and affections should be mostly where our treasure is, yes, when our all is. But how heavenly minds and heaven, loving hearts. But I will stop on this subject. I send my trunk and cloth home by Rooker. I have already sent back my surplus clothing and things to Richmond in Capt Mulls trunk. I have no news to give you every thing remains remarkably quiet along the lines. We often hear the yankees are coming, but still they don't come, but I expect they will come some of these days. We are drilling daily, and doing picket duty along the river. Our Brigade has been increased by another Regt (26th Miss), and a battalion (Alabamans) recently.[27] We had a brigade drill yesturday, and our Brigade made a very fine showing. I think we will do our whole duty should the enemy come. But I must stop talking at this rate, lest you think we are anxious to get into a fight, we are not anxious but if fighting must be done we are willing to do our part. I even pray the good Lord that we may have no more shedding of blood, but we have to say "his will be done" I am your loving husban in the dearest ties of nature, and in hope of a blissful future.

My own Dear Sarah,   Joe.

"Hope and Love" Trust in God

On Rapidan, Va.
April 24th, 1864

My Dear wife:

I have the pleasure again of dropping you a few lines informing you that I am well at present and I hope this will find you well. I have just come of picket duty and feel somewhat stupid from loosing sleep, yet I must not on this account neglect writing to my Dear Sarah. Dear Sarah, I must tell you that I put on one of my new shirts, for the first time, the other day, and I found worked on the pocket of it something I had not seen before, two little hearts locking into each other. Dear Sarah, how justly you have illustrated our connection to each other by this, for I know you intended something more than a mere ornament by this neat little needle work. Truly, Our hearts are knit to-gether in love for time and for eternity:

I can say that every thing is still quiet with us, though we are looking every day for the storm of war to commence. The roads are getting very dry now, and if the yankees intend to move upon us, they will probably soon commence moving. We have every thing in readiness now for active campaigning. We sent off our tents yesturday and are now fairly out of doors to take the weather as it comes. There is but one tent allowed to a Regt. now, and that one is for the Col. I think we will have active operations in this army ere long if the weather keeps dry. All our men are in good spirits, and if you could see the jolity and merriment among us, you would think that fighting was the least thing in our thoughts. You must not understand me to mean that a reckless spirit is excessive amongs us, I only mean that our men are full of life. On the other hand, a deep religious feeling still pervades our Brigade, and I hope the good Lord will continue to bless us. The general impression seems now to prevail among our people and soldiers that this summer will be the end of the war. I do not pretend to offer a prediction, but I must confess that I am more hopeful now than I have been for a long time. With Gods continued blessings I have no doubt as to our final success. We all expect hard fighting this summer, but if we are true to ourselves and to our God, we will obtain our independence. May the God of hosts be with us in this coming struggle, and give us victory that may bring us speedy peace.

Monday morning, 25 — We had rain last night, and our shelter, consisting of a few boards and a blanket, kept most of the rain off us. It has cleared away this morning — And the spring birds are merily chanting their sweet songs. Spring with its birds and blossoms and all its sweet associations, is beginning. All is gladness and joy around, yet my heart is moaning and sorrowful for its mate. I am, as ever, Dear Sarah, yours in hope and love.

My own Dear Sarah,   Joe.

7. From the Wilderness to Globe Tavern, May–August 1864

"An attack is looked for at any time"

In February 1864, greatly impressed by Ulysses S. Grant's success in the West, President Lincoln placed him in command of all Union forces. Lincoln had been trying to find a general who understood that the key to victory was the destruction of the Southern armies, and with Grant he believed he had found his man. The new lieutenant general's main priority would be to destroy Lee's Army of Northern Virginia. Although Major General George Meade remained in command of the Army of the Potomac, Grant decided to make the Eastern Theater his seat of operations.[1]

Grant wanted to prevent the Rebels from being able to reinforce each other, so he implemented a plan to coordinate Federal advances against the Confederacy on numerous fronts. George Meade was to strike the Army of Northern Virginia, while Major General William Tecumseh Sherman assaulted General Joseph E. Johnston's army in the West. Sherman was also ordered to pierce the interior of the Confederacy and destroy whatever war resources he could lay his hands on.[2]

As the two main Federal armies attacked the foremost Confederate forces, Major General Benjamin Butler's Army of the James was ordered to cut the railroad between Richmond and Petersburg in order to threaten the Confederate capital from the south. Major General Franz Sigel's forces in the Shenandoah Valley and West Virginia were to move up the valley and keep Rebel forces there occupied while cutting Lee's communications to the area. Grant's last move planned for Major General Nathaniel Banks' Army of the Gulf to advance toward and capture Mobile, Alabama, then move north toward either Selma, Alabama, or Atlanta, Georgia. Though these three commanders ultimately failed to achieve what their commander had desired, Meade and Sherman continued to whittle away slowly at the Confederacy's capacity to wage war.[3]

170

General Lee had done what he could to prepare his army for the Federal offensive. On May 2, Lee met with his principal lieutenants atop Clark's Mountain. Lee informed his corps commanders that he believed the Federals were preparing to commence operations against the Army of Northern Virginia. The commanding general felt that the Union army would cross the Rapidan at either Germanna Ford or Ely's Ford, and he advised his subordinates that they should have their men ready to move. Longstreet agreed, stating, "We cannot afford to underrate him [Grant] and the army he now commands ... we must make up our minds to get into line of battle and to stay there; for that man will fight us every day and every hour till the end of this war." Longstreet, who had been friends with Grant at West Point, and best man at the Federal general's wedding, understood how effective Grant could be.[4]

The Army of Northern Virginia's weakened command structure had not changed since Gettysburg. Many unqualified and inexperienced officers remained in charge of thousands of soldiers. Yet, even though leadership had been diluted, the fighting units had grown in combat experience. Davis's brigade had improved tremendously since the spring of 1863. Not only did the influx of additional troops add to the overall strength of the brigade, but also the unit had gained valuable battlefield experience at Gettysburg and in engagements at Falling Waters and Bristoe Station. Davis and his men now had a better understanding of combat, and though many of the men still feared the deadly reality of battle, they had experienced it and knew now what to expect. Joseph Hoyle, who had led Company F at Gettysburg, was one of these officers who had grown since joining the army and was more prepared for the campaigns he and his men would face in 1864.[5]

As the roads began to dry, soldiers on both sides of the Rappahannock focused their thoughts on the upcoming campaign, wondering if they would live to see another winter. On the night of May 1, the men of Davis's brigade held a prayer meeting to invoke the blessings of God. The horrors of Gettysburg, Bristoe Station, and other battles still resonated in the minds of the fighting men, and so the hope that God would protect them in combat was a popular inspiration as the storm of more skirmishes approached.

The following day, Federal movements began to alarm the Confederate high command. On May 2, Confederate observers informed General Lee that Grant was preparing to move the Army of the Potomac. Lee, having witnessed the Federal preparations himself, agreed. The only question was in which direction would Grant strike. He received his answer shortly before midnight on May 3 when the Federals, 115,000 strong, moved southeast in an attempt to surprise Lee. Realizing that his foe was on the move, the Confederate commander began to concentrate his forces. Unsure of where Grant intended to cross, Lee was forced to keep his army spread out to oppose the Federals wherever they chose to ford the river. Confederate generals Ewell and Hill had their corps in position along the Rapidan, but Longstreet's troops were still stationed near Gordonsville. With Longstreet more than twenty miles away, as a delaying action Lee ordered Ewell and Hill to advance closer to where the Union army was crossing.[6]

A. P. Hill had been ordered to march east following the Orange Plank Road. Ewell was moving in the same direction on the Orange Turnpike just north of the Orange Plank Road. By the evening of May 4, the 55th North Carolina, with the rest of Davis's brigade, now under the command of John Stone, camped near New Verdiersville, Virginia. The following day at about 3:30 P.M., the 55th engaged the Federals under the command of Brigadier General George W. Getty, which was part of Major General Winfield Scott Hancock's II Corps. Getty's Federal troops continued to assault Heth's position, but were never able to push the Confederates beyond the crest of the hill in front of their line. Shortly after Getty's troops had begun their assault, Major General David B. Birney's division, posted on the right, and Brigadier General Gershom Mott's division, positioned on Getty's left, joined in the attack.[7]

After hours of desperate fighting, the battle around the Orange Plank Road ended in a stalemate. Although outnumbered, the 55th North Carolina had held its ground and helped save Hill's flank from being turned by Hancock. The regiment had over 200 of its men killed, wounded, or reported missing. Joseph J. Hoyle's Company F suffered over 50 percent in casualties during the first day of the battle of the Wilderness, but the fighting that started on May 5 would last almost continually throughout most of the summer of 1864.[8] The unit's historian, Lieutenant Charles M. Cooke, described the situation as the fighting ended on May 5.

> The order for the charge was not given, and about sunset the firing had nearly ceased in our front, and Thomas' Georgia Brigade of Wilcox's division came in and relieved us, and we were sent to the right of the road where we rested for the night. We had held the enemy in check. Not one yard of our line had given away one foot during the three hours the fearful onslaughts had been made upon us,[9]

On May 6, the Federals attacked again and this time succeeded in forcing the 55th North Carolina back. The previous day's fighting had left the regiment ill-prepared to face another assault, but the men rallied and returned to the line later in the day.[10] Ten members of the 55th, including Sergeant Westly A. Williams of Company F, had their names placed on the Confederate Roll of Honor for acts of courage and bravery in the face of the enemy during the two days of fighting in the Wilderness.[11]

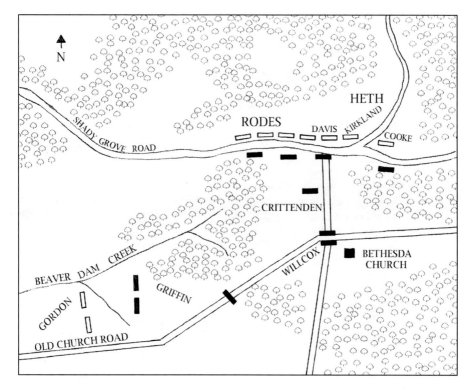

Heth's location on the evening of June 2, 1864.

As Longstreet had predicted, Grant did not intend to quit until he had defeated Lee's Army. On May 7, the Federals attempted to move around Lee's right flank, a move Grant would continue throughout the Overland campaign. The 55th North Carolina saw action on May 10 at Talley's Mill, near the Bloody Angle on May 12, and then steadily until May 19 when the battles for Spotsylvania Court House ended. The Army of Northern Virginia had suffered over 12,000 in these engagements.[12]

By the end of May 1864, the 55th North Carolina began marching toward Richmond. Grant had once again made a move to the right of the Army of Northern Virginia, and Lee quickly ordered his lieutenants to march in an effort to counter the Federals. The armies met at Cold Harbor in early June and fought to another stalemate. The 55th remained behind breastworks during most of the fighting, but did participate in Major General Jubal Early's assault against the Federal right on June 2. Early was temporarily in command of the Confederate Third Corps, Hill being indisposed. During this engagement the regiment's commanding officer, Colonel Belo, was wounded and would never lead the 55th in combat again. Joseph Hoyle did not participate in the attack on June 2, having been out with skirmishers when the orders to advance had been issued.[13]

Failing to break Lee's lines at Cold Harbor, Grant decided to attempt to capture Petersburg, a vital railroad hub that, if taken, would seriously limit the Army of Northern Virginia's ability to re-supply. The 55th North Carolina was ordered to march toward Petersburg, and had reached the city by July 5. For the remaining days of July 1864, the regiment entrenched and fortified their position near Petersburg. Lieutenant Cooke described what the trench area occupied by the regiment looked like in his history of the unit.

> The part of the line occupied by our regiment was so near to that of the enemy that sharpshooting was kept up constantly between the lines with casualties of almostdaily occurrence. The enemy had a number of mortar guns planted just in rear of their lines, from which shells were discharged almost constantly night and day. As some measure of protection, the men and officers of the regiment dug holes in the side of the hill, upon which the line of our regiment was formed. The headquarters of the regiment was a hole six by nine feet square, thus made in the side of the hillwith an opening to the rear, and it was in this place that the writer, Adjutant of the regiment, received all orders from superior officers, received and made all reports and all regimental orders, and there the commanding officer and myself slept at night.[14]

Snipers and occasional mortar shells constantly harassed the men. As Earl J. Hess has noted the earthworks and entrenchments lead to "a campaign of attrition," which had a negative effect on both armies.[15] By mid–August, however, the Federals were ready to launch an offensive. Grant ordered Major General Gouverneur K. Warren to advance and destroy as much of the Weldon Railroad as possible. By 5:00 A.M. on August 18, Warren's men were near Globe Tavern, located about three miles south of Petersburg. Davis's brigade, along with Brigadier General Henry Walker's command, was ordered to attack the Federals positioned near the Davis Farm.

The 55th North Carolina, which was positioned in the center of Davis's command, advanced rapidly through a cornfield and continued through a sparse pine forest. The 55th formed a line of battle with the rest of Davis's brigade on the western side of the Petersburg and Weldon Railroad. As Davis's and Walker's men attacked Warren's forces, they succeeded in flanking Brigadier General Romeyn B. Ayres's troops. After this initial triumph, the Federals, with the help of reinforcements, were able to push the Rebels back. The Federal counterattack occurred as darkness began to envelope the surrounding area. Warren's men were able to pour a heavy and deadly fire into the Confederates. Davis's troops, able to do no more, retreated to the protection of their trenches. The battle of Globe Tavern or Davis' Farm was particularly devastating for the 55th North Carolina, which incurred almost 50 percent in casualties.[16]

Among the wounded was Joseph J. Hoyle. Lieutenant Cooke stated in his history of the 55th North Carolina that the "losses of our regiment there were relatively greater than in any other battle in which it participated." The lieutenant claimed that of the 150 men who fought in the battle, over half were killed or wounded. Cooke declared that there was "scarcely an officer or man who did not bear either in his body or clothing the marks of the terrible conflict." Hoyle had been wounded in the right leg. The wound was so severe that doctors had to amputate the leg soon after the battle. Hoyle was transported to Hospital Number 4 in Richmond, but was unable to recover from his wounds. The young lieutenant who prayed every day that he would one day see his lovely wife again died in a Richmond hospital on or around September 1, 1864. Hoyle died "while gallantly leading his company" in battle. He had commanded Company F at several bloody battles including Gettysburg. His presence would be sorely missed throughout the remaining eight months of the war. The regiment's historian paid particular reverence to Joseph Hoyle when he wrote his account years later stating "he was ever a faithful and conscientious officer." The war would continue for another eight months, but for Joseph Hoyle the end came on a warm September evening far from home.[17]

* * *

Camp on Rapidan River, Va.
May 1st, 1864

My Dear wife:

I have the pleasure again this evening of writing you a few lines informing you that I am well, and I hope this will find you enjoying the same blessings. I feel thankful that I can tell you all still remains quiet with us yet. We have been expecting a forward movement of the enemy now for some time, yet they seem slow to start, and I could sincerely hope they may not come at all, yet this can scarcely be expected according to human purposes, yet I trust in the Lord. I pray Him to avert the storm of battle, and nothing is impossible with God. But should the alwise Creator see fit to again bring us into the carnage of battle, I pray his protection and mercy to be with us. In His hands we are safe, therefore we can do nothing more than put ourselves in His care & resign ourselves, and our all to His blessing — Dear Sarah, I hope we will continue to have all your prayers. I depend a great deal on the prayers of my friends at home — I know from past experiences that God will answer fervent heart-felt prayers and I know, also, that I shall have your most hearty prayers, and I hope all the rest at home will not neglect to pray for us soldiers. I have sent a letter to Brother John Boiles from our "Christian Association" to be read to you all at St. Peters. I hope it may stir you all up to more diligence in matters of religion and prayer, and thereby do you all good, as well as result to our spiritual advantage. I must also tell you that in addition to our other meetings we are holding a prayer meeting once every week on special behalf of our country. I do think we ought to pray more for our country, and deliverence from this cruel war. We held a prayer meeting in the Brigade this, this evening on special behalf of our country. It was largely attended, and if men ever prayed in earnest, I reckon an earnest one went up, this evening, from many a soldier, that God would give us peace and independence. Will not the Lord of hosts hear our earnest supplications? O let us humble our selves before him, for our deliverence can come from none other source. Dear Sarah, you did not fully find out my puzzle sent you on the 1st of April. It is this:

"M u c h   l o v e   t o   S a r a h"
 1 2 3 4   5 6 7 8   9 10   11 12 13 14 15

As ever, yours in hope and love.
My own Dear Sarah,   Joe.

Battle Field
May 7th, 1864

My Dear wife:

I have the pleasure of dropping you a few lines this morning. The great battle commenced day before yesturday.[18] We were engaged in the evening and suffered severely. Through the goodness of God I am spared so far. A great many of our Co. are wounded. David Logan was killed and G. White is thought to be.[19] Some of the wounded are as follows: Wm. T. Williams, badly. A. McClurd, S. Hoyle, Peter White, David Brendel, Anderson Self, Robt Self, Peter Buff, David Buff, Phillip Buff, Aaron Cook, Samuel Wortman, John Ledford — and some others.[20] Very few of these men have been seen since they were wounded, so we cannot tell much about them. The following men yet safe and with the company. Capt Mull, Jno. Cline, J. R. Willis, Solmon Willis, Wesly Williams, John Dickson, Wm. Craige and others.[21] We were not engaged yesterday, though there was some hard fighting and the yankees were driven back. Firing has been going on this morning and we may go into the fight again any moment, be not troubled, trust in God. I must close as the man who caries this is starting. Yours & c.

Joe.

The following was not dated:

List of Casualties in Co. F 55th N. C. T., on the 5th of May, 1864 —
Killed — David Logan & George White — 2.
Wounded — W. T. Williams, since died,
Andrew McClurd, in side of the right breast
Peter Buff, in finger
David Buff, in arm, slight
Phillip Buff, in breast, severely
S. Martinson, in hand[22]
P. R. White in shoulder, severely
Aaron Cook, in hand, severely
F. Bracket, in knee[23]
Solomon Hoyle, in finger
Wm. Cook, in arm[24]
D. A. Brendel, in finger
Samuel Wortman, in hand
Robert Self, in shoulder
Anderson Self, in foot, slight
Jno. Ledford, in finger
Peter Shuford, in arm[25]
Joseph Canipe, in hip, slight[26]
J. S. Crow,
Henry Norman.---21.
Missing — John Mull, S. M. Wright, Jesse Tallent. — 3.[27]

These missing, I suppose, were captured. The manner and degree in which each is wounded may not be correct in each, but I have got it as near so as possible.

Whole loss 26 — We went into the fight with 50 men.[28]

May 11th, 1864

We were again engaged on the 10th (Tuesday).[29] We charged the enemy, and drove them from two lines of their breast works. Our loss was heavy again — The following is a list of casualties in our company — Killed — Jesse Cook.—1 Wounded.—John Cline, in thigh severely; Wesley Williams in side, severely; David Buff Jr. in shoulder severely, Wm. Craige, in arm, slight, Henry J. Willis, in mouth, slight.[30]—6 whole loss 7.[31]

By God's goodness I have been spared thus far. L. S. Self came through the first day safe, so did W. B. Hoyle — since then I have not seen them. A great deal of fighting has been done, and the battle is still going

on. We have driven the enemy back in almost every case in which they
have attacked us. I feel to thank God for our success thus far, and pray he
will give us complete success and speedy peace. Gamewell Gantt is safe
thus far, Mack Hoyle is wounded slightly in hip.[32] Davis came through 1st
day safe. I have but little opportunity to write, and less to send off what I
do write. I am as ever yours in hope and love.

                                                                    Joe.

                                                   Spotsylvania, C. H.
                                                      May 19th, 1864
My Dear Wife:
     I again take the pleasure of writing you a few lines, though I do not
suppose you will get what I write, as we get no letters from you. This
makes the fourth letter I have written you since the battle commenced,
now just 2 weeks. We have not done any fighting since I wrote you last,
though we are lieing in about 1000 yards of the yankee lines, and expecting
an attack at any moment.[33] We have good fortifications to protect us.
Yesturday the yankees shelled us heavily, but did us no damage. They also
made a charge on the left of our lines, and were driven back, as usual. Pray
God to be with us for our deliverence must come from him alone. As ever,
yours in hope and love.

                                                                    Joe.

                                                              May 20.
     A heavy fight took place on our left yesturday evening, but I do not
know for sure how it went, reports say our men were successful.[34] I have
been suffering with the Diarheah for several days, but I feel some better to-
day. All has been quiet along the lines to-day, though the storm of battle
may break cross at any time.

                                                                    Joe.

                                                   Near Hanover Junction
                                                      May 25th, 1864
My Dear wife:
     I again have the pleasure of dropping you a few lines, informing you
that I am well again. I have suffered a great deal from hard marching for a
few days past. I do not think I was ever nearer worn out, but we have been
resting now for a couple of days, and I am feeling about right again. I will
give you some account of our late movements. On Saturday, 21st, the yankees left Spotsylvania C. H. and moved in the direction of Fredericksburg.

That night we also left and moved in the direction of Hanover Junction. We marched nearly all night, resting only an hour or two before day. Early Sunday morning we again commenced marching and marched hard all day. We camped this night on the Central Rail Road, 10 miles above Hanover Junction. Early Monday morning we again took up the march and marched three or four miles till we crossed South Anna River, about 3 or 4 miles from the junction. Here we rested till evening, when we fell in and retraced our steps up the road 2 or 3 miles to meet the yankees who were about to strike the road at this point. A sharp fight took place here by Wilcox Division. Our Division was exposed to the shelling but was not engaged and suffered none. After night came on we fell back to the South Anna River, and took position on its east bank. Where we are now. Our army is again in position in front of Grant and tis said hard fighting was done on the right of the lines yesterday. Skirmishing is going on in our front to-day and an attack is looked for at any time. The captain has been sick since we left Spotsylvania, and I am placed in command of the company again.

Dear Sarah you must be not over anxious about me, but put your trust in the Lord, and He will do all things for the best. I know you are anxious and troubled about me, but I pray God to give you comfort and consolation in his love and goodness. I write you frequently but I do not expect you get my letters — I have got no letter from you in three weeks — you may be sure I am anxious to get one. W. B. Hoyle was well day before yesterday. L. S. Self was safe when we left Spotsylvania. Jourdan Gant was wounded and died last Saturday. You must let mother know how I am getting along still, as I shall not write to her till there is more likelyhood of letters getting through. Give my love to all, especially to your father and mother. I remain as ever, yours in hope and love.

My own Dear Sarah,　　　　　　　　　　　　　　　　　　　　　　　　　Joe.

P. S — Melvin Gant has just come down from the 34 and says L. S. Self is missing and supposed was captured in the fight day before yesterday evening.[35]

Vicinity of Richmond,
Sunday, May 29th, 1864

My Dear wife:

I wrote you last from near Hanover Junction. The enemy did not attack us there but withdrew on the morning of the 27th and commenced moving down on the Peninsula. We commenced moving down toward Richmond on the morning of the 27th also. We moved slowly all day and also yesterday, keeping opposite the enemy, and are now about 7 miles north east of Richmond, awaiting further developments of the enemy. Although we have fell back on Richmond, yet we have not been whipped back, on the other hand we have whipped the enemy whenever he has attacked us. So the yankees have got here not by driving us back but by moving around our flank. I do not see that Grant has gained any advantage, although he has got nearer Richmond, for it must be born in mind that he might have got this near by coming up the Peninsula without loosing a man, while he has already lost about 60,000 men.[36] Our soldiers are in hopeful spirits. It seems that Grant is now mustering all his strength for a final struggle, and we hope this will end the war. Let your prayers be with us, by God's continued blessings, we will be delivered from our enemies. Put your trust in God and all will be well with us. I look alone to Him for deliverence. I can tell you that Albert Ivester came to us this morning. He run away from Point Lookout on the 1st day of this month, and since then has been making his way back getting to Richmond yesterday.

Joe.

Gaines Mills
June 4th, 1864

My Dear wife:

I am thankful to be able to inform you that I am still unhurt, and in tolerable health. I have been sick some of late, but have never left the regiment. Day before yesterday evening our Brigade was engaged in bloody strife again. I was not with them during the fight having previously been sent out on the skirmish line, before the Brigade moved to attack them.[37] Our Division in conjunction with Ewells forces moved on the enemies flank, and drove them with considerable loss from their breast works. Our loss was light.[38] In our Co. were killed, none, wounded Andrew Warlich in thigh.[39] J. A. Canipe on leg, slight, Wm. Hicks on knee, slight.[40] I joined the Brig after dark, lieing in line behind the yankee breastworks. Early yesterday morning, the enemy attacked portions of our lines, but were repulsed and kept back all day our Brig. was not engaged during the day except skirmishing. Andrew Williams of my Co. was severely wounded in the thigh. No body else was hurt in our company — Cooks Brigade on our left were heavily engaged during most of the day — Their loss was not heavy — W. B. Hoyle came through safe. Before day this morning, we withdrew from our position, and are moving down to the right this morning. We are now halted at Gaines Mills, and I suppose will take position this evening or to-night. A heavy fight took place along a good portion of our lines yesterday, and the enemy were repulsed at all points. O may the

God of hosts continue to be with us, and give us such success as shall bring a speedy peace. Rufus was well this morning. I have received some letters from you, but not of late date. Give my love to all. As ever, yours in hope and love. Sarah.

Joe.

Bottom's Bridge, Va.
June 15th, 1864

My Dear wife:

This will inform you that I am not well. I have been sick several days, but have not left the Regt. I think I am improving some. We moved here day before yesterday. On Sunday night the yankees left their position near Gaine's Mills, and Monday morning our army commenced moving also. It is not yet known where they will make a show next. We are awaiting their demonstration. Your letter of the 8th was received yesterday and read with

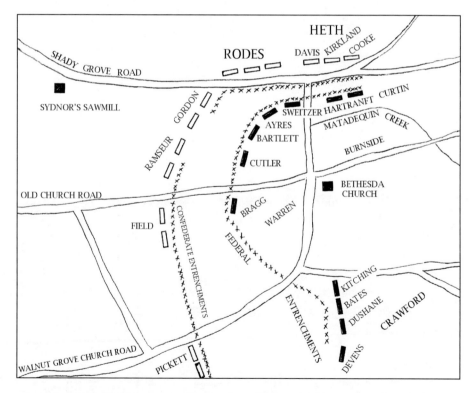

Location of Heth's brigades on the morning of June 3, 1864, as Burnside and Warren prepare to attack.

usual pleasure. Dear Sarah, you must not be troubled too much. I know these are trying and troublesome times, yet let us put our trust in God, and be patient. I hope therefore, you will not let my condition trouble you over much. The Lord will order all things for the best, and your over anxiety cant do me any good. Let us hope for the best and at the same time be prepared for the worst. I saw W. B. Hoyle this morning. He is well. I hear from Rufus every few days. He is doing well. I want a pair of socks when-ever you can send them to me. I remain as ever, yours in hope and love.

Joe.

P.S. I heard the other day that Andrew McClurd was dead.[41] He died at Charlottsville, Va. The news came tolerably straight, and I fear it is true.

Vicinity of Petersburg, Va.
June 21st, 1864

My Dear wife:

Through the mercies of God, I am still spared, and enjoying usual health. Our Brigade has not been engaged in the recent fights around Petersburg. We are on the lines between Petersburg and Richmond. The yankees are close in our front, and under cover of their gunboats. All seems to be remarkably quiet this morning. I scarcely hear even a picket gun any where. I think Petersburg is safe now, although the yankees are in shelling distance of it. The yankees seem very aderminat in their efforts, and this is by far the strongest effort they have ever made against us, but by Gods blessings we have been able to resist it successfully thus far, and I can look forward with encouragement and hope to the future. Dear Sarah, your let-ter of the 13th was received yesterday, and read with pleasure. I am glad that you can repose your trust in God, and I pray His grace may continue to be a sufficient support, and comforter for you. We can only say, The will of the Lord be done. I hope you will not fail to write regularly. I write you often and am sorry you do not get my letters more regularly. Give my love to all. As ever, yours in hope & love.

My own Dear Sarah,   Joe.

I wrote you recently to send me a pair of socks. I want them colored.

Near Petersburg, Va.
July 5th, 1864

My Dear wife:

This will inform you that we have again changed positions. Day before yesterday we left the north side of the James River and are now in position on the right of the lines around Petersburg, near the Weldon Rail

Road. The enemy is about a mile off at this point, but further to our left. The lines are in close proximity and picket firing is constantly going on. Though this has been the condition for some time now, and I think it doubtful whether Grant makes another general attack from his present lines. We are having very dry and hot weather for some time now, and suffer a great deal from the heat, as we frequently have to lie in line through open fields exposed to the sun. And when we march, the dust is excessively hard on us. I do hope, and pray, this hard campaign will soon end, and with it this cruel war also. And I must say that I now look forward to the future with some emotions of encouragement and renewed hope. I have just heard that the yankees have been in Morganton, and at Camp Vance. I do not know whether it is true or not, but if the yankees get among you up there, you must all act the part of soldiers, and they will not find it convenient to stay with you long.[42] Let us be patient, and trust a just and merciful God for the issue and our deliverence will come. I saw W. B. Hoyle yesturday safe and well. I received a letter from W. R. Self bearing date of the 27th inst. He was then at Stanton, and well. My respects to all — As ever, yours in hope & love.

My own Dear Sarah,   Joe

July 7 — This morning leaves me well. Nothing unusual has occurred.

Vicinity of Petersburg, Va.
July 11th, 1864

My Dear wife:

I take the opportunity of dropping you a few lines, informing you that I am well. Though it is little encouragement to write when it is so uncertain about letters going through. I have received no letter from you in several weeks now. Though I hope I shall ere long as the trains are now running through again. Nothing of interest has occurred since I last wrote you. We have been on the lines around Petersburg till yesturday evening when we moved down the Weldon Rail Road a few miles in order to guard it while trains are passing. We continue to have dry and hot weather. Things are suffering for rain very much. I saw Rufus yesturday evening — Doing well. W. B. Hoyle is also doing well. Please write me if Linsay will still remain at the mills, and also how all things are getting along. Say also whether J. C. Willis is exempt again or not, and give me a history of things generally. I have nothing of any interest in the way of news to write you, hence the brevity of this letter. I await with much anxiety the next move of the yankee army. I do not think it probable that they will attack us again from their present lines. With reliance on the strong army of Jehovah, we must await the issue, at the same time praying the mercies of God. I remain as ever yours in hope & love. My own Dear Sarah.

Joe.

Near Petersburg, Va.
July 18th, 1864

My Dear wife:

I have the pleasure of dropping you a few lines this morning, informing you that I am well, and I hope this will find you enjoying the same blessing. I received your kind letter of the 22nd June, a day or two since. Though it was old yet I was glad to get it and read it with pleasure. I hope I shall get others from you in a few days, as the mail now come through. I have no news of importance to write you. We are still in our old position near Petersburg, and nothing unusual has occurred since I last wrote you. There is no telling what turn affairs will assume next. We have had a good deal of exciting news of our troops in Maryland of late. But after getting near Washington, they have now fallen back on this side of the Potomac. I am not able to say what they have accomplished, though it is said they have secured a large number of beeves etc, and suffered small loss. I hope all has been done for the best, and I pray the good Lord will so direct us as to insure a speedy peace. The great burden of my prayer (and I reckon of every other soldier) is that this cruel war may speedily end. We are all tired, yet we are not out of heart. We look to the future with hope, and, with reliance on the strong arm of God, expect deliverence. May it be his good pleasure to give us this deliverence soon. I hope you will continually ask for this deliverence from this cruel war in your prayers. It is needless for me to say that I would be glad to see you, for you know this is always my most ardent desire, and could I anticipate a definite time when I would be permitted to unite in presence with you again, it would almost make me forget present afflictions. But God only knows the future, and we must be content to abide His righteous will. I am, as ever, yours in hope & love. My own Dear Sarah.

Joe.

Near Petersburg, Va.
July 25th, 1864

My dear wife:

This will inform you that I am in usual health, and hope this may find you well. We are still occupying our old position here. Nothing unusual is occurring along the lines. We are having some rain now. The weather is remarkably cold for the season. It rained last night and I got up this morning pretty well soaked and almost frozen. The sun is shining out now and I think I will dry off during the day. I wrote you and Rooker a few days since to fix me up a box of provisions and send it to me or for Rooker to bring it. I want you to hurry it up and have Rooker to start with it at once. It will only take him 2 days to come here. If he comes tell him to bring all he can for the company and he shall be paid all expenses. His trip shall not cost him one cent. We will pay all expenses. I have some bad news for McClurd, which you will let them know. James McClurd and Jack Towry were tinkering with a loaded shell (which had failed to burst when thrown) when it bursted and killed them both.[43] James belonged to Capt. Hoyles Co. of the 34th.[44] This occurred last Friday. A. R. Rice from that Co. told me of it yesturday.[45] Write me how you are all getting along at St. Peter's. Also let me know when and where the next quarterly meeting will be held. As ever, yours in hope & love. My own Dear Sarah. Joe.

Trenches near Petersburg, Va.
Aug. 8th, 1864

My Dear wife:

Your kind letter of the3rd inst is just to hand, and gave me pleasure, as usual to hear from you. I was sorry to hear that you did not think Rooker able to bring me a box, but soldiers have long since learned how to endure disappointments, and so we must be content with such things as we have. But I hope you may meet up with an opportunity to send me something. If we remain here, A. P. Ivester can bring something. If you send I want a bottle of vinegar. And Sarah, as to you coming out here I did not mean that. I know you could not come now without injury to yourself, and besides we are in no condition now for you to come. You may be sure I would be glad to see you, but you cannot come to see me now. We have not changed our position since I last wrote you. The yankees shell us occasionally, and Wm. Craige was wounded day before yesterday evening from a shell. He had gone out to the sinks (about 100 yards from the breast works) when a shell, thrown over, burst near him, and a ball from it struck him on the nose, tearing away that part of his nose nearest his forehead, passing diagonally just over the right eye. The eye was not injured, I don't consider the wound dangerous, but it will not doubt give him a good deal of pain. He is now sent to Richmond. We are still having very warm weather, and suffer a good deal from heat; however we have plenty of water of a fair quality, and we have no right to grumble at our position, as others on other parts of the line are seeing a great deal harder times. On some parts of the line a person can not raise his head above the works day nor night without being exposed to bullets. I have not seen Rufus in a good while, though I heard from him yesturday. He is all right. I wish you would give me the Brigade & Division that Wm. R. Self is in, as I want to write to him. Have not seen Wm. B. Hoyle in several days. His Regt. is on the lines where they have to <u>lie</u> <u>low</u>.

Tuesday, 9th — Dear Sarah, this morning finds me well as usual, and I hope it may find you well. I pray the good Lord may keep you in his love, and that it may be his good pleasure that we may again soon join each other in presence to live to-gether again. God grant us this earthly good. But I must close. My love to all. I am, Dear Sarah, as ever, yours in hope & love. My own Dear Sarah.

Joe.

Near Petersburg, Va.
Aug. 16th, 1864

My Dear wife:

I have the pleasure of dropping you a few lines, informing you that I am well as usual, and I hope this may find you well. Your kind letter of the 7th is to hand and was read with pleasure as usual. I have nothing new in the way of military matters. Things continue to wear their usual aspect around here. We are having a good deal of rain now, but the dry weather has already cut crops very short hereabout. Dear Sarah I will have to cut this letter short in order to get it off this morning. But I have nothing to write that would interest you. I pray we may be permitted to see each other in the flesh again. But we can do nothing more than consign us to the will of him who directs all things, not forgetting however that He is ever ready to hear and answer the prayer of faith. I am, as ever, yours in hope & love. My own Dear Sarah.

Joe.

Richmond, Va.
Genl Hospital No. 4
Aug — 30th 1864

My dear wife:

I again drop you a few lines informing you that I am bad of sick. I cant say I am improving. My leg took some infomations yesturday morning but has got right again I hope. May God do all right. Sarah come and see me. My love to mothers & all. I cant write any more now. As ever yours in hope and love,

Joe
Sarah

Epilogue: Death

"I pray we may be permitted to see each other in the flesh again."

Joseph J. Hoyle died in the hospital on September 1, 1864. He was twenty-six years old. He would never have the opportunity to see his "most earthly desire" again. The Confederacy had no formal system of informing family members of a soldier's death so this sad duty normally fell to a close friend. It is not known who informed Sarah that Joseph had died in Hospital Number 4 in Richmond, Virginia, but at some point his body was brought back to her. Joseph J. Hoyle is buried at St. Peter's Methodist Church in Shelby, North Carolina, near his beloved wife Sarah.[1]

The religious beliefs of many Americans at the time made the news of a "good death" an absolute and religion was an important part of Southern family life. To question death was to question the wisdom of God, and consequently, although anguished over the loss of loved ones, people accepted that the end of one's life was part of a virtuous existence. Many individuals believed if a soldier died nobly in battle he was promised life after death in heavenly glory. If Sarah and Joseph's family members believed this they would have at least been comforted by his last actions as a fighting man in the Confederate Army. As the regimental historian, Charles M. Cooke, who included few personal references of officers or enlisted men's deaths in his history, wrote years later, "Lieutenant J. J. Hoyle, of Company F, was killed while gallantly leading his company; he was ever a faithful and conscientious officer."[2]

Sarah struggled with the grief the war had laid upon her doorstep. The sorrow the loss of her husband and brothers brought, most likely stayed with her for the rest of her years, but life goes on and soon she was able to pick up the pieces of her shattered dreams and begin anew. She married Able Hallman, a Confederate veteran who served with Company I, 11th North Carolina. The couple had one child, J. Albert Hallman, born in 1871. Sarah died on July 2, 1929, and is buried in the St. Peter's Methodist Church Cemetery.

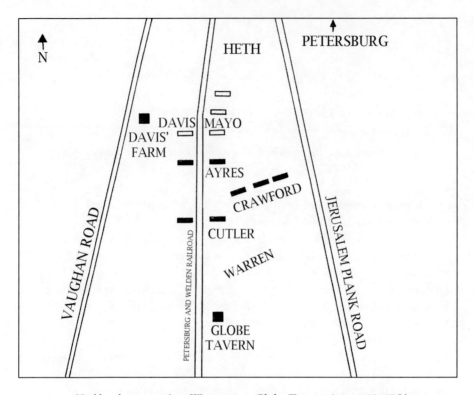

Heth's advance against Warren near Globe Tavern, August 18, 1864.

Based on documentation from other soldiers wounded on the battlefield, the agonizing and sad experiences of Joseph J. Hoyle's last weeks can be ascertained. As he and his men made the fateful charge at Globe Tavern Hoyle, as the regimental historian states, was leading the way, most likely encouraging his troops to press on and cover the ground between their works and the Federal line as quickly as possible. At some point a Union rifleman found his mark and hit Lieutenant Hoyle in the right leg. Falling to the ground the courageous officer may still have been pushing his command forward with words of support. Possibly he was able to make his way back to Confederate lines, or if too injured to move, would have remained on the battlefield until the firing and confusion happening all around him subsided and assistance came to carry him to safety.

Hoyle's initial reaction to being shot was probably shock. After all one of the greatest fears of combat is being wounded during the engagement and the impact of the bullet may have spun him around knocking him off his feet. He most likely ripped his pants open around the wound area to determine the severity of the injury. Depending on the wound Joseph may have thought of death or focused on the horrors he had seen first hand in August 1863, and would most likely glimpse again, occurring at army hospitals. There would have been little if any pain initially; the first physical discomfort associated with being shot was a "peculiar tingling" feeling emanating from the wounded area. As time past, however, and the numbness subsided, pain began to slowly increase. Loss of blood would have made the young officer thirsty, making the need for water a primary concern.[3]

When Joseph finally arrived at the regimental aid station, located close to the field of battle, his wound would have been cleaned and dressed then assessed by the surgeon as to the seriousness of the injury. It can be assumed that the medical staff at the aid station believed Hoyle had a better than average chance of surviving because he was then transported to one of the division or corps hospitals. There the better qualified surgeons would work on the wound and prepare him to be moved to Richmond for recovery. The treatment he received would not have resembled modern medical procedures, the Civil War era still being in, as one historian puts it, "the tail end of medical dark ages." But it was not as backwards as some have come to believe. For example the image of suffering soldiers having to have limbs removed or other inflictions being treated without the use of anesthesia is not always accurate. Of the men cared for during the Civil War only a relatively small percentage received no anesthesia to dilute their pain. However, shortages of medical supplies, especially in the South during the last year of the conflict, may have meant Hoyle received little or no medicine to dull the pain during his time in the care of a Confederate medical staff.[4]

At one point while at the division or corps hospital one or more of the surgeons working on Hoyle determined that his wound was severe enough to warrant the amputation of his right leg. If this was the case, the medical staff most likely believed the young lieutenant had no chance of surviving the injury without the procedure. The fact that he had to have his leg removed provides some information on the damage caused by the bullet wound he received at Globe Tavern. This course of action was often taken if there was extensive bone or joint damage. The injury would not heal unless all of the bone fragments were removed. The type of bullet used during this time jumbled around in the body and carried pieces of dirt or clothing deep into the wound. The foreign materials forced into the body could cause more concerns and sometimes fatal infections.[5]

After the short, but rough ambulance ride to Richmond, Hoyle was placed in Hospital Number 4. It was there that he wrote his final letter to his much loved and cherished wife. In his barely legible final letter, the pain he was enduring was evident in comparison to his earlier, more styled writings. Possibly too ill to write, he dictated his words to another. He may or may not have known he was dying at the time he wrote his final words. His simple letter may have been an attempt to delay the grief he knew his wife would endure upon hearing of his death. It is not known if Hoyle died in the company of friends or alone, but his passing so far from home was hard to accept for his family. The thought of the impersonal death her loving husband experienced proved to be one more sad reality for Sarah Hoyle. Like so many young men who fought in the Civil War, Joseph J. Hoyle never came home.

Appendix A: Miscellaneous Undated Letters

The following letters were among the Hoyle Papers at Duke University; however, they were not dated.

> To My Own Dear Sarah
> A heart so true so pure as thine
> Should never sorrow now,
> Could I sway Fates destined hand
> Joy ever to thee should flow.
>
> When first in heart we joined
> How unmixed wer our joys,
> But time has brought the bitter kind
> And now the cup's mixed with alloy.
>
> My Dearest Sarah now alone must be
> How wearisom the hours pass away.
> O, had I wings, I now would see
> My Dearest one, before another day.
>
> To join thee again in union sweet
> Is ever my prayer and ardent wish.
> O the joy when thee again I meet
> Tis enough, no fuller earthly joy I wish
> Love is pure—God is love
>
> Joe

To The Absent Members of Co "F" 55th N.C. Regt.

All men belonging to this company (Capt. Mulls) now at home whose furloughs have expired will report to camp, immediately in person, or through the Medical Department (C. S. A.) at Charlotte N.C. No more doctor's certificates will be taken. Also this is made to include all prisoners payrolled and delivered previous to 1st Sept, 1863. On failure to comply with this order, the absentee will be considered a deserter and dealt with accordingly. This is fair warning.

J. J. Hoyle, 1st Lt.
Comdg — Co. "F" 55th N.C. Regt.

My Dear Sarah,

I am truly glad to hear your ardent wishes that I might be enabled to enter the ministry. You know that this has been my inclination for several years' and if it had not been for this cruel war I would have been a preacher ere this. And I am now more firmly resolved to enter the ministry than ever, if the good Lord sees proper to bring me through this war. Sarah, I want to enjoy as much of God and heaven as I can while I stay here on earth, and I believe I can best serve my Heavenly Master by being a minister of His blessed gospel. I am glad you give me the time of the quarterly meeting, and I thought I would write to your preacher, Brother Hoyle, and make an effort to come home and apply for licens at that meeting, but we are now ordered off to Fredericksburg, I suppose, and I do not expect I can possibly get off. If we had staid here, I believe I could have gotten off. So I scarcely by know whether to write to brother Hoyle or not. But if I do not get off this time which I can hardly expect, I wish you would let me know still of the quarterly meetings. I hope God will see fit to let me engage in this my long desired calling. And I am truly glad that I have the wishes and prayers of my dearest one on earth in this behalf. Sarah, I would to God that I could have the pleasure of talking to you about this matter. But let us hope in God, and give him all our love. I remain, as ever, yours in hope and love.

Mrs. S. A Hoyle   Joe

Dear wife,

I have seen P. P Mull about that note and he says it is at his home. So you will get J. A. Mull to go up again and look it up, telling him to tell Peters wife if the note is not delivered up I will not pay interest upon it any longer. She can have the note found if she will and she will be acting very mean if she does not. I have told Peter to write to his wife about it. Write me about it as soon as you make an effort about it. Dear Sarah, I do not know where we will settle down, though I expect somewhere in this country. Direct your letters still to Franklin Depot. This is written very badly, and you will have trouble in reading it, but it is the best I can do under the circumstances. I remain as ever your loving husband, the boys are well.[1]

S.A. Hoyle   Joe

Appendix B: Regimental Roster for the Field and Staff Officers of the 55th North Carolina State Troops and Company F

FIELD AND STAFF OFFICERS
(Some of the men listed in this section also appear in company rosters)

Colonel

John Kerr Connally— Served as regimental colonel until being wounded at Gettysburg on July 1, 1863.

Lieutenant Colonels

Alfred H. Belo— Served as the regiment's Assistant Quartermaster, and as Major until being promoted to Lt. Colonel on July 3, 1863. Wounded at Gettysburg on July 1, 1863; returned to duty in January 1864, and was given command of the regiment. Wounded in the left arm at Cold Harbor on June 2, 1864, and did not return to command of the 55th.

Abner S. Calloway— Resigned on January 12, 1863.

Maurice T. Smith— Killed at Gettysburg on July 1, 1863.

Major

James S. Whitehead— Died on August 7, 1862. The cause of death was not reported.

Adjutants

1st Lt. Charles M. Cooke— Served as acting Adjutant from June 1864 through April 9, 1865.

1st Lt. Charles R. Jones— Served as acting Adjutant for several months after July 1, 1863.

1st Lt. Henry T. Jordan— Appointed Adjutant on November 18, 1862, and served until being captured at Gettysburg on July 1, 1863. Remained at Johnson's Island until March 14, 1865.

1st Lt. William H. Young— Resigned on or about November 1, 1862.

Assistant Quartermasters

George Washington Blount— Appointed Assistant Quartermaster on May 20, 1862. Dismissed prior to November 1, 1862.

William P. Webb— Appointed Assistant Quartermaster on April 30, 1863. Relieved from duty and served as Assistant Quartermaster in the Forge Bureau in Georgia. Had served as the 55th North

Carolina's Assistant Commissary of Substance from November 18, 1862, through April 30, 1863.

Chaplains

Issac G. Connalay— Appointed on an unspecified date.

William B. Royall— Served as Chaplain from November 18, 1862, through July 24, 1863.

Surgeons

Benjamin T. Green— Served as Surgeon from November 18, 1862, until being captured at Gettysburg on or about July 5, 1863. He returned to duty sometime after November 1863 and served until April 9, 1865.

James A. Smith— Served as Surgeon from May 19, 1862, through November 1, 1862.

Assistant Surgeons

Isaac G. Cannady— Served as Assistant Surgeon from May 20, 1862, through April 9, 1865.

W. T. Parker— Date of appointment not reported. Captured at Gettysburg on or about July 5, 1863. Paroled in November 1863, but no further service record exists.

Hospital Stewards

A. J. Stone— Appointed Hospital Steward on an unspecified date and served until being transferred to the 48th North Carolina State Troops Regiment sometime between July and October 1864.

Peterson Thorp, Jr.— Appointed Hospital Steward sometime between July and October 1864 and served until April 9, 1865.

Ensign

Marlin B. Galloway— Appointed Ensign on April 27, 1864, and served until being killed during the battle of the Wilderness on May 5, 1863.

Sergeants Major

Jesse Allen Adams— Served as acting Sergeant Major from May or June 1863 until being wounded and captured at Gettysburg on July 1, 1863. Paroled in August 1863 and returned to duty. Appointed to Sergeant Major sometime between July and October 1864 and served until April 9, 1865.

William N. Holt— Served as Sergeant Major from May or June 1862 through May 8, 1863, when he was promoted to 3rd Lt. Company H.

Quartermaster Sergeants

Alonzo H. Dunn— Served as Quartermaster Sergeant until his death on July 12, 1862. The cause of death was not reported.

Henry S. Furman— Appointed Quartermaster Sergeant on October 7, 1862.

Commissary Sergeant

William B. Royal— Served as Commissary Sergeant from sometime after October 1863 until April 9, 1865.

Ordnance Sergeant

J. W. C. Young— Served as Ordnance Sergeant from November 19, 1862, until April 9, 1865.

Band

Henry C. Adcock— Surrendered at Appomattox.

Rufus M. Beam— Surrendered at Appomattox.

Francis N. Bernard— Captured at Tabernacle Church, Virginia, April 3, 1865.

John Paul Bernard— Paroled on or around April 14, 1865.

William H. Cleland— Paroled at Houston, Texas, on or about August 4, 1865.

Jacob C. Ellington— Captured at Petersburg, Virginia, April 3, 1865.

George Lewis Falls— Surrendered at Appomattox.

Eugene Geauffretean— Captured at Tabernacle Church, Virginia, April 3, 1865.

William H. Horne— Surrendered at Appomattox.

Charles E. Jacke— Deserted on or about April 4, 1865.

Jacob C. Pearson— Surrendered at Appomattox.

William H. Rowland— Surrendered at Appomattox.

William H. Shelly— Captured near Sutherland's Station, Virginia, April 2, 1865.

Burton P. Summerell— Surrendered at Appomattox.

Allen H. Taft— Paroled on or around April 14, 1865.

Henry C. Turnage— Surrendered at Appomattox.

Archibald A. Tyson— Survived the war.

ROSTER OF COMPANY F

Officers

Capt. Peter M. Mull
Capt. Godfrey E. Taft
2nd Lt. Henry Cline
1st Lt. Joseph J. Hoyle
1st Lt. William H. Hull
2nd Lt. Peter P. Mull
3rd Lt. Eli Newton
1st Lt. Archibald H. A. Williams

Noncommissioned Officers and Privates

Pvt. William P. Bigham
Pvt. Jacob A. Bivens
Pvt. Peter M. Bivens
Pvt. Daniel W. Boyles
Pvt. William M. Boyles
Pvt. Williamson F. Brackett
Pvt. Zachariah Brackett
Pvt. Sidney Bradshaw
Pvt. David A. Brendle
Pvt. Wesley M. Brendle
Brittain (first name and rank not listed)
Pvt. Aaron Buff
Pvt. Christopher Buff
Pvt. David Buff Jr.
Pvt. David Buff Sr.
Pvt. James Buff
Pvt. Peter Buff
Pvt. Philip Buff
Pvt. David A. Bumgarner
Pvt. William P. Bumgarner
Pvt. Massenburg Burton

William Burton (rank not listed)
Pvt. Adam Canipe
Pvt. Albert Canipe
Pvt. Daniel E. Canipe
Pvt. David Canipe
Pvt. John A. Canipe
Pvt. Joseph Canipe
Pvt. Maxwell Canipe
Pvt. Noah J. Canipe
Pvt. William R. Chapman
Pvt. John Carpenter
1st Sgt. John Cline
Pvt. Aaron Cook Jr.
Pvt. Aaron Cook Sr.
Pvt. Harrison Cook
Pvt. Jesse Cook
Pvt. Noah W. Cook
Pvt. William Cook
Pvt. William Craig
Pvt. John S. Crow
Pvt. John R. Dickson
Pvt. William Downs
Pvt. John F. Elmore
Pvt. William Elmore
Pvt. William M. Freeman
Pvt. Jacob A. Gales
Pvt. Joseph C. Gantt
Pvt. James C. Goodson
Pvt. Miles Goodson
Sgt. Ephraim Gross
Pvt. Robert J. Hicks
Pvt. William H. Hicks
Pvt. Eli Hoyle

Pvt. Henry Hoyle
Pvt. Joel Hoyle
Pvt. Joseph Hoyle
Pvt. Levi Hoyle
Pvt. Robert D. Hoyle
Pvt. Solomon Hoyle
Pvt. Hiram Hudson
Pvt. John D. Hudson
Pvt. Thomas Huffman
Pvt. Benjamin Hull
Sgt. Albert P. Ivester
Pvt. Allen R. Johnson
Pvt. Andrew J. Johnson
Pvt. James M. Keever
Cpl. Julius A. Kennedy
Pvt. Peter Lail
Pvt. John Ledford
Pvt. William Ledford
Pvt. David Logan
Pvt. H. Loman
Pvt. Robert A. McCall
Pvt. Andrew McClurd
Pvt. Wade McClurd
Pvt. Jonathan McNeely
Pvt. Zachariah D. McNeilly
Pvt. Samuel McNeilly
Pvt. Leander M. Martin
Pvt. Ezra Mull
Pvt. John M. Mull
Pvt. Alfred Newton
Pvt. Eli Newton
Pvt. George A. Newton
Pvt. Henry Norman
Pvt. Robert H. Norman
Pvt. Alfred G. Peeler
Pvt. Lafayette Pope
Pvt. Joseph Prewit
Peter Prewitt (rank not listed)
Pvt. James T. Price
Pvt. Caleb Randall
Pvt. William S. Seagle
Pvt. Anderson Self

Sgt. Isaac R. Self
Pvt. Jacob R. Self
Pvt. Robert Self
Pvt. Rufus Self
Pvt. William J. Self
Pvt. Daniel F. Shuford
Pvt. Henry P. Shuford
Pvt. Peter M. Shuford
Pvt. John Smith
Pvt. James P. Stamey
Pvt. John Swink
Pvt. William N. Swink
Pvt. Robert Swofford
Pvt. Aaron Tallent
Pvt. Jesse E. Tallent
Pvt. David W. Turner
Pvt. James Turner
Pvt. James P. Walker
Sgt. Andrew Warlick
Pvt. David P. Warlick
Pvt. Noah B. Warlick
Pvt. George White
Cpl. Peter R. White
Cpl. Stephen J. White
Pvt. Andrew P. Williams
Sgt. Westly A. Williams
Pvt. William T. Williams
Pvt. Henry J. Willis
Pvt. Jacob B. Willis
Pvt. James Willis
1st Sgt. James R. Willis
Pvt. John Y. Willis
Pvt. Robert H. Willis
Pvt. Samuel O. Willis
Pvt. Solomon Willis
Pvt. Thomas Willis
Pvt. Levi Wise
Pvt. Major Wortman
Pvt. William S. Wortman
Pvt. Silas M. Wright
Pvt. Samuel Young

Appendix C: Field and Staff Officers and Men from Company F Who Died from Disease While Serving with the 55th North Carolina

Field and Staff Officers

Maj. James S. Whitehead, August 1862
Capt. Albert E. Upchurch, Co. A, 1863, (POW)
2nd Lt. Benjamin J. Blount, Co. H, 1863, (POW)
1st Lt. Elbert B. Salmons, Co. I, 1862
2nd Lt. William H. Webb, Co. K, 1863, (POW)

Noncommissioned Officers and Privates

Pvt. Daniel W. Boyles, 1863
Pvt. Zachariah Bracket, 1864
Pvt. Aaron Buff, 1864
Pvt. Adam Canipe, 1862
Pvt. Albert Canipe, 1862
Pvt. John F. Elmore, 1862
Sgt. Ephraim Gross, 1862
Pvt. Levi Hoyle, 1862

Pvt. Robert D. Hoyle, 1862
Pvt. Hiram Hudson, 1864
Pvt. Andrew J. Johnson, 1863
Pvt. Robert A. McCall, 1862
Pvt. Zachariah D. McNeilly, 1864
Pvt. John M. Mull, 1865, (POW)
Pvt. George A. Newton, 1863
Pvt. Lafayette Pope, 1862
Pvt. James Price, 1862
Pvt. Caleb Randall, 1862
Pvt. William S. Seagle, 1863, (POW)
Pvt. Robert Self, 1865, (POW)
Pvt. John Swink, 1863, (POW)
Pvt. William N. Swink, 1863, (POW)
Pvt. David W. Turner, 1863, (POW)
Pvt. James Turner, 1863
Pvt. David P. Warlick, 1862
Pvt. James Willis, 1863
Pvt. John Y. Willis, 1862
Pvt. Samuel O. Willis, 1865, (POW)
Pvt. Major Wortman, 1862

(POW) indicates that the particular soldier died while in a Union prison camp.

This list of soldiers is not intended to infer that the above listed soldiers were the only members of the 55th North Carolina to die from disease during the Civil War. There are many individual records that do not explain the cause of death, and so it can be assumed that at least a portion of those soldiers died from diseases as well.

Appendix D: Field and Staff Officers and Men from Company F Who Were Killed in Action or Reported Missing in Action While Serving with the 55th North Carolina State Troops

Field and Staff Officers

Lt. Col. Maurice T. Smith, Gettysburg
Ens. Marlin B. Galloway, Wilderness
Capt. George A. Gilreath, Co. A, Gettysburg
1st Lt. William Hunt Townes, Co. D, Globe Tavern
2nd Lt. William S. Wilson, Co. E, Gettysburg (missing in action and presumed dead)
1st Lt. Joseph J. Hoyle, Co. F, Globe Tavern
2nd Lt. Mordecai Lee, Co. G, Gettysburg
Capt. Edward Fletcher Satterfield, Co. H, Gettysburg

Noncommissioned Officers and Privates

Pvt. William M. Boyles, Gettysburg
Pvt. Williamson F. Brackett, Gettysburg
Pvt. Jesse Cook, Talley's Mill
Pvt. John D. Hudson, Petersburg
Pvt. Benjamin Hull, Spotsylvania
Pvt. David Logan, Wilderness
Pvt. Andrew McClurd, Wilderness
Pvt. Samuel McNeily, Gettysburg
Pvt. Ezra Mull, Petersburg
Pvt. William J. Self, Gettysburg
Pvt. Robert Swofford, Gettysburg (MIA)
Pvt. George White, Wilderness
Pvt. Andrew P. Williams, Cold Harbor
Pvt. William T. Williams, Wilderness
Pvt. Thomas Willis, Gettysburg
Pvt. Levi Wise, Falling Waters
Pvt. Samuel Young, Washington, NC

Notes

Introduction

1. Earl J. Hess, *Pickett's Charge—The Last Attack at Gettysburg* (Chapel Hill: University of North Carolina Press, 2001), 333–335.

2. His mother, Susan's, maiden name is Mull, sister of Peter M. Mull, who served with Joseph in Company F. Joseph's other siblings were Barbara, Margaret, John, and Sarah. B. Rondal Mull and Mable M. Mull, *Mull: A History and Genealogical Record of the Mull Family in North Carolina* (Franklin, NC: Genealogy Publishing Services, 1997); Federal Census 1840, 1850, and 1860.

3. The English surname Hoyl is derived from the German Heyl, though why the "e" was added at the end is not known. Elizabeth Hoyle Rucker, *The Genealogy of Peiter Heyl and His Descendants, 1110–1936* (Shelby, NC: Zolliecoffer Jenks Thompson, 1938), 22, 27–28, 31.

4. Rucker, *The Genealogy of Peiter Heyl*, 31–36, 162; Lee B. Weathers, *The Living Past of Cleveland County: A History* (Shelby, NC: Star, 1956), 18–20.

5. Weathers, *The Living Past of Cleveland County*, 3, 7, 18, 21, 33; Guion Griffs Johnson, *Ante-Bellum North Carolina: A Social History* (Chapel Hill: University of North Carolina Press, 1937), 187–188.

6. S. Arnold Ramey, *Cleveland County North Carolina Marriages: 1851–1868* (Lattimore, NC), 26. For letters, see Joseph J. Hoyle to Sarah A. Self, December 1858 to July 1860. For an overview of the life of Southern women in this period see Sally G. McMillen, *Southern Women: Black and White in the Old South* (Wheeling IL: Harlan Davidson, 1982).

7. Annie Self Arnold, *Some Descendants of Old Robert Selfe* (Salem, MA: Higginson Book Company, 2004), 13–16; Military Service Records (Microfilm M270) North Carolina State Archives, Division of Archives and History, Raleigh, NC.

8. Both teaching certificates, a copy of Joseph Hoyle's valedictorian speech, and examples of his lessons can be found in his letters. The lesson plans offer a wonderful view of education in the South during the mid-19th Century and can be found in the letters as well, specifically the years 1858 through 1861. Joseph J. Hoyle Papers, Perkins Library Manuscripts Department, Duke University, Durham, NC.

9. A. B. Hayes to Joseph J. Hoyle, December 17, 1860, Joseph Hoyle Papers.

10. There are several excellent studies about the causes that led to the Civil War. Among the best are David M. Potter's *The Impending Crisis, 1848–1861* (New York: Harper & Row, 1976); William W. Freehling's *The Road to Disunion: Secessionists at Bay, 1776–1854* (Oxford University Press, 1990), and his second volume, *The Road to Disunion: Secessionists Triumphant, 1854–1861* (Oxford University Press, 2007). Only eleven states seceded from the Union, but the Confederacy eventually admitted two others: Missouri and Kentucky.

11. William C. Harris, *North Carolina and the Coming of the Civil War* (Raleigh: North Carolina Department of Culture and History, 1988), 1–4, 8.

12. Harris, *North Carolina and the Coming of the Civil War*, 6–8; Eugene D. Genovese, *The Political Economy of Slavery* (New York: Vintage, 1967), 250.

13. Barrett, *North Carolina in the Civil* War, 15–17; Harris, *North Carolina and the Coming of the Civil War*, 15–20; Genovese, *The Political Economy of Slavery*, 194–195; Allan Nevins, *Ordeal of the Union: Fruits of Manifest Destiny, 1847–1852* (New York: Charles Scribner's Sons, 1947), 315–318.

14. Harris, *North Carolina and the Coming of the Civil War*, 25–30; Allan Nevins, *Ordeal of the Union: A House Dividing, 1852–1857* (New York: Charles Scribner's Sons, 1947), 316–317. Joseph Hoyle's region had remained firmly behind the Democratic Party throughout the 1850s, continuing to elect Democrat Francis Burton Craige to represent their district in the House of Representatives from 1853 until the state seceded from the United States in 1861. Craige was the delegate who at the North Carolina Secession Convention introduced the Ordinance of Secession. Craige would continue to represent his district in the Provisional Confederate Congress, but would decline to run for office in the regular Confederate Congress. Ezra J Warner and W. Buck Yearns, *Biographical Register of the Confederate Congress* (Baton Rouge: Louisiana State University Press, 1975), 63–64; Joel D. Treese, ed., *Biographical Directory of the American Congress, 1774–1996* (Alexandria, VA: CQ Staff Directories, 1997), 875.

15. Harris, *North Carolina and the Coming of the*

Civil War, 51–56; Barrett, *North Carolina in the Civil War*; William S. Powell, *North Carolina Through Four Centuries* (Chapel Hill: University of North Carolina Press, 1989), 347. Victor Davis Hanson, *Carnage and Culture: Landmark Battles in the Rise of Western Power* (New York: Random House, 2002), 21. These numbers vary, but most sources agree that about 40,000 of North Carolina's soldiers died during the war from combat, combat-related wounds, and disease. In all, one in four Confederate deaths were from North Carolina.

16. Rucker, *Genealogy of Peiter Heyl*, 16, 39.

17. Emory M. Thomas, *The Confederate Nation: 1861–1865* (New York: Harper & Row, 1979), 152–156. For a list of other exemptions see James M. McPherson, *Battle Cry of Freedom: The Civil War Era* (New York: Oxford University Press, 1988), 430–431.

Chapter 1

1. Bell Irvin Wiley, *The Life of Johnny Reb: The Common Soldier of the Confederacy* (Indianapolis: Bobbs-Merrill, 1943).

2. Bell Irvin Wiley, *The Life of Billy Yank: The Common Soldier of the Union* (Indianapolis: Bobbs-Merrill, 1952).

3. Pete Maslowski, "A Study of Morale in Civil War Soldiers," *Military Affairs* 34 (December 1970), 122–126.

4. Samuel A. Stouffer et al., *The American Soldier: Studies in Social Psychology in World War II* (Princeton: Princeton University Press, 1949).

5. Michael Barton, *Goodmen: The Character of Civil War Soldiers* (London: Pennsylvania State University Press, 1981).

6. Barton, *Goodmen: The Character of Civil War Soldier.* 4.

7. James I. Robertson, *Soldiers Blue and Gray* (Columbia: University of South Carolina Press, 1988), viii.

8. Reid Mitchell, *Civil War Soldiers* (New York: Viking, 1988), vii.

9. Reid Mitchell, *The Vacant Chair: The Northern Soldier Leaves Home* (New York: Oxford University Press, 1993).

10. James M. McPherson, *For Cause and Comrades: Why Men Fought in the Civil War* (New York and Oxford: Oxford University Press, 1997).

11. James M. McPherson, *What They Fought for, 1861–1865* (Baton Rouge: Louisiana State University Press, 1994).

12. Paddy Griffith, *Battle Tactics of the Civil War* (New Haven, CT: Yale University Press, 1989).

13. Joseph Allan Frank, *With Ballot and Bayonet: The Political Socialization of American Civil War Soldiers* (Athens: University of Georgia Press, 1998), vii.

14. John Keegan, *The Face of Battle* (New York: Viking, 1976).

15. Earl J. Hess, *The Union Soldier in Battle: Enduring the Ordeal of Combat* (Lawrence: University Press of Kansas, 1997), x–xi.

16. Grady McWhiney and Perry D. Jamieson, *Attack and Die: Civil War Military Tactics and the Southern Heritage* (Tuscaloosa, AL: University of Alabama Press, 1982).

17. Paddy Griffith, *Battle Tactics of the Civil War* (New Haven, CT: Yale University Press, 1989).

18. Gerald F. Linderman, *Embattled Courage: The Experience of Combat in the American Civil War* (New York: The Free Press, 1987).

19. Joseph Allan Frank and George A. Reaves, *"Seeing the Elephant": Raw Recruits at the Battle of Shiloh* (New York: Greenwood Press, 1989).

20. Eric T. Dean, *Shook Over Hell: Post-Traumatic Stress, Vietnam, and the Civil War* (Cambridge: Harvard University Press, 1997).

21. Benjamin Quarles, *The Negro in the Civil War* (Boston: Little, Brown, 1953).

22. Dudley Taylor Cornish, *The Sable Arm: Negro Troops in the Union Army, 1861–1865* (New York: Longmans, Green, 1956).

23. Ira Berlin, ed., *Freedom's Soldiers: The Black Military Experience in the Civil War* (Cambridge: Cambridge University Press, 1982).

24. Joseph T. Glatthaar, *Forged in Battle: The Civil War Alliance of Black Soldiers and White Officers* (New York: The Free Press, 1992).

25. Charles Kelly Barrow, J. H. Segars, and R. B. Rosenburg., eds., *Forgotten Confederates: An Anthology About Black Southerners* (Atlanta: Southern Heritage Press, 1995), 3.

26. Richard Rollins, ed., *Black Southerners in Gray: Essays on Afro-Americans in the Confederate Armies* (Redondo Beach, California: Rank and File Publications, 1994).

27. *Ibid.*, 1.

28. Barrow, Segars, and Rosenburg, *Forgotten Confederates.*

29. Noah Andre Trudeau, *Like Men of War: Black Troops in the Civil War, 1862–1865* (New York: Little, Brown, 1998).

Chapter 2

1. Grady McWhiney and Perry D. Jamison, *Attack and Die: Civil War Military Tactics and the Southern Heritage* (Tuscaloosa: University of Alabama Press, 1982); John Hope Franklin, *The Militant South, 1800–1861* (Cambridge, MA: Harvard University Press, 1956).

2. Mark A. Weitz, "Drill, Training, and the Combat Performance of the Civil War Soldier: Dispelling the Myth of the Poor Soldier, Great Fighter," *The Journal of Military History* 62 (April 1998): 272–275; Jeffrey M. Girvan, *The 55th North Carolina in the Civil War: A History and Roster* (Jefferson, NC: McFarland, 2006), 6–7.

3. David G. Chandler, *The Military Maxims of Napoleon* (London: Greenhill Books, 1987), 74; Weitz, "Drill, Training, and Combat Performance of the Civil War Soldier," 275; Anthony Kellett, *Combat Motivation: The Behavior of Soldiers in Battle* (Boston: Kluwer Nijhoff Publishing, 1982), 41.

4. Kellett, *Combat Motivation*, 41–46; Richard

Notes. Chapter 3

Holmes, *Acts of War: The Behavior of Men in Battle* (New York: The Free Press, 1985), 36, 43; Keegan, *The Face of Battle*, 320–321; Hess, *The Union Soldier in Battle*, 115.

5. Stuart Wright, ed., *Memoirs of Alfred Horatio Belo: Reminiscences of a North Carolina Volunteer* (Gaithersburg, MD: Olde Soldier, n.d.), 20; Girvan, *The 55th North Carolina*, 32–34.

6. Girvan, *The 55th North Carolina*, 32–34; Douglas Southall Freeman, *Lee's Lieutenants: A Study in Command*, 3 vols. (New York: Charles Scribner's Sons, 1946), 2: 487–488.

7. Charles M. Cooke, "Fifty-fifth Regiment," in *Histories of the Several Regiments and Battalion from North Carolina in the Great War, 1861–1865*, Walter Clark., ed., 5 vols (Goldsboro, NC: Nash Brothers, 1901), 3: 292; Girvan, *The 55th North Carolina*, 33–35.

8. Kellett, *Combat Motivation*, 42–43.

9. S. L. A. Marshall, *Men Against Fire: The Problem of Command in Future War* (Alexandria: Byrd Enterprises, 1961), 148–149.

10. C. Day Lewis, ed., *The Collected Poems of Wilfred Owen* (New York: New Directions Books, 1963), 55.

11. Marshall, *Men Against Fire*, 184; Drew Gilpin Faust, "Christian Soldiers: The Meaning of Revivalism in the Confederate Army," *Journal of Southern History* 53 (February 1987), 64; Samuel J. Watson, "Religion and Combat Motivation in the Confederate Armies," *The Journal of Military History*, 58 (January 1994): 29–31.

12. Frank L. Owsley, *Plain Folk of the Old South* (Baton Rouge: Louisiana State University Press, 1982), 97–98; Linderman, *Embattled Courage*, 9; Watson, "Religion and Combat Motivation in the Confederate Armies," 34–35; Steven Woodworth, "The Meaning of Life in the Valley of Death," 42 (December 2003), 56–59.

13. Marshall, *Men Against Fire*, 44; Kellett, *Combat Motivation*, 222–223; S. Kirson Weinberg, "The Combat Neuroses," *The American Journal of Sociology* 51 (March 1946): 471; Joseph J. Ondishko, Jr., "A View of Anxiety, Fear, and Panic," *Military Affairs* 36 (April 1972): 58–59; Hess, *The Union Soldier in Battle*, 6–7.

14. Kent Gramm, ed., *Battle: The Nature and Consequences of Civil War Combat* (Montgomery: University of Alabama Press, 2008), 27–28; Kellett, *Combat Motivation*, 135–136; Keegan, *The Face of Battle*, 173.

15. Gramm, *Battle*, 19–20; Dave Grossman, *On Killing: The Psychological Costs of Learning to Kill in War and Society* (New York: Little, Brown, 1995), 74–75. Hess, *The Union Soldier in Battle*, 45–49; Keegan, *The Face of Battle*, 140–141.

16. Stephen Berry, "When Metal Meets Mettle: The Hard Realities of Civil War Soldiering," *North & South* 9 (August 2006), 14–17; Peter Carmichael, "The Manly Art of Staying Put," *Civil War Times* 42 (December 2003), 36–39.

17. Grossman, *On Killing*, 2, 231–240; Eric T. Dean, Jr., "His Eyes Indicated Wildness and Fear," *North & South* 9 (August 2006), 62–69.

18. Holmes, *Acts of War*, 109–113.

19. Keegan, *The Face of Battle*, 296–297; Hanson, *Carnage and Culture*, 6–8; Hess, *The Union Soldier in Battle*, 194–195.

20. Gordon C. Rhea, *The Battles for Spotsylvania Court House and the Road to Yellow Tavern, May 7–12, 1864* (Baton Rouge: Louisiana State University Press, 1997), 3.

21. McPherson, *Battle Cry of Freedom*, 742–743.

22. David J. Eicher, *The Longest Night: A Military History of the Civil War* (New York: Simon & Schuster, 2001), 663–664; Joseph T. Glatthaar, *General Lee's Army: From Victory to Collapse* (New York: The Free Press, 2008), 364–365; Freeman, *Lee's Lieutenants*, 3:346–348.

23. James I. Robertson, Jr., *General A. P. Hill: The Story of a Confederate Warrior* (New York: Random House, 1987), 251–252;

24. Gordon C. Rhea, *The Battle of the Wilderness, May 5–6, 1864* (Baton Rouge: Louisiana State University Press, 1994), 188–194; Noah Andre Trudeau, "A Frightful and Frightening Place," *Civil War Times Illustrated* 38 (May 1999), 46–47.

25. Girvan, *The 55th North Carolina*, 96; Rhea, *The Battle of the Wilderness*, 194–196.

26. Gordon C. Rhea, *Carrying the Flag: The Story of Private Charles Whilden, the Confederacy's Most Unlikely Hero* (New York: Basic Books, 2004), 123–124; Girvan, *The 55th North Carolina*, 96–97.

27. Cooke, "Fifty-fifth Regiment," 304.

28. Rhea, *The Battle of the Wilderness*, 223–229; Cooke, "Fifty-fifth Regiment," 304.

29. Cooke, "Fifty-fifth Regiment," 304.

30. Rhea, *The Battle of the Wilderness*, 229; Girvan, *The 55th North Carolina*, 98–99.

Chapter 3

1. T. H. Pearce, *They Fought: The Story of Franklin County Men in the Years 1861–1865* (Adams Press, 1969), 45; Emory M. Thomas, *The Confederate Nation: 1861–1865* (New York: Harper & Row, 1979), 152–153.

2. Pearce, *They Fought*, 49; Manarin and Jordan, eds., *North Carolina Troops*, 13: 349, 485.

3. "Obituary of Lt. Sidney Smith Abernethy," *Confederate Veteran* 7 (1899), 301.

4. Robert K. Krick, *Lee's Colonels: A Biographical Register of the Field Officers of the Army of Northern Virginia* (Dayton, OH: Morningside Bookshop, 1979), 86; Stuart Wright, ed., *Memoirs of Alfred Horatio Belo: Reminiscences of a North Carolina Volunteer* (Gaithersburg, MD: Olde Soldier Books, n.d.), 12, n43.

5. James S. Whitehead Diary, Division of Archives and History, Raleigh, North Carolina; Manarin and Jordon, eds. *North Carolina Troops*, 13: 430, 476.

6. Wright, *Belo*, 12–13; Krick, *Lee's Colonels*, 44–45; Charles M. Cooke, "Fifty-fifth Regiment," in *Histories of the Several Regiments and Battalions from North Carolina in the Great War, 1861–1865*,

Walter Clark, ed., 5 vols (Goldsboro, NC: Nash Brothers, 1901), 3: 306–307.

7. James K. Wilkerson to his parents, June 28, 1862, Wilkerson Papers, Perkins Library Manuscript Department, Duke University, Durham, NC.

8. For a better understanding of Lee's strategic plans in June 1862 see Joseph L. Harsh, *Confederate Tide Rising: Robert E. Lee and the Making of Southern Strategy, 1861–1862* (Kent, OH: Kent State University Press, 1998).

9. John G. Barrett, *North Carolina as a Civil War Battleground, 1861–1865* (Raleigh: North Carolina Department of Cultural Resources, 1980), 15, 17.

10. Barrett, *The Civil War in North Carolina*, 66–69; James M. McPherson, *Ordeal by Fire: The Civil War and Reconstruction* (New York: University of Oxford Press, 1992), 180–181. For more on McClellan's overall plans for Burnside see Ethan S. Rafuse, *McClellan's War: The Failure of Moderation in the Struggle for the Union* (Bloomington & Indianapolis: Indiana University Press, 2005), 169, 185–186.

11. Barrett, *North Carolina as a Civil War Battleground*, 43–44; Rafuse, *McClellan's War*, 203, 232, 241–242.

12. The regiment's baptism of fire occurred on August 7, 1862. The 55th North Carolina was sent to prevent the Federals from landing a reconnaissance party and reconnoitering the area around Kinston. The 55th formed in a line of battle on the south side of the Neuse River, about seven miles from Kinston. The Federal gunboat *Ellis* positioned itself directly across from the regiment and proceeded to fire on the Confederate line. Private Solomon Hoyle of Company F was the only member of the regiment wounded during the barrage.

13. Camp Mangum was located about four miles east of Raleigh, North Carolina.

14. Hoyle is referring to either Privates James Calloway Goodson or Miles Goodson, both farmers living in Catawba County, North Carolina, before enlisting. Information regarding the members of the 55th North Carolina was obtained from the compiled Service Records, Fifty-Fifth Infantry, (microfilm version, M270, Reels 514–518) North Carolina Department of Archives and History, Raleigh, North Carolina, and Louis H. Manarin and Weymouth T. Jordan, Jr., *North Carolina Troops, 1861–1865: A Roster*, 15 vols. (Raleigh, NC: Division of Archives and History, 1966–2004), Volume 13 (Jordan has been compiling the remaining units and will complete the series with another volume. He compiled volumes 12 through 15).

15. Private John S. Crow was a farmer living in Cleveland County, North Carolina, before enlisting in the Confederate Army on April 19, 1862, at age 20. Private Crow was wounded in the face during the battle of the Wilderness on May 5, 1864, but returned to duty sometime before July 1, 1864. He surrendered with other members of the 55th North Carolina at Appomattox Court House, Virginia, on April 9, 1865. Private William Elmore was a farmer living in Cleveland County before enlisting in the

army on April 19, 1862, at age 26. He was captured at Gettysburg on July 1, 1863, and confined at Fort Delaware, Delaware, until being transferred to Point Lookout, Maryland, on October 20, 1863. After spending seven months as a prisoner of war, William Elmore joined the 1st U.S. Volunteer Infantry Regiment after taking the Oath of Allegiance on January 30, 1864.

16. Private William Craig was a farmer living in Cleveland County before enlisting in the army on April 19, 1862, at age 40. Private Craig was discharged sometime in the fall of 1862, possibly because of his age, but reenlisted on March 14, 1863. He was captured at Gettysburg on July 1, 1863, and sent to Fort Delaware. Private Craig was transferred to a hospital at Chester, Pennsylvania, in August 1863, and paroled for exchange on September 23, 1863. He returned for duty on an unspecified date. Craig was wounded at Petersburg, Virginia, on August 6, 1864, and hospitalized at Richmond. He returned for duty sometime before November 1, 1864. He survived the war.

17. Private Robert Self was a farmer from Cleveland County before enlisting in the army on May 3, 1862, at age 22. Private Self fought throughout the war until being captured at Hatcher's Run, Virginia, on April 1, 1865. He died at Point Lookout on July 2, 1865; Private Jacob A. Gales was a farmer living in Cleveland County before enlisting in the army on May 10, 1862, at age 22. He was discharged for disability before June 1862.

18. Private Jacob R. Self and Corporal Isaac R. Self were brothers from Cleveland County. They both worked as farmers before enlisting in the army together on April 19, 1862. These two soldiers were Joseph Hoyle's wife's brothers. Jacob, known as "Rooker," joined the Confederate Army at age 21, and was promoted to Corporal sometime in September or October 1862. During the autumn months of 1862 Rooker was home on sick-furlough, and then again in the autumn of 1863. He was reduced in rank sometime in 1863 and was discharged on April 21, 1864, because of the disability caused by his wounds. It is unknown where he was wounded. Isaac Self was 20 when he enlisted. He was mustered in as a Corporal and then promoted to Sergeant in September or October 1862. Isaac was captured at Gettysburg on July 1, 1863. He spent the remaining years of the war as a prisoner at Fort Delaware. He was released from prison on June 7, 1865, after taking the Oath of Allegiance to the United States.

19. A group of soldiers that eat together.

20. Sergeant James R. Willis was a farmer in Cleveland County before enlisting on April 24, 1862, at age 33. Sergeant Willis was wounded at Globe Tavern, Virginia, in August 1864, but returned for duty and surrendered with the 55th North Carolina at Appomattox Court House, on April 9, 1865. Sergeant John Cline was a farmer from Cleveland County before enlisting on April 19, 1862, at age 30. Sergeant Cline was captured at Gettysburg on July 1, 1863, but returned to service sometime after being paroled in August 1863. He

was promoted to 1st Sergeant before November 1863, and was wounded at Spotsylvania Court House, Virginia, on May 12, 1864. He left the service in October 1864, most likely because of the wounds he received in May. Private Robert H. Willis was a farmer living in Cleveland County before enlisting on April 19, 1862, at age 22. He was captured at Gettysburg on July 1, 1863, and remained a prisoner of war until taking the Oath of Allegiance on June 7, 1865. Private Solomon Willis was a farmer living in Cleveland County before enlisting on April 19, 1862, at age 32. Solomon was captured near Sutherland's Station, Virginia, on April 2, 1865, and was released after taking the Oath of Allegiance on June 22, 1865. (It is interesting to note that Sarah Willis, Solomon's wife, stated in a pension application that her husband had been killed in action.) Corporal Julius A. Kennedy was a farmer living in Cleveland County before enlisting as a Corporal on April 19, 1862, at age 28. Corporal Kennedy was wounded at Globe Tavern, Virginia, in August 1864 and captured in a hospital in Richmond on April 3, 1865. Kennedy was released from prison on June 16, 1865, after taking the Oath of Allegiance. Private Jesse Cook was a farmer in Cleveland County before enlisting on April 19, 1862, at age 30. Private Cook was killed in action at Talley's Mill, Virginia, on May 10, 1864. Private William J. Self was a farmer in Cleveland County before joining the service on April 24, 1862, at age 22. Private Self was killed in action at Gettysburg on July 1, 1863.

21. Hoyle is referring to Major General George B. McClellan's Peninsular Campaign, which began on March 17, 1862, when the Army of the Potomac began moving to the Virginia peninsula between the James and York rivers. By May 17, 1862, several Federal gunboats, including the ironclads USS *Monitor* and *Galena*, were within ten miles of Richmond, and by the third week of May McClellan had 105,000 men in position northeast of the Confederate capital. For a concise overview of the Peninsula Campaign, see David J. Eicher, *The Longest Night*, 268–297. For a more in-depth view of the Peninsular campaign, see Stephen W. Sears, *To the Gates of Richmond: The Peninsula Campaign* (New York: Ticknor & Fields, 1992)

22. Captain Peter M. Mull served as a Private in Company K, 1st Regiment North Carolina Infantry (6 months) before being appointed Captain of Company F, 55th North Carolina State Troops Regiment on April 1, 1862. He helped organize Company F, and Joseph Hoyle was one of his recruits. He was severely wounded in the head and chest during the battle at Washington, North Carolina, on September 6, 1862. He spent the remaining months of 1862 hospitalized, and served intermittently throughout the remainder of the war due to numerous hospitalizations. As a result of his sporadic duty, Joseph Hoyle became Company F's de facto commanding officer. Captain Peter M. Mull survived the war.

23. The 55th North Carolina was trained in the art of military formations and fighting techniques

by Lieutenant Sidney Smith Abernethy. Abernethy had served with the 30th North Carolina Regiment as an officer before becoming the 55th's drillmaster. "Obituary of Lt. Sidney Smith Abernathy," *Confederate Veteran*, 7 (1899), 301.

24. Bell Irvin Wiley, one of the best-known scholars of the Civil War soldier, asserted that food "was undoubtedly the first concern of Johnny Reb." At the start of the war Confederate soldiers received adequate supplies of food, but as the conflict raged on the men serving in the army found themselves eating less and less. By the spring of 1862, Confederate officials were forced to reduce the rations supplied to each soldier. Although Confederate generals, including Robert E. Lee and P. G. T. Beauregard, ordered increases in the daily ration, the Confederate government was logistically unable to comply. As the war went on, the daily ration continued to dwindle. Bell Irvin Wiley, *The Life of Johnny Reb: The Common Soldier of the Confederacy* (Baton Rouge: Louisiana State University Press, 1992), 90–91.

25. Private John Y. Willis was a farmer from Cleveland County before enlisting in the army on May 10, 1862, at age 27. Private Willis died of febris fever on December 24, 1862, in a hospital in Petersburg, Virginia. Private William P. Bigham was a farmer from Cleveland County before joining the service on April 19, 1862, at age 18. Private Bigham was captured at Gettysburg, Pennsylvania, around July 4, 1863. After spending several months in Federal prisons, Bigham was released in February 1864 after taking the Oath of Allegiance. He then joined Company D, 1st U.S. Volunteer Infantry.

26. At this time, Joseph Hoyle did not know what letter his company would be designated as. Company F was mustered into state service on May 30, 1862, at Camp Mangum.

27. Religion was very important to many Civil War soldiers. The majority of soldiers were Christians, predominately Protestant. Joseph Hoyle was a devout Methodist, and many of his letters make references to his faith in Jesus Christ. Several scholarly works have been published that describe the religious world of the common soldier during the Civil War, the most recent being Steven E. Woodworth, *While God Is Marching On: The Religious World of Civil War Soldiers* (Lawrence: University Press of Kansas, 2001). Another study that reviews religion in the Confederate armies is William J. Jones, *Christ in the Camp: Or, Religion in the Confederate Army* (Richmond, 1887), Chandra Manning also address this in her study of why the war was fought, *What This Cruel War Was Over*, 141– 144; see also Drew Gilpin Faust's essay "Christian Soldiers: The Meaning of Revivalism in the Confederate Army," *The Journal of Southern History*, 58 (February, 1987): 63–90.

28. On May 10, 1862, President Davis sent his wife, Varina, and their four children to Raleigh. Varina Davis and her children first stayed at the Yarborough Hotel and then moved to the campus of St. Mary's School. President Davis's family would, except for one brief visit to Richmond, re-

main in Raleigh until August 1862. William J. Cooper, Jr., *Jefferson Davis, American* (New York: Knopf, 2000), 388.

29. Corporal Lemuel S. Self was a farmer from Cleveland County before he enlisted in the 34th North Carolina State Troops Regiment. He served in Company F of that regiment, which was also known as the Floyd Rifles. He was captured at the North Anna River, Virginia, on May 23, 1864, and confined at Point Lookout, where he died on October 3, 1864. The cause of his death was not reported. He was also Joseph Hoyle's brother-in-law.

30. Colonel John Kerr Connally was from Yadkin County, North Carolina. He had previously served as Captain of Company B, 21st North Carolina State Troops Regiment, which had been the 11th Regiment North Carolina Volunteers. Connally was appointed Colonel of the 55th North Carolina on May 19, 1862. He was wounded in the left arm and right hip at Gettysburg on July 1, 1863, while carrying the regiment's flag. His left arm was amputated and he was captured near Cashtown, Pennsylvania, on July 5, 1863. After spending several months in a Federal hospital, he was confined, first at Fort McHenry, Maryland, and then Point Lookout. Connally was paroled and exchanged in March 1864, and later served as a commanding officer of a brigade of Junior Reserves.

31. Commissaries were in charge of making sure the company was adequately supplied. Hoyle's duties included distributing rations and ensuring that his company received necessary supplies. For a brief overview of the commissary officer's duties see Robert E. L. Krick, *Staff Officers in Gray: A Biographical Register of the Staff Officers in the Army of Virginia* (Chapel Hill: University of North Carolina Press, 2003), 28–35.

32. Hoyle is referring to the battle of Fair Oaks, also called Seven Pines, which was fought near Richmond on May 31 and June 1, 1862. Each side claimed victory; however, Confederate casualties were slightly higher. During the two days of fighting the Confederates suffered 980 killed, 4,749 wounded, and 405 missing; Union loses were 790 killed, 3,594 wounded, and 647 missing. The most significant event that occurred as a result of the battle was the wounding of General Joseph E. Johnston. Johnston had been the commander of the Army of Northern Virginia since the first battle of Bull Run. During the action on May 31, Johnston was shot in the right shoulder and hit in the chest by a shell fragment. Although Johnston would return to active duty, his days as the Army of Northern Virginia's commander were over. Johnston was replaced briefly by Major General Gustavus W. Smith, but President Davis, who had been at the battle in person, felt Smith not up to the challenge and replaced him with General Robert E. Lee. This change in command would forever alter the way the Army of Northern Virginia fought. Eicher, *The Longest Night: A Military History of the Civil War*, 278–280.

33. Joel Hoyle was a Corporal at the time this letter was written, but he was reduced to the rank of Private in the fall of 1862. He was a farmer living in Cleveland County when he enlisted on April 19, 1862, at age 22. He was captured at Gettysburg on July 1, 1863, and confined to a Federal prison until January 1864. After taking the Oath of Allegiance, he joined Company C of the 1st U.S. Volunteer Infantry Regiment.

34. During the first few months of service it was not uncommon for as many as half the men of a regiment, and sometimes even more, to be incapable of performing their duties because of sickness and disease. Farmers were especially prone to contract diseases because their immune systems were not prepared to ward off sickness. Also, physical examinations were not required by the Confederate government until the fall of 1862; thus, men unfit for service were often the first to contract diseases. However, the Confederate armies needed soldiers, so even after these examinations were in effect, many men unfit for service were admitted to the ranks. Wiley, *The Life of Johnny Reb: The Common Soldier of the Confederacy*, 244–245.

35. Hoyle received his state bounty of $50 on June 2, 1862. Also, he and most of the men in Company F received a jacket, cap, and blanket. *Peter Mull Record Book, North Carolina Department of Archives and History, Raleigh, North Carolina.* Private Berryman H. Self was living in Lincoln County, North Carolina, when he enlisted in the army on July 4, 1862, at age 28. Berryman served in Company G, 57th North Carolina State Troops Regiment, and was Joseph Hoyle's brother-in-law. He was hospitalized in Richmond, Virginia, on November 22, 1862, with aphonia and pneumonia. Berryman died in the hospital on December 23, 1862. He was the first of Sarah Hoyle's brothers to die during the war.

36. The soldiers of the 55th received their arms on June 28, 1862.

37. Salas Proctor was a 39-year-old farmer from Cleveland County. According to the 1860 Federal Census, he owned land valued at $1300.

38. William Royal was the 55th's acting chaplain at this time and was officially appointed to the post in November 1862. Royal resigned in July 1863 due to illness.

39. Joseph Hoyle to "Mr. Editor," June 11, 1862, *Spirit of the Age*, June 16, 1862.

40. Disease, as mentioned above, racked both the Union and Confederate armies. By the end of the war nearly 200 men that served with the 55th North Carolina are known to have died from disease.

41. Some of the "influences" Hoyle is referring to were gambling, card playing, drinking, theft, not honoring the Sabbath, and the use of profanity. For a better understanding of the vices that plagued the Confederate armies, see Bell Irvin Wiley, *The Life of Johnny Reb: The Common Soldier of the Confederacy* 36–58.

42. James K. Wilkerson to his parents, June 28, 1862, James K. Wilkerson Papers, Perkins Library Manuscripts Department, Duke University, Durham, NC.

43. As mentioned above the Confederate government passed the first of three conscription acts on April 16, 1862. William C. Davis, *Look Away! A History of the Confederate States of America* (New York: The Free Press, 2002), 226; Thomas, *The Confederate Nation: 1861–1865*, 152–155.

44. Private John F. Elmore joined the regiment on July 14, 1862, at age 18, but died in a hospital in Petersburg, Virginia, in December 1862 of typhoid pneumonia.

45. Free blacks and runaway slaves often assisted the Union Army in scouting areas they were familiar with. In July 1862, the U.S. Congress passed a bill that gave the President the power to enlist "persons of African descent" for any war service they were capable of performing. Often, however, Confederate soldiers executed blacks caught assisting Union forces; it is not known how the Confederate government felt about this practice. On December 24, 1862, President Davis issued a general order requiring all former slaves captured in arms to be sent to state officials for trial. McPherson, *Battle Cry of Freedom: The Civil War Era*, 498, 566. Major-General Ambrose E. Burnside commanded a Federal expedition in February 1862 and captured Confederate positions on Roanoke Island. During the next several weeks the Federals gained control of North Carolina ports for 150 miles up and down the North Carolina sounds. By July 20, 1862, Burnside, who left the Carolina coast on July 6 with 7000 soldiers, had been ordered to assist McClellan in Virginia, and one of his former divisional commanders, Brigadier-General John G. Foster, was in command of the Department of North Carolina — nicknamed the Coast Division — and had begun sending reconnaissance teams out to learn the topography of the Carolina coastal region. John G. Barrett, *The Civil War in North Carolina* (Chapel Hill: University of North Carolina Press, 1963), 66–69; John S. Carbone, *The Civil War in Coastal North Carolina* (Raleigh: Division of Archives and History North Carolina Department of Cultural Resources, 2001), 67.

46. This movement of troops, which occurred earlier in July, left only two infantry regiments, one cavalry regiment, and three artillery units in North Carolina. Barrett, *The Civil War in North Carolina*, 128–129.

47. 3rd Lieutenant Eli Newton was a carpenter in Cleveland County before enlisting in April 1862, at age 27. Newton resigned on or about July 23; however, his resignation was rejected. He resigned again on October 20, 1862, and it was accepted on November 6, 1862. Newton reenlisted as a private in Company F. He was wounded at Gettysburg on July 1, 1863, but returned to duty. Newton was wounded again at Suffolk, blinded in the right eye, sometime before March 4, 1864, when he was discharged because of his injury.

48. The Confederate Congress abolished the election of officers in February 1865. Glatthar, *General Lee's Army*, 199.

49. 1st Lieutenant William H. Hull was a farmer living in Catawba County before enlisting at age 35. He was appointed 1st Lieutenant on April 1, 1862. Hull resigned on August 15, 1862, because of a "want of education." His resignation was accepted on August 28, 1862.

50. This letter refers to the same events mentioned in Hoyle's July 27 letter.

51. Hoyle is referring to one of several Federal reconnaissance missions of the Trenton-Pollocksville region and the area between Washington and Greenville, North Carolina, ordered by General Foster. These expeditions achieved very little for the Federal forces stationed in North Carolina. Barrett, *The Civil War in North Carolina*, 131–132.

52. Hoyle is referring to what is known as the Second Bull Run, or to Southerners as Second Manassas, campaign, which occurred northwest of Richmond. By August 14, 1862, Major General John Pope, commanding the newly organized Army of Virginia, had moved his Federal forces (containing about 55,000 troops) toward the Virginia Central Railroad. General McClellan had also begun removing troops from the peninsula to reinforce Pope; however, some historians assert that McClellan purposely moved at a slow pace to prevent his being in position to assist Pope. General Lee understood that if McClellan's soldiers reached Pope before he had time to attack, his outnumbered troops would be overwhelmed. By August 14, Lee had begun his move to strike Pope. Lee hoped to hit Pope before the Federal armies could merge. John J. Hennessy, *Return to Bull Run: The Campaign and Battle of Second Manassas* (New York: Simon & Schuster, 1993); Douglass Southall Freeman, *R.E Lee: A Biography*, 4 vols. (New York: Charles Scribner's Sons, 1934–1935), 2: 271–273; Eicher, *The Longest Night: A Military History of the Civil War*, 318–323. For a more in-depth study of Lee's overall strategy see Joseph L. Harsh, *Confederate Tide Rising: Robert E. Lee and the Making of Southern Strategy, 1861–1862*. For morale effects of the battle in the North see Hennessy, *Return to Bull Run*, and for a reexamination of how disastrous the battles were for the Union forces in 1862 see William Marvel, *Lincoln's Darkest Year: The War in 1862* (New York: Houghton Mifflin, 2008).

53. Berry, op. cit. Corporal William R. Self was a farmer from Catawba County when he enlisted on July 4, 1862, at age 26. He joined the 57th Regiment with his brother Berryman, and served in Company E. William Self was wounded in the head or neck at Fredericksburg, Virginia, on December 13, 1862, but returned to duty sometime before January 1, 1863. He was wounded in the foot at Gettysburg on July 1, 1863, while courageously carrying the regiment's flag. He was hospitalized in Richmond and returned to duty sometime in November or December 1863. Corporal Self was wounded a third time, this time in the left thigh at Lynchburg, Virginia, on or about June 18, 1864. He was captured at Winchester, Virginia, on July 20, 1864, and was confined at a Federal hospital there. He was exchanged on an unspecified date. William R. Self survived the war; he was Joseph Hoyle's brother-in-law.

54. Sergeant Roderick M. Sherrill enlisted in the Confederate Army on July 24, 1861, at age of 23. He served with Company D, 1st North Carolina Regiment, and died on September 8, 1862, of typhoid fever.

55. Terrisa was Sarah Hoyle's 29-year-old sister.

56. Private Amzi A. Bost was a farmer living in Catawba County when he enlisted on July 4, 1862, at age 32. He served in Company E, 57th North Carolina State Troops Regiment. Private Bost was captured at Chancellorsville, Virginia, on the 3rd or 4th of May 1863, and confined at Fort Delaware. He was transferred to City Point, Virginia, for exchange, and died in a hospital at Winchester, on or about July 29, 1863. The cause of his death was not reported; Private Jethro Calvin Bost was a farmer living in Catawba County before enlisting on July 4, 1862, at age 26. He was killed at Gettysburg on or about July 2, 1863, reportedly while carrying the regimental flag.

57. 2nd Lt. Henry Cline was a farmer living in Cleveland County before enlisting at age 24. Cline resigned his commission on January 5, 1863. The reason was not reported, but a note on his letter stated he was "deficient in education" and unable to perform his duties properly. Private Wade McClurd was a blacksmith living in Cleveland County before enlisting on April 19, 1862, at age 22. McClurd spent most of the war as a regimental blacksmith and mechanic. He survived the war.

58. St. Peter's Methodists Church, Cleveland County, North Carolina.

59. On the night of August 22, 1862, J. E. B. Stuart, Robert E. Lee's flamboyant cavalry commander, attempted to destroy the bridge over Cedar Run, near Catlett Station, Virginia. Had he been successful, this would have caused General Pope at least a two-day delay by interrupting the Federal supply line. Heavy rain prevented Stuart and his troops from destroying the bridge. The Confederates did, however, capture about 500 horses and mules, several hundred prisoners, supplies, a Federal payroll chest containing thousands of dollars, and General Pope's dress uniform coat and papers. Hennessy, *Return to Bull Run*, 74–79; Emory Thomas, *Bold Dragon: The Life of J. E. B. Stuart* (New York: Harper & Row, 1986), 145–147.

60. Confederate General Braxton Bragg moved his Army of Tennessee into Chattanooga late in July 1862, and by late August he marched through middle Tennessee. By September 5, 1862, General Bragg declared the whole of the state of Tennessee to be back under Confederate control. Shortly after this, he began his invasion of Kentucky. Although hoping for the same success he found in Tennessee, General Bragg, lacking confidence in himself and his army and primarily because the Western Confederate command was not unified as in the East, retreated into Tennessee after the stalemate at Perryville on October 8, 1862. General Bragg's decision to withdraw is considered one of the more controversial decisions of the war in the West. Herman Hattaway, *Shades of Blue and Gray: An Introductory Military History of the Civil War* (Columbia: University of Missouri Press, 1997), 100–103. For a more in-depth view of General Bragg see Grady McWhiney, *Braxton Bragg and Confederate Defeat: Field Command*, vol. 1, (New York: Columbia University Press, 1969). For an understanding of the command problems in the Confederate's Western armies, see Steven E. Woodworth, *Jefferson Davis and His Generals* (Lawrence: University Press of Kansas, 1990), and William J. Cooper, Jr., *Jefferson Davis: American* (New York: Knopf, 2000).

61. Private Samuel Young was a farmer living in Catawba County, North Carolina, before enlisting on April 22, 1862, at age 21. He was killed during the battle at Washington, North Carolina, on September 6, 1862.

62. Private Andrew McClurd was a farmer living in Cleveland County before enlisting on May 3, 1862, at age 21. He was wounded in the right shoulder during the battle of the Wilderness on May 5, 1864. He was hospitalized in Charlottesville, Virginia, and died of his wounds on May 30, 1864.

63. Hoyle is referring to General Lee's first invasion of the North, which resulted in the Antietam campaign. Shortly after defeating General Pope at Second Manassas, General Lee urged Jefferson Davis to support his plan to invade the North. Davis agreed and on September 4, 1862, Lee's Army of Northern Virginia began moving northward. Lee hoped to capitalize on the momentum he had achieved as a result of Second Manassas, realizing a victory on Northern soil might possibly gain foreign recognition for the Confederacy. Also, he hoped to give Virginia farmers time to harvest their crops and recruit Marylanders into his army. Eicher, *The Longest Night*, 335–337; Douglas Southall Freeman, *Lee's Lieutenants*, 3 vols. (New York: Charles Scribner's Sons, 1942–1944), II, 144–146. For an overall view of the Antietam Campaign see Stephen W. Sears, *Landscape Turned Red: The Battle of Antietam* (New Haven, CT: Ticknor & Fields, 1992), and James V. Murfin, *The Gleam of Bayonets: The Battle of Antietam and Robert E. Lee's Maryland Campaign, September 1862* (New York: Thomas Yoseloff, 1965). For a comprehensive study of Lee's strategy during the Antietam campaign see Joseph L. Harsh, *Taken at the Flood: Robert E. Lee & Confederate Strategy in the Maryland Campaign of 1862* (Kent, OH: Kent State University Press, 1999).

64. Weymouth T. Jordan, Jr., states that the 55th suffered more casualties than Joseph Hoyle listed, including seven men killed or mortally wounded, eight wounded, eleven captured and one missing. Louis H. Manarin and Weymouth T. Jordan, Jr., *North Carolina Troops, 1861–1865: A Roster*, 15 vols. (Raleigh, NC: Division of Archives and History, 1966–2004), 13: 353.

65. Private Samuel Young of Company F was killed during the battle; Private Brison W. Weaver was a farmer living in Cleveland County before enlisting on March 29, 1862, at age 32. He was killed during the battle at Washington, North Carolina, on May 6, 1862; Private Thomas Mitchum was a farmer living in Cleveland County before enlisting on March 29, 1862, at age 32. During the battle at

Washington, North Carolina, he was wounded in the arm, but returned for duty on an unspecified date. He was wounded in the arm again and captured during the Battle of the Wilderness on May 5, 1864. After being hospitalized, Private Mitchum was sent to Fort Delaware prison until being released on June 7, 1865, after taking the Oath of Allegiance. Private James P. Roach was a farmer living in Cleveland County before enlisting on March 29, 1862, at age 22 in March 1862. He was wounded in the side, back, and thigh at Washington, North Carolina, and was captured. He died of his wounds; the date and location of his death were not reported. Private Burrel M. White was a farmer living in Cleveland County before enlisting on March 29, 1862, at age 20. He was reported missing after the battle at Washington, North Carolina, but returned for duty on an unspecified date. He was reported missing at Gettysburg on July 1, 1863, and died sometime before June 11, 1864. The date, location, and cause of his death were not reported. Sergeant Thomas Greene was a farmer living in Cleveland County before enlisting on May 6, 1862, at age 30. Sergeant Greene was captured at Washington, North Carolina, on September 6, 1862. On September 23, 1862, he was imprisoned at Fort Columbus, New York Harbor, and exchanged on October 6, 1862. He returned for duty on an unspecified date and was captured at Falling Waters, Maryland, on July 14, 1863. He was sent first to Old Capital Prison, Washington, D.C., before being transferred to Point Lookout, Maryland, on August 8, 1863. On August 18, 1864, he was transferred to Elmira, New York, and then paroled on October 11, 1864, and transferred for exchange. He died on October 13, 1864 at Port Royal, South Carolina. The cause of his death was not reported. Private John Lewis of Company G, and Private Thomas Hall of Company I were also killed during the battle at Washington, North Carolina. Private Lewis was a farmer before enlisting in the army in Johnston County, North Carolina, on April 9, 1862, at age 19. He was wounded in the head and captured at Washington on September 6, 1862. He died sometime before November 17, 1862. The date and location of his death were not reported. Private Thomas Hall was a farmer living in Wake County, North Carolina, before enlisting on May 12, 1862, at age 49. Private Hall fractured his right thigh during the battle at Washington, North Carolina, and was captured by the Federals. He died sometime after, probably from his wounds. The date and place of his death were not recorded.

Chapter 4

1. James K. Wilkerson to his father, October 13, 1862, Wilkerson Papers.

2. Cooke, "Fifty-fifth Regiment," 290; James K. Wilkerson to his father, October 31, 1862, Wilkerson Papers.

3. *North Carolina Standard* (Raleigh), December 16, 1862.

4. Gary W. Woodward to his father, March 6, 1863, Hugh Buckner Johnston Collection, PC 206, Division of Archives and History, Raleigh, NC, Manarin and Jordan, eds. *North Carolina Troops*, 13: 357–358.

5. Steven A. Cormier, *The Siege of Suffolk: The Forgotten Campaign, April 11–May 4, 1863* (Lynchburg, VA: H. E. Howard, 1989), 5–7; Douglas Southall Freeman, *Lee's Lieutenants: A Study in Command*, 3 vols. (New York: Charles Scribner's Sons, 1946), 2: 468.

6. Jeffry D. Wert, *General James Longstreet: The Confederacy's Most Controversial Soldier* (New York: Simon & Schuster, 1993), 227–29; Cormier, *The Siege of Suffolk*, 16–18.

7. *OR* (Army), 18: 338–340.

8. Private John M. Mull was a farmer living in Catawba County before enlisting in the Confederate army on May 3, 1862, at age 32. John Mull served in the regimental band, and was captured during the battle of the Wilderness on May 5, 1864. He was imprisoned at Point Lookout until being transferred to Elmira, New York, at the end of July 1864, where he died of chronic diarrhea on June 20, 1865.

9. The Federals had about 11,500 troops stationed in Suffolk at this time. Steven A. Cormier, *The Siege of Suffolk: The Forgotten Campaign, April 11–May 4, 1863* (Lynchburg, VA: H. E. Howard, 1989), 7.

10. 2nd Lieutenant Abner B. Hayes was a farmer living in Caldwell County when he enlisted on July 15, 1861, at age 21. He was wounded at Bristoe Station, Virginia, on October 14, 1863, and died in the hospital in Richmond on or about June 7, 1864, of his wounds.

11. Rufus Self was Joseph Hoyle's brother-in-law. He enlisted in the Confederate Army on October 7, 1862, at age 18. Wounded at Gettysburg on July 3, 1863, Rufus spent several months in various hospitals. In May and June 1864, he was assigned to work with the division commissary. He returned to regular duty on an unspecified date. He was captured at or near Sutherland's Station, Virginia, on April 2, 1865. Rufus was released on June 6, 1865, after taking the Oath of Allegiance.

12. About a week after the Confederate Congress passed the first conscription bill on April 16, 1862, they added a supplementary law specifying several exempt categories including state civil officials, telegraph operators, river and railroad workers, miners, clergymen, teachers, hospital workers, apothecaries, and several categories of industrial laborers. Those operating mills were included, but Joseph Hoyle was already in the service before the exemption took effect. His wife and friends sent a petition to the secretary of war in November 1862, but were not successful in getting Joseph Hoyle exempted from service.

13. Confederate officials long hoped Great Britain and France would recognize the Confederacy and help pressure Lincoln's administration to reach a peaceful settlement that would ensure Southern independence. Although discussed widely by both

governments, foreign recognition never occurred. After Lee's victory at Chancellorsville in May 1863, the French thought about finally recognizing the Confederacy, but Napoleon III would not act without British consent, which never came about, partly because of anti–French sentiments. James M. Mc-Pherson, *Battle Cry of Freedom*, 650–651.

14. Sergeant Peter P. Mull, Joseph Hoyle's mother's brother, was a tanner living in Burke County, North Carolina, before enlisting on May 1, 1862, at age 31. He was appointed 2nd Lieutenant in March 1863, and was wounded and captured at Gettysburg on or around July 3, 1863. After spending time in the hospital at Chester, Pennsylvania, he was transferred to the Federal prison at Johnson's Island, Ohio, in September 1863. Mull was paroled and exchanged in March 1865. He survived the war. Peter P. Mull was also the cousin of Captain Peter M. Mull and Private Ezra Mull.

15. Fort Caswell was built on Oak Island by the United States Army between 1826 and 1838, as part of the buildup of coastal defenses after the War of 1812. Named for North Carolina's first governor, Richard Caswell, the fort was an enclosed pentagonal casement fortification built to help guard Old Inlet. The Confederates blew up Fort Caswell on January 17, 1865, to prevent the Federals from capturing it intact. Chris E. Fonvielle, Jr., *The Wilmington Campaign: Last Rays of Departing Hope* (Campbell, CA: Savas, 1997), 31, 33, 312.

16. This letter was not found in the Joseph J. Hoyle Papers.

17. Hoyle is referring to 3rd Lieutenant Archibald Hunter Arrington Williams. Lt. Williams had served as a Private in Company H, 12th North Carolina Troops Regiment before being appointed 3rd Lieutenant of Hoyle's company on November 6, 1862. Williams was wounded in the head at Gettysburg on July 3, 1863, and returned to duty on an unspecified date. Williams was promoted to 1st Lieutenant on September 3, 1864, after Joseph Hoyle's death. He was wounded in the right hand on September 27, 1864, and hospitalized in Richmond; the location of his wounding is not listed. He was paroled at Greensboro, North Carolina, on May 3, 1865. He survived the war.

18. Mary Self was William R. Self's wife.

19. Benjamin T. Green previously served as the Surgeon of the 15th North Carolina Troops Regiment before being appointed to the 55th on November 18, 1862. He was captured at Gettysburg on or about July 5, 1863, while tending to wounded soldiers. He spent time in various Federal prisons from July through November 1863. He was paroled and exchanged on November 23, 1863, and returned for duty on an unspecified date. Doctor Green surrendered at Appomattox Court House, Virginia, on April 9, 1865.

20. Nicholas Williams Lillington was appointed 2nd Lieutenant on October 1, 1862. However, his service record indicates that he served with Company H, 55th North Carolina Troops Regiment, and not Company F. He may have transferred to Company H after November 1862. Captain Lilling-

ton, who was a Lieutenant at the time, was wounded in the head at Suffolk on May 1, 1863. He returned for duty on an unspecified date and was wounded again in the thigh at Gettysburg on July 1, 1863. He was promoted to Captain on July 3, 1863. He returned for duty again on an unspecified date, but was hospitalized in Richmond in May 1864, with chronic diarrhea. He spent most of the remaining months of the war in various hospitals. He survived the war.

21. Burnside was soundly defeated at Fredericksburg on December 13, 1862. Union casualties totaled 12,653 (1284 killed in action, 9600 wounded, and 1769 captured or missing). Confederate losses totaled 5309 (595 killed in action, 4061 wounded, and 653 captured or missing). Also, Burnside was at Falmouth, Virginia, during this time, having given testimony to the Committee on the Conduct of the War on December 18, 1862. George C. Rabel, *Fredericksburg! Fredericksburg!* (Chapel Hill: University of North Carolina Press, 2002), 288–289; William Marvel, *Burnside* (Chapel Hill: University of North Carolina Press, 1991), 206–207.

22. The other two times being the battles of First and Second Manassas.

23. Mary Emaline Mull was married to Joseph's uncle Peter P. Mull. The couple lived in Burke County and had eight children. B. Rondal Mull and Mable M. Mull, *Mull: A History and Genealogical Record of the Mull Family in North Carolina* (Franklin, NC: Genealogy Publishing Services, 1997), 56.

24. Hoyle could be referring to one of several men who served with the 55th North Carolina. The Muster roll for Company C lists six Carpenters, at least three of whom lived in Cleveland County before enlisting. Also, Private John Carpenter served briefly with Company F before transferring to Company B and then obtaining a substitute to take his place in the ranks.

25. Private Robert J. Hicks was born in Mecklenburg County, Virginia, but was living in Catawba County, North Carolina, where he worked as a farmer before enlisting on April 22, 1862, at age 20. Records indicate he surrendered at Appomattox Court House on April 9, 1865.

26. During his January 1863 message to the First Confederate Congress, President Jefferson Davis requested that the exemption law passed in October 1862 be revised. On May 1, 1863, the Confederate Congress enacted a new exemption law, but the changes applied only to the overseer provision and to calm the outrage of the non-slaveholders and those owning fewer than twenty slaves. The revision was also implemented to ensure that needed grain and other provisions would continue being supplied unhindered. Herman Hattaway and Richard E. Beringer, *Jefferson Davis, Confederate President* (Lawrence: University Press of Kansas, 2002), 201–202.

27. Private Christopher Buff was a farmer living in Cleveland County before enlisting on April 19, 1862, at age 22. Private Buff was wounded at Wash-

ington, North Carolina, on September 6, 1862, and returned for duty on an unspecified date. He spent much of 1864 in various hospitals for different ailments. Private Buff was captured at or near Sutherland's Station, Virginia, on April 2, 1865. He was confined at Point Lookout Prison on April 5, 1865, and then released on June 23, 1865, after taking the Oath of Allegiance.

28. Private James Willis was a farmer living in Cleveland County before enlisting on October 8, 1862, at age 17. He died on January 31, 182_, of an unspecified disease.

29. These prisoners were most likely from the recent battle at Fredericksburg. During the war, Confederates captured and held approximately 210,000 Federal prisoners, and the Union about 220,000. Transporting POWs become a problem, as neither side had adequate prison facilities. Because of the lack of suitable prisons and transportation, both Union and Confederate governments set up a system to parole prisoners. Eventually, this system was altered to include exchanges, set up on a parity of grades. For example, one general was equal to sixty privates; a major general would be exchanged for forty privates. By the end of the war the Confederates had paroled and exchanged about 152,000 Federal prisoners of war. Primarily due to the fact that Confederate leaders refused to recognize black soldiers and refused to include them in exchanges, the United States War Department suspended the prisoner exchange system in the spring of 1863. Eicher, *The Longest Night,* 628–629.

30. Private Ezra Mull, Captain Peter M. Mull's brother and 2nd Lieutenant Peter P. Mull's cousin, was a farmer living in Cleveland County before enlisting in the army on April 24, 1862, at age 34. Ezra was mustered into the service as a Sergeant, but was reduced in rank sometime between January and October 1863. Private Mull helped recruit men for Company F in May and June of 1864. He was wounded near Hatcher's Run, Virginia, on February 5, 1865, and died on or around the same date.

31. The long roll signaled that the men needed to prepare for action.

32. Peter Mull never really recovered from the wounds he received at Washington, North Carolina, and so after being promoted to 1st Lieutenant on March 11, 1863, Joseph Hoyle commanded Company F until his death in September 1864.

33. During the Civil War, as in most wars, fellow soldiers held men who shirked duty and found ways to avoid combat in very low esteem. Joseph Allan Frank and George A. Reaves assert that the tendency for Civil War soldiers to be less tolerant of cowards and shirkers than veterans of the Second World War may have a direct correlation with the fact that most Civil War units were from particular towns or counties and so soldiers did not want their hometown to be associated with those who were, as they perceived them, less honorable men. Joseph Allan Franks and George A. Reaves, *"Seeing the Elephant": Raw Recruits at the Battle of Shiloh* (Urbana and Chicago: University of Illinois Press, 2003), 135–136.

34. Throughout the war President Davis invoked the grace of God in assisting the Confederate cause. On February 27, 1863, Davis informed the Confederate Congress that March 27, 1863, would be a day of prayer and fasting throughout the South. James D. Richardson, *The Messages and Papers of Jefferson Davis and the Confederacy: Including Diplomatic Correspondence, 1861–1865,* Vol. 1 (New York: R. R. Bowker, 1966), 324–325.

35. Private Thomas Willis was a farmer living in Cleveland County before enlisting in the army on May 10, 1862, at age 20. He was killed at Gettysburg on July 1, 1863.

36. Brigadier General Joseph R. Davis was President Jefferson Davis's nephew, the son of Isaac Davis. Joseph Davis was a successful Mississippi lawyer and farmer, and served as a secessionist Democrat in the state Senate in 1860 before joining the Confederate Army in April 1861. He first served as a lieutenant colonel of the 10th Mississippi Infantry Regiment, and then became aide-de-camp to President Davis in August 1861. He was promoted to brigadier general on September 15, 1862. Joseph R. Davis served in the Army of Northern Virginia until surrendering at Appomattox on April 9, 1865. The 55th North Carolina officially joined Davis's brigade on April 7, 1863. Jon L. Wakelyn, *Biographical Dictionary of the Confederacy* (Westport, CT: Greenwood Press, 1977), 163; *OR* (Army) 18: 910; Cooke, "Fifty-fifth Regiment." 290–291.

37. Major General George Pickett graduated last in his class at West Point in 1846. Pickett fought during the Mexican War and resigned his U.S. Army commission in 1861, and joined the Confederate Army. He first served as a colonel of Virginia troops before being promoted to brigadier general in February 1862. He fought under Longstreet throughout the war until he was relieved from command by General Lee on April 6, 1865, and is best known for his fateful charge at Gettysburg on July 3, 1863. Major General John Bell Hood graduated from West Point in 1853, and resigned from the U.S. Army in 1861 to volunteer for service in the Confederate Army. Hood was promoted to brigadier general in March 1862, and served with distinction during the Seven Days and at Second Manassas. He lost an arm while leading his division at Gettysburg, and lost his right leg at Chickamauga. President Davis, seeking a general with an offensive spirit, promoted Hood to Lieutenant General on February 8, 1864. Hood was given command of the Army of Tennessee and fought in the Western Theatre during some of the war's most horrific fighting. He surrendered to Federal authorities in May 1865. Major General Micah Jenkins, who graduated from the South Carolina Military Academy in 1855, was an ardent secessionist and helped organize a regiment to serve with the Confederate Army. He served with distinction at First Manassas, Williamsburg, and Seven Pines. Jenkins was promoted to brigadier general in July 1862, and continued to serve under Longstreet until he was mortally wounded at the Wilderness on May 6, 1864. All three were divisional commanders serving in

Longstreet's First Corps at the time this letter was written. Wakelyn, *Biographical Dictionary of the Confederacy*, 238–239, 253–254, 347; Also see Freeman, *Lee's Lieutenants*, vols. 1–3.

38. The act of hiring a substitute, a person to serve as one's representative when conscripted, was rooted in European tradition and used during the Revolutionary War, and thus many politicians, both North and South, viewed the practice as a citizen's right. In the South the price for a substitute soared to over $1000, but in the North the government placed a cap on the cost at $300; this, Republicans insisted, was to ensure that the average man could afford a substitute. This practice led to many soldiers, fighting in both armies, to claim the war a "rich man's war and poor man's fight." Many soldiers fighting for the Union and for the Confederacy were bitterly opposed to the practice of hiring a substitute. The Confederate government repealed the use of substitutes in December 1863, making all men ages 18 to 45 eligible for conscription. In 1864, the conscription age changed again to 17 to 50. This was primarily implemented because of the need for more troops, not as a reaction to dissatisfied soldiers. McPherson, *Battle Cry of Freedom*, 600–605; Thomas, *The Confederate Nation: 1861–1865*, 152–156.

39. Hoyle is referring to the battle that occurred in and around Chancellorsville, Virginia, May 2–6, 1863. Major General Joseph Hooker, commanding the Army of the Potomac, began his advance on Richmond on April 27, 1863. Hooker's plan called for the 1st and 6th corps to advance across the Rappahannock River just south of Fredericksburg. As this force moved on Lee south of Fredericksburg, the Federal 5th, 11th, and 12th corps marched northwest to Kelly's Ford to attack the Army of Northern Virginia's left flank. Unprepared and caught off guard, Lee assumed that the threat on Fredericksburg was not immediate and ordered the bulk of his forces to Chancellorsville. On the evening of May 1, 1863, Lee met with Lieutenant General Thomas "Stonewall" Jackson, then commanding the Army of Northern Virginia's Second Corps. Lee and Jackson devised a plan to once again split the already divided army and send some 26,000 troops on a march to attack the Federal right flank, leaving just 17,000 to defend against the bulk of the Union Army. This audacious plan worked, and Jackson's force, striking the Union 11th Corps at about 5:20 P.M. on the afternoon of May 2, 1863, crushed the Federal right flank. Darkness and quick responses by several Federal commanders checked the Confederate tide. By 9:00 P.M., the Union Army had set up a defensive line near Hazel Grove. Jackson, hoping to stop the Federals from being able to retreat across the Rappahannock at United States Ford, rode into the darkness to reconnoiter the area. As he and several of his staff rode back toward their own line, members of the 18th North Carolina opened fire believing the riders to be Union cavalry. Jackson and several of his aides were hit in the melee. General Thomas "Stonewall" Jackson was hit three times and had to have his left arm ampu-

tated. Eight days later, on May 10, 1862, he died of pneumonia. Although the loss of Jackson would be devastating to the Confederacy, Lee was able to defeat Hooker and force the Federals to retreat back across the Rappahannock. The Army of the Potomac would not pose a serious threat to Lee's army in Virginia until the spring of 1864. T. Harry Williams, *Lincoln and His Generals* (New York: Vintage Books, 1952), 235–242; Eicher, *The Longest Night*, 475–489; Freeman, *Lee's Lieutenants*, 2, 529–583. For a definitive study of the Chancellorsville campaign see Stephen W. Sears, *Chancellorsville* (Boston: Houghton Mifflin, 1996).

40. Private Noah W. Cook was a farmer residing in Cleveland County before enlisting in the army on April 19, 1862, at age 19. The wound he received at Suffolk, causing his right leg to be amputated, resulted in his being discharged for reason of disability on October 1, 1864.

Chapter 5

1. Cormier, *Siege of Suffolk*, 308–310.
2. James K. Wilkerson to his parents, June 10, 1863, Wilkerson Papers.
3. *Ibid.*; Freeman, *R. E. Lee*, 3: 27.
4. Girvan, *The 55th North Carolina in the Civil War*, 42–46.
5. *Ibid.*, 46–47; Terrence J. Winschel, "Part 1, Heavy was Their Loss: Joe Davis's Brigade at Gettysburg," No. 2 (January 1990) *The Gettysburg Magazine*, 8. There are many excellent studies of the Gettysburg campaign. For the first day of the battle see especially Harry F. Pfanz *Gettysburg—The First Day* (Chapel Hill: University of North Carolina Press, 2001), and David G. Martin, *Gettysburg, July 1* (Conshohocken, PA: Combined Books, 1995). The works published on the entire battle are too numerous to list, but the best operational study is Edwin B. Coddington, *The Gettysburg Campaign: A Study in Command* (Dayton, OH: Morningside Press, 1979). For a specific study of corps command on the Confederate side see the essay "Confederate Corps Leadership on the First Day at Gettysburg: A.P. Hill and Richard S. Ewell in a Difficult Debut," in Gary W. Gallagher, *Lee and His Generals in War and Memory* (Baton Rouge: Louisiana State University Press, 1998).
6. *OR* (Army), 27, 2: 650–651.
7. The death of Stonewall Jackson.
8. Sergeant Thomas S. Shuford, a farmer from Cleveland County, was killed at Chancellorsville on May 3, 1863. He was nominated for the Badge of Distinction for gallantry at Chancellorsville.
9. Hoyle is referring to the Rev. Richard Baxter's book *Saint's Rest*, first published in 1650.
10. Hoyle is referring to Chaplain Thomas Dwight Witherspoon, who lived in Oxford, Mississippi, and was captured at Gettysburg on July 5, 1863. Witherspoon was later paroled and exchanged. He surrendered with the 42nd Mississippi at Appomattox Court House on April 9, 1865.
11. Corporal Julius A. Kennedy was a farmer liv-

ing in Cleveland County before enlisting in the army on April 19, 1862, at age 28. Corporal Kennedy spent much of his first year of the war on sick furlough or in hospitals. He was wounded in the shoulder at Globe Tavern on August 18, 1864. He returned to duty prior to November 1, 1864, and was captured in a Richmond hospital on April 3, 1865, and confined at Newport News, Virginia. Corporal Kennedy was released on June 16, 1865, after taking the Oath of Allegiance.

12. After the death of Stonewall Jackson, General Lee reorganized the Army of Northern Virginia into three corps, each with three divisions. Lieutenant General James Longstreet remained in command of the First Corps, and Lieutenant General Richard S. Ewell was placed in command of Jackson's old Second Corps. Lee placed his ablest division commander, Lieutenant General A. P. Hill, in charge of the newly organized Third Corps. Major General Henry Heth was given command of one of Hill's divisions, which contained the brigades of brigadier generals James Johnston Pettigrew, James J. Archer, Joseph R. Davis, Colonel John M. Brockenbrough, and Joseph R. Davis. Major General Henry Heth graduated from West Point in 1842, and served in the United States Army during the Mexican War. Henry Heth, *The Memoirs of Henry Heth*, edited by James L. Morrison, Jr. (Westport, CT: Greenwood Press, 1974), 172n; Freeman, *Lee's Lieutenants*, 2, 709–711; Wakelyn, *Biographical Dictionary of the Confederacy*, 227–228.

13. Major General Hooker had received intelligence that Lee's army was on the move north, and so on June 13, 1863, he ordered the Army of the Potomac to pursue. Major General John Sedgwick's Sixth Corps, stationed near Fredericksburg, began moving north during the evening of June 13, 1863. Stephen W. Sears, *Gettysburg* (Boston and New York: Houghton Mifflin, 2003), 84–85; James I. Robertson, *General A. P. Hill: The Story of a Confederate Warrior* (New York: Random House, 1987), 200.

14. The Gettysburg campaign began on June 3, 1863, with Lieutenant General Richard S. Ewell's corps marching to Culpeper, Virginia. Confederate cavalry units screened Ewell's movements as he marched his command north, reaching just north of Front Royal by June 12. On June 14 and 15, Ewell captured Winchester, Virginia, and most of the Federals stationed there. Along with the 4,000 prisoners (not 12,000 as Hoyle asserted), the Second Corps obtained 300 loaded wagons, 23 cannon, and a large quantity of supplies. In addition to Ewell's success, Major General Robert Rodes's divisions of Ewell's corps captured another 200 prisoners, 5 artillery pieces, and about 6,000 bushels of grain at Martinsburg, Virginia, on June 15. Harry W. Pfanz, *Gettysburg: The First Day*, 5–6; Herman Hattaway and Archer Jones, *How the North Won: A Military History of the Civil War* (Urbana: University of Illinois Press, 1983), 398.

15. Hoyle is referring to the Chancellorsville battlefield.

16. Hoyle was not the only member of the 55th

to comment about the welcome the regiment received while marching through Charles Town, Virginia (Charleston, West Virginia). Captain Howell G. Whitehead, of Company E, also expressed his gratitude for the citizens of the town in his diary. Howell G. Whitehead Diary (typescript), Civil War Roster Project Document No. 0696, North Carolina Division of Archives and History, Raleigh, NC.

17. Hoyle is accurate on all of these men accept William Craig, who was captured on July 1, 1863, and survived the war. William Craig, Thomas Willis, and William J. Self have been noted above. Private Williamson F. Brackett was a farmer residing in Cleveland County before enlisting in the army on April 19, 1862, at age 18.

18. Eli Newton was wounded in the arm or hand on July 1, 1863. Private John Smith was a farmer living in Catawba County before enlisting in the army on May 10, 1862, at age 35. He was discharged on May 28, 1862, for being overage. Smith then reenlisted as a substitute for C. C. Atwater. He was wounded in the hand at Gettysburg on July 1, 1863, and hospitalized in Richmond on July 14. He returned to duty on an unspecified date and was wounded at the Wilderness, Virginia, on May 5, 1864. He was hospitalized in Charlotte, North Carolina, and returned to duty on July 12, 1864. He survived the war. Private Robert Swofford worked as a farmer in Cleveland County before enlisting in the army on May 13, 1862, at age 17. He was wounded in the arm on July 1, 1863, and reported missing. Private Daniel Canipe worked as a farmer and lived in Cleveland County before enlisting in the army on May 13, 1862, at age 27. He was wounded in the chest at Gettysburg on July 1, 1863, and captured, probably on July 5, 1863, when the Federals attacked the retreating Confederate wagons near Cashtown or near Greencastle, Pennsylvania. Daniel was transferred to the hospital at Davids Island, located in New York Harbor, and then paroled and exchanged at City Point, Virginia, on September 16, 1863. He returned to duty on an unspecified date. He was captured near Hatcher's Run, Virginia, on March 31, 1865, and imprisoned at Point Lookout, Maryland. Daniel Canipe was released on June 24, 1865, after taking the Oath of Allegiance. Private John Anderson Canipe was a farmer living in Cleveland County before enlisting in the army on April 19, 1862, at age 27. John was wounded in the jaw at Gettysburg on July 1, 1863, and captured. He was sent to the hospital at Davids Island, New York Harbor until being paroled on August 24, 1863, and exchanged at City Point a few days later. He did not return to duty until November 4, 1864, after spending time in hospitals and at home on sick furlough. He surrendered with his regiment on April 9, 1865, at Appomattox Court House. Private Samuel McNeily was a farmer living in Cleveland County before enlisting in the army on March 17, 1863, at age 40. He was wounded in the chest at Gettysburg on July 1, 1863, and captured on that day or a few days later, possibly at Cashtown or Greencastle. He was sent to the hospital at Davids Island, New York Harbor, where he

died on August 3, 1863, of his wounds. Private Jonathan McNeely was a farmer living in Cleveland County before enlisting in the army on May 3, 1862, as a substitute. He was wounded in the shoulder at Gettysburg on July 1, 1863, and captured on that day or a few days later. He was sent to the hospital at Davids Island, New York Harbor. He was paroled and exchanged in September 1863. He returned to duty on an unspecified date. Jonathan McNeely was furloughed in January 1865, because of the wound he received at Gettysburg. Private Aaron Cook, Jr., was a farmer living in Cleveland County before enlisting in the army on May 3, 1862, at age 18. Private Cook was wounded in the leg at Gettysburg on July 1, 1863, and captured on or about the same date. He was sent to a hospital in Chester, Pennsylvania, and paroled for exchange in September 1863, at City Point, Virginia. He surrendered at Appomattox Court House, on April 9, 1865. Private Henry Norman worked as a farmer and lived in Cleveland County before enlisting in the army on May 10, 1862, at age 26. He was wounded in the left arm and the groin at Gettysburg on July 1, 1863. Private Norman was hospitalized in Richmond, and returned for duty prior to May 1864. He was wounded in the finger at the Wilderness, on May 5, 1864. He retired to the Invalid Corps on February 21, 1865.

19. 1st Sergeant John Cline was captured on July 1, 1863, and sent to Fort Delaware, Delaware. He was paroled for exchange at the end of July 1863. Sergeant Isaac R. Self, Hoyle's brother-in-law, was captured on July 1, 1863, and confined at Fort Delaware, Delaware, on July 8, 1863. He was released on June 7, 1865, after taking the Oath of Allegiance. Corporal Albert P. Ivester, was captured at Gettysburg on July 1, 1863, and imprisoned at Fort Delaware. He was transferred to Point Lookout on October 20, 1863, and escaped from prison on March 11, 1864. He returned to duty on March 29, 1864, and was promoted to Sergeant on October 17, 1864. Ivester surrendered with the 55th on April 9, 1865, at Appomattox Court House. Private David A. Bumgarner was a farmer living in Cleveland County before enlisting in the army on April 19, 1862, at age 18. He was captured at Gettysburg on July 1, 1863, and confined at Fort Delaware, until being transferred to Point Lookout on October 20, 1863. Bumgarner died at Point Lookout on August 10, 1863; the cause of his death was not reported. Private Wesley M. Brendle was a farmer living in Lincoln County, North Carolina, before enlisting in the army on May 13, 1862, at age 20. He was captured at Gettysburg, on July 1, 1863, and confined at Fort Delaware until being transferred to Point Lookout on October 20, 1863. He was paroled and exchanged in March 1865, and sent to a hospital in Richmond. He survived the war. Private Peter M. Bivens was a farmer living in Lincoln County before enlisting in the army on April 22, 1862, at age 20. He was captured on July 1, 1863, at Gettysburg, and imprisoned at Fort Delaware until being transferred to Point Lookout in October 1863. Bivens died at Point Lookout on February 19, 1864. The cause of his death was not reported. Private William Elmore was a farmer living in Cleveland County before enlisting in the army on April 19, 1862, at age 26. William Elmore was captured at Gettysburg on July 1, 1863, and confined at Fort Delaware until being transferred to Point Lookout on October 20, 1863. He was released on or about January 30, 1864, after he agreed to take the Oath of Allegiance and join the United States Army. He served in Company G, 1st Regiment U.S. Volunteer Infantry. Private Hoyle (previously mentioned) was captured at Gettysburg on or about July 1, 1863, and imprisoned at Fort Delaware. Private Joel Hoyle was captured at Gettysburg on July 1, 1863, and confined at Fort Delaware. Private Robert H. Norman was farmer living in Cleveland County before enlisting in the army on May 13, 1862, at age 30. He was captured at Gettysburg on July 1, 1863, and imprisoned at Fort Delaware, until being transferred to Point Lookout on October 20, 1863. Robert Norman was paroled then exchanged on September 22, 1864, and returned for duty in October 1864. He was retired from field duty in February 1865, and detailed to work with the hospital department. He was captured near Sutherland's Station, Virginia, on April 2, 1865, and released at the end of June 1865, after taking the Oath of Allegiance. Private Peter Lail was a farmer living in Burke County before enlisting in the army on February 9, 1863, at age 18. He was captured at Gettysburg on July 1, 1863, and confined to Fort Delaware, until he was released on June 7, 1865, after taking the Oath of Allegiance. Private William S. Seagle was a farmer living in Catawba County before enlisting in the army on April 22, 1862, at age 18. William Seagle was captured at Gettysburg on July 1, 1863, and confined to Fort Delaware. He was transferred to a hospital in Chester, Pennsylvania on August 10, 1863, and died ten days later either of chronic diarrhea or debilitas. Private William N. Swink was a farmer living in Burke County before enlisting in the army on February 9, 1863, at age 21. He was wounded and captured at Gettysburg on July 1, 1863, and confined to Fort Delaware. He died on August 24, 1863, at Fort Delaware of rubeola. Private John Swink was a farmer living in Burke County before enlisting in the army on February 9, 1863, at age 24. He was captured at Gettysburg on July 1, 1863, and imprisoned at Fort Delaware, where he died on August 31, 1863, of rubeola. Private David W. Turner was a farmer living in Cleveland County before enlisting in the army on February 23, 1863, at age 34. He was captured at Gettysburg on July 1, 1863, and imprisoned at Fort Delaware. Private Turner was transferred to a hospital at Chester, Pennsylvania, on July 19, 1863, and died a few weeks later on August 2, 1863, of chronic diarrhea and general debility. Private Robert H. Willis (previously mentioned) was captured at Gettysburg on July 1, 1863, and confined at Fort Delaware, until being released on June 7, 1865, after taking the Oath of Allegiance. Private Samuel O. Willis was a farmer living in Cleveland County before enlisting in the army on May 10, 1862, at age

26. He was captured at Gettysburg on July 1, 1863, and confined at Fort Delaware, until being transferred to Point Lookout on October 30, 1863. Samuel Willis died at Point Lookout on May 9, 1865, of chronic dysentery. Private Noah J. Canipe was a farmer living in Cleveland County before enlisting in the army on May 13, 1862, at age 18. He was captured at Gettysburg on July 1, 1863, and confined to Fort Delaware, until being transferred to Point Lookout on October 20, 1863. Noah Canipe was paroled, although the date of his parole is not reported. He died at Petersburg, Virginia, sometime during the winter of 1863; the cause of death was not reported. Private Noah B. Warlick was a farmer living in Cleveland County before enlisting in the army on May 10, 1862, at age 22. He was captured at Gettysburg on July 1, 1863, and confined at Fort Delaware until being transferred to a hospital at Chester, Pennsylvania, on August 10, 1863. Noah Warlick was paroled and then exchanged on September 23, 1863, and returned for duty on an unspecified date. He was wounded in the right leg near Petersburg on October 1, 1864, and had to have the leg amputated. He was furloughed, most likely because of his disability, on November 22, 1864. He survived the war. Private Stephen J. White was a farmer living in Cleveland County before enlisting in the army on April 24, 1862, at age 26. He was captured at Gettysburg on July 1, 1863, and confined at Fort Delaware, until transferred to Point Lookout on October 20, 1863. Private White was paroled and then exchanged on March 20, 1864, and returned to duty on an unspecified date. White was promoted to Corporal on October 17, 1864, and surrendered with the regiment at Appomattox Court House, on April 9, 1865.

20. Lieutenant Colonel Maurice T. Smith was killed during the first day of fighting at Gettysburg. Colonel John K. Connally, as mentioned above, was shot several times while leading his regiment in battle on July 1, 1863. He was captured by the Federals on July 5, 1863, and first sent to a hospital at Gettysburg, and then transferred to a hospital in Baltimore, Maryland, early in August 1863. In October of the same year, Connally was transferred to Fort McHenry Prison in Maryland, and on January 23, 1864, he arrived at Point Lookout, Maryland. Colonel Connally was paroled for exchange on March 3, 1864, and then sent to a Confederate hospital in Danville, Virginia. Connally never returned to duty with the 55th North Carolina, but in November 1864 he was given command of a brigade of Junior Reserves stationed at Wilmington, North Carolina, and commanded these troops during the Wilmington campaign of 1864 and 1865. He resigned his command over a disagreement about his status as a Junior Reserve officer on February 9, 1865. His resignation was accepted on March 7, 1865. Chris Fonvielle, Jr., *Last Rays of Departing Hope*, 141, 166.

21. Private Alfred Newton was a farmer living in Cleveland County before enlisting in the army on April 24, 1862, at age 26. He was wounded at Gettysburg on July 3, 1863, but returned for duty. It is not known if he survived the war. Private Rufus

Self, as previously mentioned, was wounded in the right hand at Gettysburg on July 3, 1863. Private William Murkson Boyles was a farmer living in Catawba County before enlisting in the army on April 22, 1862, at age 22. He was wounded at Gettysburg on July 3, 1863, and returned to duty on an unspecified date. He was again wounded at Globe Tavern, Virginia, on August 18, 1864, in the left leg. His leg was amputated and he died in a hospital in Petersburg, on September 13, 1864. Private Harrison Cook was a farmer living in Cleveland County before enlisting in the army on February 25, 1863, at age 17. He was wounded in the wrist at Gettysburg on July 3, 1863. He returned to duty on an unspecified date, and deserted to the Federals on or around March 16, 1865. He was confined at Washington, D.C., until being released on an unspecified date after taking the Oath of Allegiance.

22. For 2nd Lieutenant Peter P. Mull see above. Private James Calloway Goodson was a farmer living in Catawba County before enlisting in the army on May 10, 1862, at age 19. He was wounded in the left hip at Gettysburg on July 3, 1863, and captured on or around the same day. He was hospitalized at Chester, Pennsylvania, and then transferred to Point Lookout on October 2, 1863. He was paroled and exchanged in March 1864, and returned for duty before June 30, 1864. He was captured near Hatcher's Run, Virginia, on March 31, 1865, and confined again at Point Lookout. Goodson was released on June 27, 1865, after taking the Oath of Allegiance. Private Anderson Self was a farmer living in Cleveland County before enlisting in the army on February 19, 1863, at age 35. He was wounded in the left thigh at Gettysburg on July 3, 1863, and captured on or about the same day. He was transferred to a hospital at Davids Island on July 20, 1863. He was paroled and exchanged on August 28, 1863. He returned to duty on an unspecified date and was wounded in the foot at the Wilderness on May 5, 1864. He returned to duty before June 30, 1864, and surrendered with the regiment at Appomattox Court House, on April 9, 1865.

23. For a comprehensive study of Lee's retreat from Gettysburg, including insight into the experiences of those men of the 55th North Carolina wounded at Gettysburg, read Kent Masterson Brown, *Retreat from Gettysburg: Lee, Logistics, and the Pennsylvania Campaign* (Chapel Hill: University of North Carolina Press, 2005); Girvan, *The 55th North Carolina in the Civil War*, 71–75.

24. Private Levi Wise was a farmer living in Catawba County before enlisting in the army on April 24, 1862, at age 35. He was killed at Falling Waters, Maryland, on July 14, 1863. Private James P. Stamey was a millwright living in Catawba County before enlisting in the army on April 22, 1862, at age 43. He was captured at Falling Waters, on July 14, 1863, and imprisoned at Point Lookout. He was paroled and exchanged in February 1865. He survived the war. Private Daniel Franklin Shuford was a farmer living in Catawba County before enlisting in the army on April 22, 1863, at age 26. He was

captured at Falling Waters, on July 14, 1863, and confined at Point Lookout. Shuford was paroled and exchanged in March 1864. He was captured at or near Sutherland's Station, on April 2, 1865. Shuford was again confined at Point Lookout until being released on June 20, 1865, after taking the Oath of Allegiance.

25. Hoyle failed to list the following members of his company that were wounded or captured at Gettysburg, July 1–3, 1863. Private William P. Bigham was captured on or around July 4, 1863. Private Massenburg Burton was wounded and captured, and Private Allen Richard Johnson was captured.

26. The action at the railroad cut, which Hoyle is eluding to, is summarized in an account of the battle written by then Major Rufus R. Dawes of the 6th Wisconsin, and in a history of that regiment focusing on the Gettysburg campaign. See Rufus R. Dawes, *Service with the Sixth Wisconsin Volunteers* (Madison: State Historical Society of Wisconsin, 1962), and Lance J. Herdegen and William J. K. Beaudot, *In the Bloody Railroad Cut at Gettysburg* (Dayton, OH: Morningside, 1990).

27. In his influential study of the nature of battle, John Keegan asserts that it is the soldier's "right to flight" that makes combat bearable for most fighting men. This illuminating viewpoint offers insight into the minds of those who, after crossing a field of about a mile in length on July 3, 1863, realized their only chance to fight another day was to retreat. John Keegan, *The Face of Battle* (New York: The Viking Press, 1976), 309.

28. The Official Records indicate that Davis's brigade as a whole suffered 897 casualties, while the 55th North Carolina's casualties totaled 198: 39 killed and 159 wounded. *OR* (Army), 27 2: 333. The problem with the Official Records is that the figures do not include those missing in action. Captain Robert W. Thomas of Company K, who temporarily commanded the 55th from August 1863 through January 1864, compiled a list of the regiment's losses at Gettysburg and had the statistics published by the *Weekly State Journal*, a Raleigh newspaper. Captain Thomas's figures totaled 377 casualties, with 34 killed, 159 wounded, and 184 missing. R. W. Thomas to the *Weekly State Journal*, (Raleigh) August 12, 1863. Another study of regimental losses at Gettysburg asserts that the 55th North Carolina suffered 55 killed, 143 wounded, and 22 missing — making the total 220. John W. Busey and David G. Martin, *Regimental Strengths and Losses at Gettysburg* (Highstown, NJ: Longstreet House, 1986), 290.

29. As Company F's acting commanding officer, Joseph Hoyle most likely had to write many letters similar to this one to Mrs. Wise.

Chapter 6

1. James I. Robertson, *General A. P. Hill: The Story of a Confederate Warrior* (New York: Random House, 1987), 230–232. Douglas Southall Free-

man, in his magisterial work on the Army of Northern Virginia, argues that President Davis's proclamation did not have much of an effect on motivating deserters to return to the army. *Lee's Lieutenants: A Study in Command,* vol. 3, 218–219.

2. Barrett, *The Civil War in North Carolina,* 171–172; Joseph Allan Frank, *With Ballot and Bayonet: The Political Socialization of American Civil War Soldiers* (Athens, GA: University of Georgia Press, 1998), 97–98; Girvan, *The 55th North Carolina in the Civil War,* 76–77.

3. Frank, *With Ballot and Bayonet,* 97–98; Girvan, *The 55th North Carolina in the Civil War,* 76–77; "Convention of N.C. Troops," *Spirit of the Age,* August 24, 1863; Manning, *What This Cruel War Was Over,* 141–144. For more on William Woods Holden and Zebulon B. Vance, see William C. Harris, *William Woods Holden: Firebrand of North Carolina Politics* (Baton Rouge: Louisiana State University Press, 1987), and Clement Dowd, *Life of Zebulon B. Vance* (Charlotte, NC: Observer, 1897).

4. Manarin and Jordan, *North Carolina Troops,* 13: 388–390; Mitchell, *Civil War Soldiers,* 37–38.

5. Cooke, "Fifty-fifth Regiment," 302–303; Manarin and Jordan, *North Carolina Troops,* 13: 389; William D. Henderson, *The Road to Bristoe Station: Campaigning with Lee and Meade, August 1–October 20, 1863* (Lynchburg, Virginia: Howard, 1987), 30–47.

6. Girvan, *The 55th North Carolina in the Civil War,* 80–81.

7. *Ibid.,* 84–86.

8. Wiley, *The Life of Johnny Reb,* 180–182; Woodworth, *While God Is Marching On,* 230.

9. Alarmed by the number of desertions, General Lee advised President Davis to offer amnesty to all deserters who returned to their respective regiments, excluding those twice convicted of desertion. In response, Davis pardoned all those who were either on trial or already serving sentences for desertion. General Lee also reinstated the furlough system to boost morale. Lieutenant Hoyle is correct in his account with regard to numbers. The furlough system set up at this time established furloughs at the rate of two for every 100 men present for duty. Robert E. Lee, *Lee's Dispatches: Unpublished Letters of General Robert E. Lee, C. S. A. to Jefferson Davis and the War Department of the Confederate States of America, 1862–65,* edited by Douglas Southall Freeman, (New York: G. P. Putnam's Sons, 1957), 124; Freeman, *Lee's Lieutenants,* vol. 3, 218; Hattaway and Beringer, *Jefferson Davis, Confederate President,* 235–236.

10. The Confederate postal system continued to be slow throughout the war. However, Postmaster General John H. Reagan was an effective administrator and his leadership was crucial in the overall ability of the Confederate government to regulate mail delivery. Although hampered by many obstacles, including the war and constant interruptions of postal routes, the Confederate postal service remained in operation throughout the conflict and

enabled soldiers at the front to receive much-needed comfort from their loved ones. Hattaway and Beringer, *Jefferson Davis, Confederate President*, 51–52, 337–338.

11. Hoyle is referring to the Peace Movement in North Carolina, which began to gain momentum in the summer of 1863. Nearly 100 peace demonstrations occurred throughout the Old North State during these months. Primary concerns for the peace advocates were the conscription laws, the suspension of *habeas corpus*, and a general desire for the war to end. William Woods Holden, owner of the popular Raleigh newspaper the *Raleigh Standard*, called for all Confederate states to convene a peace conference to negotiate an end to the war. Opposition to this peace movement in North Carolina was headed by Zebulon B. Vance, himself a former Confederate officer. Both Vance and Holden threw their hats in the ring and hoped to be elected governor of North Carolina. Near the end of August 1863, the soldiers from North Carolina, serving in the Army of Northern Virginia, banded together and threw their support behind Vance. The Tar Heel troops held a convention and each North Carolina regiment sent delegates to vote on a series of resolutions. Lieutenant Thomas J. Hadley of Company A, and Lieutenant Charles R. Jones of Company G, represented the 55th North Carolina. The resolutions passed by the delegates included an assertion that the soldiers would only accept an honorable peace and repudiated the voices of all those in their home state whose actions cast "a chill and gloom" on the fighting men. With the support of the troops, who were able to vote by proxy, Zebulon Vance was elected governor of North Carolina in 1863. His election was a clear mandate from the Old North State's fighting men that they wanted to continue the war until independence was achieved. "Convention of N.C. Troops," *Spirit of the Age*, August 24, 1863; Joseph Allan Frank, *With Ballot and Bayonet: The Political Socialization of American Civil War Soldiers* (Athens, GA: University of Georgia Press, 1998), 97–98. For a view of the effects of the peace movement on the Army of Northern Virginia, see Freeman, *Lee's Lieutenants*, vol. 3, 217–218.

12. At the beginning of the war Confederate privates received $11 per month. The amount was raised to $18 per month in June 1864. Corporals were paid $13 per month and 1st Sergeants received $20 a month at the beginning of the war. Although soldiers and officers were to receive pay on a monthly basis, usually the men had to wait months before receiving any money. Mark Mayo Boatner III, *The Civil War Dictionary*, rev. ed., (New York: McKay, 1988), 624–625.

13. Major General George G. Meade, commander of the Army of the Potomac, had planned to force Lee and his army back to Richmond by initiating a series of battles that were to be fought between Fredericksburg and Richmond. By September 8, 1863, Meade had definitive intelligence that Lieutenant General James Longstreet's corps had been sent to Tennessee to reinforce General Braxton Bragg's army. Meade, realizing Longstreet's departure presented an opportunity to attack a much-weakened Army of Northern Virginia, began moving his cavalry forces across the Rappahannock followed by the II Corps, commanded by Major General Governeur K. Warren. A few days later, on September 16, Meade ordered five more Federal corps (I, III, V, VI, and the XII) to cross the Rappahannock River, positioning each near Culpeper, Virginia. Henderson, *The Road to Bristoe Station*, 30–47; Eicher, *The Longest Night*, 596–597.

14. Corporal William B. Hoyle was a miller living in Cleveland County when he enlisted on August 16, 1862, at age 27. He served with Company I, 48th North Carolina State Troops Regiment. Corporal Hoyle was wounded in the left shoulder at Fredericksburg on December 13, 1862. William Hoyle was wounded again in the knee at Bristoe Station on October 14, 1863, and returned to duty on an unspecified date. He was wounded a third time at Reams' Station, Virginia, on August 24, 1864, and furloughed soon after. He survived the war. William B. Hoyle was married to Joseph Hoyle's wife's sister, Terrisa.

15. On August 17, 1863, General Lee wrote a message to President Davis discussing desertions. In this message General Lee expressed the opinion that the president had done all he could to convince deserters to return to their commands without the fear of punishment, but since pardons did not work as well as expected, "the rigid enforcement of the death penalty" had to be implemented to stem the tide of desertion. Robert E. Lee, *Lee's Dispatches*, 122–124.

16. The 55th North Carolina belonged to Lieutenant General Ambrose P. Hill's Third Corps, Army of Northern Virginia. A. P. Hill was a Virginian and graduated from West Point in 1847. He saw limited action during the Mexican War, but fought well in the Seminole War in Texas and Florida. Hill resigned from the United States Army in March 1861, and became the Colonel of the 13th Virginia Volunteers. He moved swiftly up the ranks until being appointed Lieutenant General in May 1863, after the death of Stonewall Jackson. When General Lee divided the Army of Northern Virginia into three corps, Hill was given command of the Third Corps. Although his service as a corps commander was tainted by mistakes in judgment, Hill served well until being killed near Petersburg on April 2, 1865. Wakelyn, *Biographical Dictionary of the Confederacy*, 228. For a more in-depth study of A. P. Hill, see James I. Robertson Jr., *General A. P. Hill: Confederate Warrior* (New York: Random House, 1987).

17. Brigadier General John R. Cooke's brigade, which consisted of the 15th, 27th, 46th, and 48th North Carolina regiments, was officially added to Heth's division on May 30, 1863. However, fearing Federal advances around Richmond, the unit remained near the Confederate capital until being sent to Gordonsville, Virginia, on September 25, 1863. Freeman, *Lee's Lieutenants*, Vol. 3, 243n.

18. Private Eli Hoyle was a farmer living in Cleveland County before enlisting in the army on

April 19, 1862, as a substitute, at age 56. He was wounded at Bristoe Station on October 14, 1863, and was transferred to a hospital in Richmond. Private Hoyle was discharged from the army on March 27, 1864, because of disability from wounds. No official casualty report was filed for the 55th North Carolina, but Louis Manarin and Weymouth Jordan, Jr., assert that the regiment suffered 3 killed and 2 captured. Davis's brigade reported 8 killed, and 37 wounded at Bristoe Station. Manarin and Jordan, eds., *North Carolina Troops,* 13: 389.

19. Although by this time deserters were being shot, both of these men apparently were pardoned or received light sentences because they returned to duty by May 1864. Private John Smith is mentioned above; Private John Ledford was a farmer living in Cleveland County before enlisting in the army on October 11, 1862, at age 33. John Ledford was reported as a deserter on May 29, 1863. He was wounded in the hand at the Wilderness on May 5, 1864, and hospitalized at Lynchburg, Virginia. Private Ledford died on June 10, 1864, of his wounds.

20. Private George W. Pearsall of Company G was among the members of the 55th North Carolina who were sick. In a letter to his wife, he informed her that he was not feeling well and had a severe cough. Pearsall indicated that the lack of quality food contributed to his poor health. Many Confederates stationed along the Rapidan River received limited rations of bread and salted meat, which resulted in scurvy and a general drop in the health of many soldiers. To remedy their lack of food, many soldiers made salads from green weeds and dandelions. George W. Pearsall to his wife, February 15, 1864, George W. Pearsall Papers, North Carolina Division of Archives and History, Raleigh, North Carolina; William M. Dame, *From the Rapidan to Richmond and the Spotsylvania Campaign* (Baltimore: Green-Lucas, 1920), 59; Wright, *Belo,* 24.

21. On February 6, 1864, the Army of the Potomac advanced across the Rapidan at Morton's Ford, but Confederate artillery fire and swift resistance forced the Federals back across the river that evening. Eicher, *The Longest Night,* 633–634.

22. Major General Cadmus M. Wilcox graduated from West Point in 1846, and served in the United States Army during the Mexican War. He served in the Army of Northern Virginia throughout the war and surrendered with Lee at Appomattox. Wakelyn, *Biographical Dictionary of the Confederacy,* 438.

23. The Rev. B. Tucker Lacy was the unofficial chaplain of the Second Corps, Jackson's former corps. He was a friend of Stonewall Jackson, and had met the general in Lexington, Virginia. Lacy was born in 1819, in Prince Edward County, Virginia, and had attended Washington College, and Union Theological Seminary. In January 1863, he visited General Jackson and hoped to be assigned a position as a regimental chaplain. He was astonished when Jackson appointed him as an unofficial chaplain of the entire Second Corps. Lacy proved to be a good administrator and fulfilled all of Jack-

son's expectations. James I. Robertson, Jr., *Stonewall Jackson: The Man, The Soldier, The Legend* (New York: Macmillan, 1997), 683–684.

24. Private Alfred G. Peeler was a farmer living in Cleveland County before enlisting in the army on February 27, 1863, at age 37. He was captured near Hatcher's Run, Virginia, sometime between March 25 and 31, 1865. Private Peeler was confined at Point Lookout until his release on June 8, 1865, after taking the Oath of Allegiance.

25. Private Joseph C. Gantt was a farmer living in Cleveland County before enlisting in the army on January 10, 1864, at age 17. He was captured near Hatcher's Run on March 25, 1865, and confined at Point Lookout. Private Gantt was released on June 27, 1865, after taking the Oath of Allegiance.

26. Lieutenant Colonel Alfred Horatio Belo joined the 55th as Assistant Quartermaster in November 1862, after serving as a Captain in the 21st North Carolina State Troops Regiment. He was appointed Major on March 10, 1863, and was wounded in the left leg at Gettysburg on July 1, 1863. Belo was appointed Lieutenant Colonel on July 3, 1863, but was unable to return to duty until January 1864, at which time he assumed command of the 55th North Carolina. He was wounded in the left arm at Cold Harbor, Virginia, on June 2, 1864, and did not return to command of the regiment. In 1865, Belo attempted to join Confederate forces serving west of the Mississippi River under the command of General Kirby Smith, but they had surrendered before his arrival. He took the Oath of Allegiance in Texas, on April 25, 1865. Wright, *Belo,* 27–34; Robert K. Krick, *Lee's Colonels,* 44–45.

27. The 26th Mississippi and the 1st Confederate Battalion had been assigned to Lieutenant General Leonidas Polk's command were serving in the Western Theater before President Davis requested their transfer to his nephew's brigade. The two units joined Davis's brigade in April 1864. Colonel A. E. Reynolds commanded the 26th Mississippi; and the Confederate Battalion, which consisted of men from Alabama, was under the charge of Lieutenant Colonel G. H. Forney. *OR* (Army), 32, 3: 672.

Chapter 7

1. Brooks D. Simpson, *Ulysses S. Grant: Triumph over Adversity, 1822–1865* (Boston and New York: Houghton Mifflin, 2000), 257, 263–264; Mary Drake McFeely and William S. McFeely, eds., *Ulysses S. Grant: Memoirs and Selected Letters* (New York: Library of America, 1990), 477–478.

2. McPherson, *Battle Cry of Freedom,* 722; Mark Grimsley, *And Keep Moving On: The Virginia Campaign, May–June 1864* (Lincoln: University of Nebraska Press, 2002), 2–3.

3. Simpson, *Ulysses S. Grant,* 268–270; McPherson, *Battle Cry of Freedom,* 722.

4. Robertson, *General A. P. Hill,* 251; Freeman, *Lee's Lieutenants,* 3: 342–45; Simpson, *Ulysses S. Grant,* 287–88.

5. To read more on unit cohesion and how

combat experience can effect soldiers in battle units, see Marshall, *Men Against Fire*, 123–125; Ondishko, Jr., "A View of Anxiety, Fear and Panic," 59–60.

6. Girvan, *The 55th North Carolina in the Civil War*, 94–95; Noah Andre Trudeau, "A Frightful and Frightening Place," *Civil War Times Illustrated* (May 1999), 44–45.

7. Girvan, *The 55th North Carolina in the Civil War*, 97–98; Cooke, "Fifty-fifth Regiment," 304. Colonel John Stone of the 2nd Mississippi was left in command of the brigade when Joseph R. Davis left to attend the funeral of President Jefferson Davis' son in Richmond, Virginia.

8. Cooke, "Fifty-fifth Regiment," 305; Stuart, *Belo*, 24–25; Girvan, *The 55th North Carolina in the Civil War*, 98–100. The losses suffered by the Federals in front of the 55th North Carolina's line were also heavy. Cooke stated that 157 Union soldiers lay dead before their line. Grimsley, *And Keep Moving On*, 42–47.

9. Cooke, "Fifty-fifth Regiment," 305.

10. Although the battle lines on the evening of May 5, 1864, remained close the men in the 55th North Carolina, and other units in Davis's brigade stacked their rifles and rested. S. L. A. Marshall, in his landmark study *Men Against Fire* described this phenomenon of fighting men resting, eating, and even sleeping when immediate combat had ended, even though the threat of sudden attack loomed. Marshall, *Men Against Fire*, 144–145.

11. *OR* (Army), 36, 1: 1100.

12. Manarin and Jordan, *North Carolina Troops*, 13: 401–406. The first phase of the Overland campaign, full of movement and frontal assaults ended around Petersburg when the campaign turned into trench warfare. Earl J. Hess, *Trench Warfare Under Grant and Lee: Field Fortifications in the Overland Campaign* (Chapel Hill: University of North Carolina Press, 2007), 206–208.

13. Charles R. Jones, "Historical Sketch of the 55th North Carolina," *Our Living and Our Dead*, April 22, 1874; Freeman, *Lee's Lieutenants*, 3: 501–3; Morrison, ed., *The Memoirs of Henry Heth*, 188–89; Cooke, "Fifty-fifth Regiment," 306. Gordon C. Rhea, *Cold Harbor: Grant and Lee, May 26–June 3, 1864* (Baton Rouge: Louisiana State University Press, 2002), 301.

14. Cooke, "Fifty-fifth Regiment," 307.

15. Hess, *Trench Warfare Under Grant and Lee*, 208.

16. Girvan, *The 55th North Carolina in the Civil War*, 123–127; Cooke; "Fifty-fifth Regiment," 309–10; *OR* (Army), 42,1: 471–72.

17. Cooke, "Fifty-fifth Regiment," 310.

18. For more on the battle of the Wilderness, see Gordon Rhea *The Battle of the Wilderness: May 5–6, 1864* (Baton Rouge: Louisiana State University Press, 1994; Edward Steere, *The Wilderness Campaign* (Harrisburg, PA: Stackpole, 1960); Noah Andre Trudeau, *Bloody Roads South: The Wilderness to Cold Harbor, May–June, 1864* (Boston: Little, Brown, 1989); Mark Grimsley, *And Keep Moving On: The Virginia Campaign, May–June 1864* (Lincoln: University of Nebraska Press, 2002).

19. Private David Logan was a farmer from Cleveland County, who enlisted in the army on August 20, 1863, at age 43. He was killed at the Wilderness on May 5, 1864. Private George White was a farmer from Cleveland County who enlisted in the army in 1861, and served with the 34th North Carolina State Troops Regiment before joining the 55th on April 19, 1862. He was killed at the Wilderness on May 5, 1864.

20. Andrew McClurd, Solomon Hoyle, Anderson Self, Robert Self, Aaron Cook, and John Ledford have already been noted. Private William T. Williams was a millwright living in Lincoln County, North Carolina, before enlisting in the army on May 10, 1862, at age 28. He was wounded in the shoulder at the Wilderness on May 5, 1864, and died shortly thereafter. Private Peter R. White was a farmer living in Cleveland County before enlisting in the army on April 24, 1862, at age 21. He was wounded in the breast at the Wilderness on May 5, 1864. White returned for duty sometime before July 1, 1864. He was promoted to Corporal in October 1864, and surrendered at Appomattox Court House on April 9, 1865. He is cited on the Confederate Roll of Honor for gallantry during the battle of Globe Tavern, Virginia, August 19, 1864; Private David A. Brendle was a farmer living in Catawba County before enlisting in the army on April 24, 1862, at age 23. He was wounded at the Wilderness on May 5, 1864, and sent to a hospital in Charlotte, North Carolina. He returned to duty in August 1864, and was hospitalized in Richmond on February 7, 1865. The date and place of his wounding was not reported. He survived the war. Private Peter Buff was a farmer from Cleveland County when he enlisted in the army on April 19, 1862, at age 24. Wounded at the Wilderness on May 5, 1864, he was hospitalized in Charlottesville, Virginia. He survived the war. Private David Buff, Sr., lived and worked as a farmer in Cleveland County before enlisting in the army on February 10, 1863, at age 22. He was wounded at the Wilderness on May 5, 1864, and sent to a hospital in Liberty, Virginia. He survived the war. Private Philip Buff lived and worked as a farmer in Cleveland County before enlisting in the army on February 10, 1863, at age 19. He was wounded in the right shoulder at the Wilderness on May 5, 1864. He was hospitalized at Charlottesville, Virginia, and died there from his wounds on May 22, 1864. Private William Samuel Wortman was a farmer living in Cleveland County before enlisting in the army on February 10, 1863, at age 27. He was wounded in the hand at the Wilderness on May 5, 1864, and returned to duty sometime before July 1, 1864. He survived the war.

21. Captain Mull, John Cline, James R. Willis, Solomon Willis, and William Craig have been previously noted. Sergeant Westly A. Williams was a farmer from Cleveland County before enlisting in the army in 1861. He served as a Private in Company K, 1st Regiment North Carolina Infantry before enlisting in the 55th on May 31, 1862. He was promoted to Sergeant in May of 1863, and was commended by Colonel Connally for gallantry at

Suffolk, Virginia, May 1, 1863. He was captured at or near Sutherland's Station, Virginia, on April 2, 1865. He was confined at Point Lookout, and released on June 21, 1865, after taking the Oath of Allegiance. Sergeant Williams is cited on the Confederate Roll of Honor for gallantry displayed at the Wilderness on May 5–6, 1864. Private John R. Dickson was a blacksmith before enlisting in the army on December 24, 1863, at age 42, and died in 1865. The date, place, and cause of death were not reported.

22. Not listed on the Compiled Service Records as being a member of the 55th North Carolina.

23. Private Zachariah Bracket was a farmer from Cleveland County, when he enlisted in the army on February 21, 1863, at age 26. He was wounded in the knee at the Wilderness on May 5, 1864. He died in a hospital in Richmond in July 1864, having contracted the measles.

24. Private William Cook was a farmer living in Cleveland County before enlisting in the army on April 19, 1862, at age 27. He was wounded at the Wilderness on May 5, 1864, and returned to duty prior to June 30, 1864. He was captured at or near Sutherland's Station, on April 2, 1865, and confined at Point Lookout. Private Cook was released on June 24, 1865, after taking the Oath of Allegiance.

25. Private Peter M. Shuford was a farmer from Catawba County when he enlisted in the army on May 3, 1862, at age 24. He was wounded in the arm at the Wilderness on May 5, 1864, and returned to duty sometime before August 18, 1864. He was wounded in the forehead at Globe Tavern on August 18, 1864, and hospitalized in Richmond. He returned to duty and surrendered at Appomattox Court House on April 9, 1865.

26. Private Joseph Canipe was a farmer living in Cleveland County before enlisting in the army on May 13, 1862, at age 32. He was wounded in the hip at the Wilderness on May 5, 1864, and returned to duty sometime before July 1, 1864. Private Canipe was captured at or near Sutherland's Station, on April 2, 1865, and confined at Point Lookout. He was released on June 24, 1865, after taking the Oath of Allegiance.

27. Private Silas M. Wright was a farmer living in Cleveland County when he enlisted in the army on April 19, 1862, at age 18. He was captured at the Wilderness on May 5, 1864, and confined at Point Lookout. He was transferred to Elmira in July 1864, and released on May 29, 1865, after taking the Oath of Allegiance. Private Jesse E. Tallent was a farmer from Burke County before enlisting in the army on December 8, 1863, at age 33. He was wounded in the right shoulder and captured at the Wilderness on May 5, 1864. He was confined at Old Capital Prison, Washington, D.C., until being transferred to Fort Delaware in September 1864. He was paroled and exchanged on October 5, 1864. His right arm was reported as useless as a result of wound. He survived the war.

28. Years later, while writing his memoirs, Lieutenant General Ulysses S. Grant asserted, "More desperate fighting has not been witnessed on this continent than that of the 5th and 6th of May." Sources vary on how many casualties the Confederates suffered during the two days of fighting at the Wilderness, but recent studies place the number around 11,000. The 55th North Carolina as a whole had 43 killed, 119 wounded, 16 captured, and 4 missing. The exact totals for Company F were not reported. Mary Drake McFeely and William S. McFeely, eds., *Ulysses S. Grant: Memoirs and Selected Letters* (New York: Library of America, 1990), 534; Gordon Rhea, *The Battle of the Wilderness*, 440; James M. McPherson, *Ordeal by Fire: The Civil War and Reconstruction* (New York: McGraw-Hill, 1992), 416; Manarin and Jordan, eds., *North Carolina Troops*, 13: 401.

29. For more on the battles for Spotsylvania Court House, see William D. Matter, *If It Takes All Summer: The Battle of Spotsylvania* (Chapel Hill: University of North Carolina Press, 1988); Gordon Rhea *The Battles for Spotsylvania Court House and the Road to Yellow Tavern: May 7–12, 1864* (Baton Rouge: Louisiana State University Press, 1997); Noah Andre Trudeau, *Bloody Roads South*.

30. Jesse Cook, John Cline, Wesley Williams, and William Craig have been previously mentioned. Private David Buff, Jr., was a farmer living in Cleveland County before enlisting in the army on April 25, 1864, at age 18. He was wounded in the left shoulder at Talley's Mill, Virginia, on May 10, 1864, and hospitalized in Richmond. He was furloughed for sixty days on June 14, 1864, and retired from the service on October 1, 1864, because of the disability of his wounds. Private Henry J. Willis was a farmer living in Cleveland County before enlisting in the army on September 17, 1861, at age 16. He enlisted in Company F, 34th North Carolina Troops, but was discharged for being underage. He reenlisted in the army on February 17, 1863, as a Private in Company F, 55th North Carolina Troops. Private Willis was wounded at Talley's Mill on May 10, 1864, and reported absent on sick furlough in September 1864. He deserted to the Federals on or about March 16, 1865, and was confined at Washington, D.C. He was released in March 1865, after taking the Oath of Allegiance.

31. Manarin and Jordan assert the 55th North Carolina's losses at Talley's Mill were at least 3 killed, 3 wounded, 2 captured, and 1 missing. These figures are uncertain, but compiled from the regiment's service records. Manarin and Jordan, eds., *North Carolina Troops*, 13: 404.

32. Sergeant Maxwell H. Hoyle was a farmer living in Cleveland County before enlisting in the army on September 17, 1861, at age 20. He enlisted in Company F, 34th North Carolina State Troops Regiment. He was wounded at the Wilderness on May 5 or 6, 1864. He returned to duty, and is believed to have survived the war.

33. The 55th North Carolina was engaged in battle on May 12, 1864, although the fighting the men participated in was not very serious. Manarin and Jordan assert that at least one member of the regiment was killed during the day's fighting. Ma-

narin and Jordon, eds, *North Carolina Troops*, 13: 405.

34. Hoyle is referring to the Battle of Harris Farm, which ended with little gained by the Confederates. On May 19, 1864, the last day of the battles for Spotsylvania Court House, Lee ordered Ewell to attack the Federal position near Harris and Alsop farms. The primary reason for this attack was to ascertain if Grant had left his right flank exposed. Gordon Rhea, *To the North Anna River: Grant and Lee, May 13–25, 1864* (Baton Rouge: Louisiana State University Press, 2000), 167, 185.

35. Private Melvin Puckett Gantt enlisted in the Confederate Army, Company F, 34th North Carolina Troops on April 20, 1864. Records indicate he was present for duty through December 23, 1864. Lemeul Self was captured at the North Anna River, Virginia, on May 23, 1864. He was confined at Point Lookout and died there on October 3, 1864. The cause of his death was not reported. This was the second of Joseph Hoyle's wife's brothers to die during the war.

36. Grant's losses were actually about 40,000. In comparison, the Army of Northern Virginia had suffered about 25,500 casualties, roughly 40 percent of Lee's whole force. Gordon Rhea, *Cold Harbor: Grant and Lee, May 26–June 3, 1864* (Baton Rouge: Louisiana State University Press, 2002), 12, 16.

37. For more on the battle of Cold Harbor, see Louis J. Baltz III., *The Battle of Cold Harbor: May 27–June 13, 1864* (Lynchburg, VA: Howard, 1994); Gordon Rhea, *Cold Harbor*; Noah Andre Trudeau, *Bloody Roads South.*

38. Included in the Regiment's casualties was Lieutenant Alfred Belo. For the second time in the war, the 55th lost its commanding officer. Belo would never return to command the regiment again after June 2, 1864.

39. Corporal Andrew Warlick was a farmer living in Cleveland County before enlisting in the army on May 10, 1862, at age 28. His wounding was not reported in his records. He was promoted to Sergeant sometime between July and October 1864. He was captured near Sutherland's Station on April 2, 1865, and confined at Point Lookout until being released on June 22, 1865, after taking the Oath of Allegiance.

40. John Anderson Canipe was previously mentioned. Private William H. Hicks was a farmer living in Catawba County before enlisting in the army on February 12, 1863, at age 18. His wound was not reported. He was captured near Hatcher's Run on March 25, 1865, and confined at Point Lookout until being released on June 13, 1865, after taking the Oath of Allegiance.

41. Private Andrew McClurd did in fact die in Charlottesville on May 30, 1864.

42. On June 13, 1864, Colonel George W. Kirk, a Federal Cavalry officer, led about 300 men on a raid into western North Carolina. The force left Morristown, Tennessee, and planned to attack Morganton, North Carolina, which was located in Burke County, north of Cleveland County. By the morning of June 28, 1864, Kirk's troops had reached Camp Vance, a Confederate base used to train conscripts. The small force of Junior Reserves surrendered to Kirk's men, who then proceeded to burn the camp. Kirk's real objective was not to destroy this base, but to capture a train on the Western North Carolina Railroad and make a quick advance to Salisbury, North Carolina, to free Federal prisoners, and to possibly destroy an important railroad bridge over the Yadkin River, located north of Salisbury. Kirk and his men were opposed by home guards and prison guards, and had to retreat. He did, however, destroy a railroad depot and a few rail cars in Morganton. His raid netted 130 prisoners, and a number of horses and mules. John G. Barrett, *The Civil War in North Carolina*, 233–235.

43. Private James C. McClurd was accidentally killed near Petersburg on July 22, 1864. Enlistment information was not reported, except for the fact that he served in Company F, 34th North Carolina State Troops.

44. Captain David R. Hoyle, Captain of Company F, 34th North Carolina State Troops, was a millwright living in Cleveland County before enlisting in the army in September 1861, at age 31. He was promoted to Captain on June 27, 1862, after being wounded at Gaines' Mill, Virginia, on June 26 or 27, 1862. He resigned on November 2, 1864. The reason for his resignation was not reported.

45. Confederate Service Records for Company F, 34th North Carolina State Troops Regiment does not list A. R. Rice as serving in the unit.

Epilogue

1. Faust, *This Republic of Suffering*, 14–24.

2. *Ibid.*, 14, 24–31; Cooke, "Fifty-Fifth Regiment," 310; Owsley, *Plain Folk of the Old South*, 96–97.

3. Hess, *The Union Soldier in Battle*, 30–32; Gramm, ed., *Battle*, 69–70.

4. Gramm, ed., *Battle*, 70–75.

5. *Ibid.*, 79–81; McPherson, *Battle Cry of Freedom*, 486–487.

Appendix A

1. The boys Hoyle is referring to are most likely Sarah's brothers Rooker and Isaac.

Bibliography

Books

Allers, Ken, Jr., *The Fog of Gettysburg: The Myth and Mysteries of the Battle*. Nashville: Cumberland House, 2008.

Arnold, Annie Self. *Some Descendants of Old Robert Selfe: (Circa 1640–1717)* Salem: Higginson, 2004.

Atlas to Accompany the Official Records of the Union and Confederate Armies. Washington, DC: Government Printing Office, 1891–95.

Barrett, John G. *The Civil War in North Carolina*. Chapel Hill: University of North Carolina Press, 1963.

_____. *North Carolina as a Civil War Battlefield, 1861–1865*. Raleigh: North Carolina Department of Cultural Resources, 1980.

Barrow, Charles Kelly, J.H. Segars, and R.B. Rosenburg, eds. *Forgotten Confederates: An Anthology About Black Southerners*. Atlanta: Southern Heritage Press, 1995.

Barton, Michael. *Goodmen: The Character of Civil War Soldiers*. University Park: Pennsylvania State University Press, 1981.

_____, and Larry M. Logue. *The Civil War Soldier: A Historical Reader*. New York: New York University Press, 2002.

Beitzell, Edwin W. *Point Lookout Prison Camp for Confederates*. Abell, MD: Edwin W. Beitzell, 1972.

Beringer, Richard E., Herman Hattaway, Archer Jones, and William N. Still, Jr. *Why the Confederacy Lost the Civil War*. Athens: University of Georgia Press, 1986.

Berlin, Ira, ed. *Freedom's Soldiers: The Black Military Experience in the Civil War*. Cambridge: Cambridge University Press, 1982.

Boatner, Mark Mayo. *The Civil War Dictionary*. Rev. ed. New York: McKay, 1988.

Boritt, Gabor S. ed. *The Gettysburg Nobody Knows*. New York and Oxford: Oxford University Press, 1997.

Brock, R. A. *Appomattox Roster: A List of the Paroles of the Army of Northern Virginia*. New York: Antiquarian Press, 1962.

Brown, Kent Masterson. *Retreat from Gettysburg: Lee, Logistics, and the Pennsylvania Campaign*. Chapel Hill: University of North Carolina Press, 2005.

Brown, Maud Morrow. *The University Greys: Company A Eleventh Mississippi Regiment, Army of Northern Virginia, 1861–1865*. Richmond, VA: Garrett and Massie, 1940.

Buford, Thomas P., Thomas H. Chilton, and Ben Price, Jr., *Lamar Rifles: A History of Company G, Eleventh Mississippi Regiment, C.S.A.* Roanoke, VA: Stone Printing Company, 1902[?].

Busey, John W., and David G. Martin. *Regimental Strengths and Losses at Gettysburg*. Hightstown, NJ: Longstreet House, 1986.

Camp, Richard. D., and Eric Hammel. *Lima-6: A Marine Company Commander in Vietnam*. Pacifica, CA: Pacifica Press, 1989.

Cash, W. J. *The Mind of the South*. New York: Vintage Books, 1991

Chandler, David G., ed. *The Military Maxims of Napoleon*. London: Greenhill Books, 1987.

Clark, Walter, ed. *Histories of the Several Regiments and Battalions from North Carolina in the Great War 1861–1865*. 5 vols. Raleigh, NC: Nash Brothers, 1901.

Coddington, Edwin B. *The Gettysburg Campaign: A Study in Command*. Dayton, OH: Morningside Press, 1979.

Collins, Bruce. *White Society in the Antebellum South*. London and New York: Longman, 1985.

Cooper, William J., Jr., *Jefferson Davis, American*. New York: Knopf, 2000.

Corell, Phillip, ed. *History of the Naval Brigade: 99th N.Y. Volunteers, Union Coast Guard, 1861–1865*. New York: Regimental Veteran Association, 1905.

Cormier, Steven A. *The Siege of Suffolk: The Forgotten Campaign, April 11–May 4, 1863*. Lynchburg: Howard, 1989.

221

Cornish, Dudley Taylor. *The Sable Arm: Negro Troops in the Union Army, 1861–1865.* New York: Longmans, Green, 1956.

Dame, William M. *From the Rapidan to Richmond and the Spottsylvania Campaign.* Baltimore: Green-Lucas, 1920.

Davis, William C. *An Honorable Defeat: The Last Days of the Confederate Government.* New York: Harcourt, 2001.

_____. *Look Away! A History of the Confederate States of America.* New York: Free Press, 2002.

Dawes, Rufus R. *Service with the Sixth Wisconsin Volunteers.* Madison: The State Historical Society of Wisconsin for Wisconsin Civil War Centennial Commission, 1962.

Dean, Eric T. *Shook Over Hell: Post-Traumatic Stress, Vietnam, and the Civil War.* Cambridge: Harvard University Press, 1997.

Dowd, Clement. *Life of Zebulon B. Vance.* Charlotte: Observer Print and Publishing House, 1897.

Dowdey, Clifford. *Death of a Nation: The Confederate Army at Gettysburg.* New York: Barnes and Noble Books, 1998.

Dubin, Michael J. *United States Congressional Elections, 1788–1997: The Official Results.* Jefferson, NC: McFarland, 1998.

Early, Jubal Anderson. *Autobiographical Sketch and Narrative of the War Between the States.* Philadelphia: Lippincott, 1912.

Eaton, Clement. *A History of the Old South.* Prospect Heights, IL: Waveland Press, 1987.

Eicher, Daivd J. *The Longest Night: A Military History of the Civil War.* New York: Simon & Schuster, 2001.

Evans, Clement A., ed. *Confederate Military History.* 12 vols. Atlanta: Confederate, 1899.

Fahs, Alice, and Joan Waugh, eds. *The Memory of the Civil War in American Culture.* Chapel Hill: University of North Carolina Press, 2004.

Faust, Drew Gilpin. *This Republic of Suffering: Death and the American Civil War.* New York: Knopf, 2008.

Five Points in the Record of North Carolina in the Great War of 1861–5. Goldsboro, NC: Nash Brothers, 1904.

Foner, Eric. *The New American History.* Philadelphia: Temple University Press, 1997.

_____. *Reconstruction: America's Unfinished Revolution, 1863–1877.* New York: Harper & Row, 1988.

Fonvielle, Chris E., Jr. *The Wilmington Campaign: Last Rays of Departing Hope.* Campbell, CA: Savas, 1997.

Foster, Gaines M. *Ghosts of the Confederacy: Defeat, The Lost Cause, and the Emergence of the New South, 1865–1913.* New York & Oxford: Oxford University Press, 1987.

Fox, William F. *New York at Gettysburg.* 3 vols. Albany, NY: Lyon, 1902.

Frank, Joseph Allan. *With Ballot and Bayonet: The Political Socialization of American Civil War Soldiers.* Athens & London: University of Georgia Press, 1998.

_____, and George A. Reaves. *"Seeing the Elephant": Raw Recruits at the Battle of Shiloh.* New York: Greenwood Press, 1989.

Franklin, John Hope. *From Slavery to Freedom: A History of Negro Americans.* New York: Knopf, 1967.

_____. *The Militant South, 1800–1861.* Cambridge, MA: Harvard University Press, 1956.

_____. *Reconstruction After the Civil War.* Chicago: University of Chicago Press, 1961.

Freehling, William W. *The Road to Disunion: Secessionists at Bay, 1776–1854.* New York: Oxford University Press, 1990.

_____. *The Road to Disunion: Secessionists Triumphant, 1854–1861.* New York: Oxford University Press, 2007.

Freeman, Douglas Southall. *Lee's Lieutenants: A Study in Command.* 3 vols. New York: Charles Scribner's Sons, 1944.

_____. *R.E. Lee: A Biography.* 4 vols. New York: Charles Scribner's Sons, 1934–1935.

_____, ed. *Lee's Dispatches: Unpublished Letters of General Robert E. Lee, C.S.A. to Jefferson Davis and the War Department of the Confederate States of America, 1862–65.* New York: G.P. Putnam's Sons, 1957.

French, Samuel G. *Two Wars: An Autobiography of Gen. Samuel G. French, an Officer in the Armies of the United States and the Confederate States, a Graduate from the U.S. Military Academy West Point, 1843.* Nashville: Confederate Veteran, 1901.

Furgurson, Ernest B. *Not War but Murder: Cold Harbor 1864.* New York: Knopf, 2000.

Gallagher, Gary W. *Three Days at Gettysburg: Essays on Confederate and Union Leadership.* Kent, OH: Kent State University Press, 1999.

_____, ed. *Fighting for the Confederacy: The Personal Recollections of General Edward Porter Alexander.* Chapel Hill: University of North Carolina Press, 1989.

_____, ed. *Lee and His Generals in War and Memory.* Baton Rouge: Louisiana State University Press, 1998.

_____, ed. *The Third Day at Gettysburg and Beyond.* Chapel Hill: University of North Carolina Press, 1994.

Genovese, Eugene D. *The Political Economy of Slavery: Studies in the Economy & Society of the Slave South.* New York: Vintage Books, 1967.

Girvan, Jeffrey M. *The 55th North Carolina in the Civil War: A History and Roster.* Jefferson, NC: McFarland, 2006.

Glatthaar, Joseph T. *Forged in Battle: The Civil War Alliance of Black Soldiers and White Officers.* New York: The Free Press, 1992.

_____. *General Lee's Army: From Victory to Collapse.* New York: The Free Press, 2008.

Gramm, Kent., ed. *Battle: The Nature and Consequences of Civil War Combat.* Montgomery: University of Alabama Press, 2008.

Greene, A. Wilson. *Civil War Petersburg: Confederate City in the Crucible of War.* Charlottesville: University of Virginia Press, 2006.

Griffith, Paddy. *Battle Tactics of the Civil War.* New Haven: Yale University Press, 1987.

Grimsley, Mark. *And Keep Moving On: The Virginia Campaign, May–June 1864.* Lincoln & London: University of Nebraska Press, 2002.

_____. *The Hard Hand of War: Union Military Policy Toward Southern Civilians, 1861–1865.* Cambridge: Cambridge University Press, 1995.

Grossman, Dave. *On Killing: The Psychological Cost of Learning to Kill in War and Society.* New York: Little, Brown, 1995.

_____, with Loren W. Christensen. *On Combat: The Psychology and Physiology of Deadly Conflict in War and Peace.* Millstadt, IL: PPCT Research Publications, 2004.

Hanson, Victor Davis. *Carnage and Culture: Landmark Battles in the Rise of Western Power.* New York: Random House, 2001.

Hardy, Michael C. *The Thirty-seventh North Carolina Troops: Tar Heels in the Army of Northern Virginia.* Jefferson, NC: McFarland, 2003.

Harris, William C. *North Carolina and the Coming of the Civil War.* Raleigh: North Carolina Department of Culture and History, 1988.

_____. *William Woods Holden: Firebrand of North Carolina Politics.* Baton Rouge and London: Louisiana State University Press, 1987.

Harsh, Joseph L. *Confederate Tide Rising: Robert E. Lee and the Making of Southern Strategy, 1861–1862.* Kent, OH: Kent State University Press, 1998.

_____. *Taken at the Flood: Robert E. Lee & Confederate Strategy in the Maryland Campaign of 1862.* Kent, OH: Kent State University Press, 1999.

Haskell, Frank Aretas. *The Battle of Gettysburg.* Madison: Wisconsin History Commission, 1908.

Hassler, Warren W., Jr. *Crisis at the Crossroads: The First Day at Gettysburg.* Montgomery: University of Alabama Press, 1970.

Hassler, William W. *A. P. Hill: Lee's Forgotten General.* Richmond, VA: Garrett & Massie, 1957.

_____, ed. *One of Lee's Best Men: The Civil War Letters of General William Dorsey Pender.* Chapel Hill: University of North Carolina Press, 1965.

Hattaway, Herman. *Shades of Blue and Gray: An Introductory Military History of the Civil War.* Columbia: University of Missouri Press, 1997.

_____, and Archer Jones. *How the North Won: A Military History of the Civil War.* Urbana and Chicago: University of Illinois Press, 1991.

Hattaway, Herman, and Richard B. Beringer. *Jefferson Davis, Confederate President.* Lawrence: University Press of Kansas, 2002.

Hayes, Johnson J. *The Land of Wilkes.* Charlotte, NC: Heritage Press, 1962.

Heleniak, Roman J., and Lawrence L. Hewitt, eds. *The Confederate High Command & Related Topics: The 1988 Deep Delta Civil War Symposium.* Shippensburg, PA: White Mane, 1990.

Henderson, William D. *The Road to Bristoe Station: Campaigning with Lee and Meade, August 1–October 20, 1863.* Lynchburg, VA: Howard, 1987.

Hennessy, John J. *Return to Bull Run: The Campaign and Battle of Second Manassas.* New York: Simon & Schuster, 1993.

Herdegen, Lance J., and William J. K. Beaudot. *In the Bloody Railroad Cut at Gettysburg.* Dayton, OH: Morningside, 1990.

Hess, Earl J. *Pickett's Charge—The Last Attack at Gettysburg.* Chapel Hill: University of North Carolina Press, 2001.

_____. *Trench Warfare Under Grant & Lee: Field Fortifications in the Overland Campaign.* Chapel Hill: University of North Carolina Press, 2007.

_____. *The Union Soldier in Battle: Enduring the Ordeal of Combat.* Lawrence: University Press of Kansas, 1997.

Hill, Daniel Harvey. *Bethel to Sharpsburg: A History of North Carolina in the War Between the States.* 2 vols. Wilmington, NC: Broadfoot, 1992.

Holden, William W. *Memoirs of W. W. Holden.* Durham, NC: Seeman Printery, 1911.

Holmes, Richard. *Acts of War: The Behavior of Men in Battle.* New York: The Free Press, 1985.

Holt, Michael F. *The Fate of Their Country: Politicians, Slavery Extension, and the Coming of the Civil War.* New York: Hill and Wang, 2004.

Horn, John. *The Petersburg Campaign: The Destruction of the Weldon Railroad, Deep Bottom, Globe Tavern, and Reams Station, August 14–25, 1864.* Lynchburg, VA: Howard, 1991.

Howard, Michael. *Clausewitz.* Oxford and New York: Oxford University Press, 1983.

_____, and Peter Paret, eds. *Carl Von Clause-*

witz: On War. Princeton, NJ: Princeton University Press, 1984.

Inscoe, John C., and Gordon B. McKinney. *The Heart of Confederate Appalachia: Western North Carolina in the Civil War.* Chapel Hill: University of North Carolina Press, 2000.

Johnson, Guion Griffis. *Ante-Bellum North Carolina: A Social History.* Chapel Hill: University of North Carolina Press, 1937.

Johnson, Robert U., and Clarence C. Buel, eds. *Battles and Leaders of the Civil War.* 4 vols. New York: Yoseloff, 1956.

Keegan, John. *The Face of Battle.* New York: Viking, 1976.

Kellett, Anthony. *Combat Motivation: The Behavior of Soldiers in Battle.* Boston: Kluwer Nijhoff Publishing, 1982.

King, Henry T. *Sketches of Pitt County, 1704–1910.* Greenville, NC: Era Press, 1976.

Krick, Robert E. L. *Staff Officers in Gray: A Biographical Register of the Staff Officers in the Army of Northern Virginia.* Chapel Hill: University of North Carolina Press, 2003.

Krick, Robert K. *Lee's Colonels: A Biographical Register of the Field Officers of the Army of Northern Virginia.* Dayton, OH: Morningside Bookshop, 1979.

Ladd, David L., and Audrey J. Ladd., eds. *The Bachelder Papers: Gettysburg in Their Own Words.* 3 vols. Dayton, OH: Morningside House, 1994.

Leed, Eric J. *No Man's Land: Combat & Identity in World War I.* Cambridge: Cambridge University Press, 1979.

Linderman, Gerald F. *Embattled Courage: The Experience of Combat in the American Civil War.* New York: The Free Press, 1987.

Livermore, Thomas L. *Numbers and Losses in the Civil War in America: 1861–1865.* Boston: Houghton Mifflin, 1901.

Lonn, Ella. *Desertion During the Civil War.* New York: Century, 1928.

Love, David C. *The Prairie Guards: A History of Their Organization, Their Heroism, Their Battles and Their Triumphs.* Starkville, MS.: n.p., 1890.

Manarin, Louis H., and W. T. Jordan, Jr., eds. *North Carolina Troops 1861–1865, A Roster.* 16 vols. Raleigh: North Carolina Division of Archives and History, 1966–2007.

Manning, Chandra. *What This Cruel War Is Over: Soldiers, Slavery, and the Civil War.* New York: Knopf, 2007.

Marshall, Charles. *Lee's Aide-de-Camp: Being the Papers of Colonel Charles Marshall Sometime Aide-de-Camp, Military Secretary, and Assistant Adjutant General on the Staff of Robert E. Lee, 1862–1865.* Edited by Frederick Maurice. Lincoln: University of Nebraska Press, 2000.

Marshall, S. L. A. *Men Against Fire: The Problem of Battle Command in Future War.* Alexandria: Byrd, 1961.

Martin, David G. *Gettysburg, July 1.* Conshohocken, PA: Combined Books, 1995.

Marvel, William. *Burnside.* Chapel Hill: University of North Carolina Press, 1991.

_____ *Lee's Last Retreat: The Flight to Appomattox.* Chapel Hill: University of North Carolina Press, 2002.

_____. *Lincoln's Darkest Year: The War in 1862.* New York: Houghton Mifflin, 2008.

Mathews, Donald G. *Religion in the Old South.* Chicago: University of Chicago Press, 1977.

Matter, William D. *If It Takes All Summer: The Battle of Spotsylvania.* Chapel Hill: University of North Carolina Press, 1988.

McFeely, Mary Drake, and William S. McFeely, eds. *Ulysses S. Grant: Memoirs and Selected Letters.* New York: The Library of America, 1990.

McMillen, Sally G. *Southern Women: Black and White in the Old South.* Wheeling, IL: Harlan Davidson, 1992.

McPherson, James M. *Battle Cry of Freedom: The Civil Era.* New York and Oxford: Oxford University Press, 1988.

_____. *For Cause and Comrades: Why Men Fought in the Civil War.* New York and Oxford: Oxford University Press, 1997.

_____. *Ordeal by Fire: The Civil War and Reconstruction.* New York: McGraw-Hill, 1992.

_____. *This Mighty Scourge: Perspectives on the Civil War.* New York and Oxford: Oxford University Press, 2007.

_____. *What They Fought For: 1861–1865.* Baton Rouge: Louisiana State University Press, 1994.

McWhiney, Grady. *Braxton Bragg and Confederate Defeat: Field Command.* Vol. 1, New York: Columbia University Press, 1969.

_____, and Perry D. Jamieson. *Attack and Die: Civil War Military Tactics and the Southern Heritage.* Montgomery: University of Alabama Press, 1982

Miller, Randall M., Harry S. Stout, and Charles Reagan Wilson. eds. *Religion and the American Civil War.* New York and Oxford: Oxford University Press, 1998.

Mitchell, Reid. *Civil War Soldiers.* New York: Viking, 1988.

Morrison, James L., Jr. ed. *The Memoirs of Henry Heth.* Westport, CT: Greenwood Press, 1974.

Mull, B. Rondal, and Mable M. Mull. *Mull: A History and Genealogical Record of the Mull Family in North Carolina.* Franklin, NC: Genealogy Publishing Services, 1997.

Murray, R.L. *First on the Field: Cortland's 76th and Oswego's 147th New York State Volunteer*

Regiments at Gettysburg. Wolcott, NY: Benedum Books, 1998.

_____. *The Redemption of the "Harper's Ferry Cowards": The Story of the 111th and 126th New York State Volunteer Regiments at Gettysburg*. Wolcott, NY: 1994.

Nevins, Allan. *Ordeal of the Union*. 8 vols. New York: Charles Scribner's Sons, 1947–1971.

Nolan, Alan T. *The Iron Brigade: A Military History*. Bloomington: Indiana University Press, 1994.

Nosworthy, Brent. *The Bloody Crucible of Courage: Fighting Methods and Combat Experience of the Civil War*. New York: Carroll & Graf, 2003.

_____. *Roll Call to Destiny: The Soldier's Eye View of the Civil War*. New York: Basic Books, 2008.

Oates, William C. *The War Between the Union and the Confederacy*. New York and Washington: Neale, 1905.

Owsley, Frank L. *Plain Folk of the Old South*. Baton Rouge: Louisiana State University Press, 1949.

Palmer, Michael A. *Lee Moves North: Robert E. Lee on the Offensive*. New York: John Wiley & Sons, 1998.

Patterson, Gerard A. *Debris of Battle: The Wounded of Gettysburg*. Mechanicsburg, PA: Stackpole Books, 1997.

Pearce, T.H. *They Fought: The Story of Franklin County Men in the Years 1861–1865*. Adams Press, 1969.

Pfanz, Harry W. *Gettysburg: The First Day*. Chapel Hill: University of North Carolina Press, 2001.

Potter, David M. *The Impending Crisis: 1848–1861*. New York: Harper & Row, 1976.

___. *The South and the Sectional Conflict*. Baton Rouge: Louisiana State University Press, 1968.

Powell, William S. *North Carolina Through Four Centuries*. Chapel Hill: University of North Carolina Press, 1989.

Power, J. Tracy. *Lee's Miserables: Life in the Army of Northern Virginia from the Wilderness to Appomattox*. Chapel Hill: University of North Carolina Press, 1998.

Priest, John Michael. *Nowhere to Run: The Wilderness, May 4th & 5th, 1864*. Shippensburg, PA: White Mane, 1995.

_____. *Victory Without Triumph: The Wilderness, May 6th & 7th, 1864*. Shippensburg, PA: White Mane, 1996.

Quarles, Benjamin. *The Negro in the Civil War*. Boston: Little, Brown, 1953.

Rabel, George C. *Fredericksburg! Fredericksburg!* Chapel Hill: University of North Carolina Press, 2002.

Rafuse, Ethan S. *McClellan's War: The Failure of Moderation in the Struggle for the Union*. Bloomington and Indianapolis: Indiana University Press, 2005.

Ramey, S. Arnold. *Cleveland County North Carolina Marriages, 1851–1868*. Lattimore, NC: Ramey, 1971.

Randall, J. G. *The Civil War and Reconstruction*. Boston: Heath, 1937.

Reardon, Carol. *Pickett's Charge in History and Memory*. Chapel Hill: University of North Carolina Press, 1997.

Reid, Brian Holden. *America's Civil War: The Operational Battlefield, 1861–1863*. New York: Prometheus Books, 2008.

Rhea, Gordon C. *The Battle of the Wilderness: May 5–6, 1864*. Baton Rouge: Louisiana State University Press, 1994.

_____. *The Battles for Spotsylvania Court House and the Road to Yellow Tavern: May 7–12, 1864*. Baton Rouge: Louisiana State University Press, 1997.

_____. *Carrying the Flag: The Story of Private Charles Whilden, the Confederacy's Most Unlikely Hero*. New York: Basic Books, 2004.

_____. *Cold Harbor: Grant and Lee, May 26–June 3 1864*. Baton Rouge: Louisiana State University Press, 2002.

_____. *To the North Anna River: Grant and Lee, May 13–25, 1864*. Baton Rouge: Louisiana State University Press, 2000.

Rhodes, Robert Hunt, ed. *All for the Union: The Civil War Diary and Letters of Elisha Hunt Rhodes*. New York: Orion Books, 1985.

Richards, James D. *The Messages and Papers of Jefferson Davis and the Confederacy: Including Diplomatic Correspondence, 1861–1865*. Vol. 1 New York: Bowker, 1966.

Robertson, James I., Jr. *General A. P. Hill: The Story of a Confederate Warrior*. New York: Random House, 1987.

_____. *Soldiers Blue and Gray*. Columbia: University of South Carolina Press, 1988.

_____. *Stonewall Jackson: The Man, the Soldier, the Legend*. New York: Macmillan, 1997.

Rollins, Richard, ed. *Black Southerners in Gray: Essays on Afro-Americans in the Confederate Armies*. Redondo Beach, CA: Rank and File, 1994.

Rucker, Elizabeth Hoyle. *The Genealogy of Peiter Heyl and his Descendants, 1110–1936*. Shelby, NC: Zolliecoffer Jenks Thompson, 1938.

Rush, Richard, et al., eds. *Official Records of the Union and Confederate Navies*, 31 vols. Washington, DC: Government Printing Office, 1894–1927.

Rutkow, Ira M. *Bleeding Blue and Gray: Civil War Surgery and the Evolution of American Medicine*. New York: Random House, 2005.

Sarkesian, Sam C., ed., *Combat Effectiveness: Co-*

hesion, Stress, and the Volunteer Military. Beverly Hills: Sage, 1980.

Scott, R.N. et al., eds. *The War of the Rebellion: A Compilation of the Official Records of the Union and Confederate Armies.* 128 vols. Washington, DC: Government Printing Office, 1880–1901.

Sears, Stephen W. *Gettysburg.* Boston and New York: Houghton Mifflin, 2003.

Shay, Jonathan. *Achilles in Vietnam: Combat Trauma and the Undoing of Character.* New York: Scribner, 1994.

Sheehan-Dean, Aaron., ed. *The View from the Ground: Experiences of Civil War Soldiers.* Lexington: University Press of Kentucky, 2007.

Simpson, Brooks D. *Let Us Have Peace: Ulysses S. Grant and the Politics of War and Reconstruction, 1861–1868.* Chapel Hill: University of North Carolina Press, 1991.

_____. *Ulysses S. Grant: Triumph Over Adversity, 1822–1865.* Boston and New York: Houghton Mifflin, 2000.

Skelton, William B. *An American Profession of Arms: The Army Officer Corps, 1784–1861.* Lawrence: University Press of Kansas, 1992.

Sloan, John A. *Reminiscences of the Guilford Grays, Co. B, 27th N.C. Regiment.* Washington, DC: Polkinhorn, 1883.

Sorrell, Moxley. *Recollections of a Confederate Staff Officer.* Edited by Bell Irvin Wiley. Wilmington, NC: Broadfoot, 1987.

Speer, Lonnie R. *Portals to Hell: Military Prisons of the Civil War.* Mechanicsburg, PA: Stackpole Books, 1997.

Stubbs, Steven H. *Duty-Honor-Valor: The Story of the Eleventh Mississippi Infantry Regiment.* Philadelphia, MS: Dancing Rabbit Press, 2000.

Sword, Wiley. *Courage Under Fire: Profiles in Bravery from the Battlefields of the Civil War.* New York: St. Martin's Press, 2007.

_____. *Southern Invincibility: A History of the Confederate Heart.* New York: St. Martin Press, 1999.

Symonds, Craig L. *Gettysburg: A Battlefield Atlas.* Baltimore: The Nautical & Aviation Publishing Company of America, 1992.

Thomas, Emory M. *Bold Dragon: The Life of J. E. B. Stuart.* New York: Harper & Row, 1986.

_____. *The Confederate Nation: 1861–1865.* New York: Harper & Row, 1979.

Tidwell, William A. *Come Retribution: The Confederate Secret Service and the Assassination of Lincoln.* New York: Barnes and Noble Books, 1997.

Treese, Joel D., ed. *Biographical Directory of the American Congress, 1774–1996.* Alexandria, Virginia: CQ Staff Directories, 1997.

Trudeau, Noah Andre. *Bloody Roads South: The Wilderness to Cold Harbor, May-June, 1864.* Boston: Little, Brown, 1989.

_____. *The Last Citadel: Petersburg, Virginia, June 1864–April 1865.* Boston: Little, Brown, 1991.

_____. *Like Men of War: Black Troops in the Civil War, 1862–1865.* New York: Little, Brown, 1998.

Tucker, Glenn. *High Tide at Gettysburg: The Campaign in Pennsylvania.* New York: Bobbs-Merrill, 1958.

_____. *Lee and Longstreet at Gettysburg.* Indianapolis: Bobbs-Merrill, 1968.

Wakelyn, Jon L. *Biographical Dictionary of the Confederacy.* Westport, CT: Greenwood Press, 1977.

_____, ed. *Southern Pamphlets on Secession, November 1860–April 1861.* Chapel Hill: University of North Carolina Press, 1996.

Walker, Francis A. *History of the Second Army Corps in the Army of the Potomac.* New York: Charles Scribner's Sons, 1886.

Warner, Ezra J., and W. Buck Yearns, eds. *Biographical Register of the Confederate Congress.* Baton Rouge: Louisiana State University Press, 1975.

Warren, Robert Penn. *The Legacy of the Civil War.* Lincoln: University of Nebraska Press, 1998.

Weathers, Lee B., *The Living Past of Cleveland County: A History.* Spartanburg, SC: Reprint, 1980.

Wert, Jeffry D. *General James Longstreet: The Confederacy's Most Controversial Soldier, A Biography.* New York: Simon & Schuster, 1993.

_____. *Gettysburg: Day Three.* New York: Simon & Schuster, 2001.

Wiley, Bell Irvin. *The Life of Billy Yank: The Common Soldier of the Union.* Baton Rouge: Louisiana State University Press, 1952.

_____. *The Life of Johnny Reb: The Common Soldier of the Confederacy.* Baton Rouge: Louisiana State University Press, 1943.

_____. *The Plain People of the Confederacy.* Baton Rouge: Louisiana State University Press, 1944.

Williams, T. Harry. *Lincoln and His Generals.* New York: Vintage Books, 1952.

Wilson, Clyde N. *The Most Promising Young Man of the South: James Johnston Pettigrew and His Men at Gettysburg.* Abilene, TX: McWhiney Foundation Press, 1998.

Wilson, LeGrand James. *The Confederate Soldier.* Memphis: Memphis State University Press, 1973.

Woodworth, Steven E. *Jefferson Davis and His Generals.* Lawrence: University Press of Kansas, 1990.

_____. *While God Is Marching On: The Religious*

World of Civil War Soldiers. Lawrence: University Press of Kansas, 2001.
Woodworth, Steven E., ed. *The Loyal, True, and Brave: America's Civil War Soldiers.* Wilmington, DE: SR Books, 2002.
Wright, Stuart T. *Historical Sketch of Person County.* Danville: Womack Press, 1974.
Wright, Stuart, ed. *Memoirs of Alfred Horatio Belo: Reminiscences of a North Carolina Volunteer.* Gaithersburg, MD: Olde Soldier Books, n.d.

Manuscripts and Documents

Wilson Library, University of North Carolina, Chapel Hill:
  Mary Jeffreys Bethell Diary.
  T.L. Clingman Papers.
  Edward D. Dixon Papers.
  Satterfield and Merritt Family Papers.
  Samuel H. Walkup Papers.

Perkins Library, Duke University, Durham, NC:
  Hugh Conway Browning Papers.
  Joseph J. Hoyle Papers.
  Henry W. Jones Papers.
  Peter M. Mull Papers.
  Patterson-Cavin Family Papers.
  Samuel H. Walkup Journal.
  James King Wilkerson Papers.

Gettysburg National Military Park Library, Gettysburg, PA:
  55th Regiment File.
  July 1, 1863: Action at the Railroad Cut File.

Joyner Library, East Carolina University, Greenville, NC:
  Roach Family Papers.
  Wisconsin Historical Society, Madison:
  Edward S. Bragg Papers.

North Carolina State Archives, Division of Archives and History, Raleigh:
  1840 Federal Census.
  1850 Federal Census.
  1860 Federal Census.
  Cleveland County Marriages.
  Hugh Buckner Johnston Collection.
  Peter M. Mull Papers.
  George W. Pearsall Letters.
  David T. Toler Papers.
  Howell G. Whitehead Diary (typescript).
  Military Collection (Civil War).
  Military Service Records (Microfilm M270).
  Record of Estates, Cleveland County, 1855–1864.

Museum of the Confederacy Library, Richmond, VA:

  Henry Heth Papers.
  Joseph R. Davis Papers.

Newspapers

The Asheville Citizen (Asheville, NC)
Asheville Gazette (Asheville, NC)
Biblical Recorder (Raleigh, NC)
Galveston Daily News (Galveston, TX)
Raleigh Register (Raleigh, NC)
Spirit of the Age (Raleigh, NC)
Standard (Raleigh, NC)
Weekly State Journal (Raleigh, NC)

Articles and Periodicals

Ashe, S.A. "The First Day at Gettysburg." *Confederate Veteran* 38 (1930), 378–81.
Belo, Alfred H. "The Battle of Gettysburg." *Confederate Veteran* 8 (1900), 165–67.
Berry, Stephen. "When Metal Meets Mettle." *North & South* 9 (August 2006), 12–21.
Carmichael, Peter. "The Manly Art of Staying Put." *Civil War Times* 42 (December 2003), 32–39.
Dean, Eric T. Jr., "His Eyes Indicated Wildness and Fear." *North & South* 9 (August 2006), 60–69.
Donald, David. "The Confederate as a Fighting Man." *The Journal of Southern History* 25 (May, 1959), 178–193.
Faust, Drew Gilpin. "Christian Soldiers: The Meaning of Revivalism in the Confederate Army." *The Journal of Southern History* 53 (February 1987), 63–90.
Hankins, Samuel. "Simple Story of a Soldier — VII, VIII." *Confederate Veteran* 21 (1929), 113–15.
Harsh, Joseph L. "Battlesword and Rapier: Clausewitz, Jomini, and the American Civil War." *Military Affairs* 38 (December 1974), 133–138.
Hartwig, D. Scott. "Guts and Good Leadership; The Action at the Railroad Cut, July 1, 1863." *Gettysburg Magazine* 1 (1989), 5–14.
Jordan, Weymouth T. Jr. "North Carolinians ... Must Bear the Blame: Calumny": An Affaire d'Honneur, and Expiation for the Fifty-fifth Regiment North Carolina Troops at the Siege of Suffolk, April–May 1863." *North Carolina Historical Review* 71 (July 1994), 306–30.
Jones, Charles R. "Historical Sketch of the 55th North Carolina." *Our Living and Our Dead*, April 22, 1874.
Maslowski, Pete. "A Study of Morale in Civil War Soldiers." *Military Affairs* 34 (December 1970), 122–126.
Ondishko, Joseph J., Jr., "A View of Anxiety,

Fear and Panic." *Military Affairs* 36 (April 1972), 58–60.

Reed, Liz Carson. "Battle in Desperation," *Civil War Times Illustrated* 34 (April 1995), 32–38, 80–81.

Satterfield, John R. "Farthest at Gettysburg: The Story of a Confederate Captain." *Gettysburg Magazine* 26 (January 2002), 94–113.

"Sidney Smith Abernethy," *Confederate Veteran* 7 (1899), 301.

Trudeau, Noah Andre. "A Frightful and Frightening Place." *Civil War Times Illustrated* 38 (May 1999), 42–55.

Venable, Charles S. "The Campaign from the Wilderness to Petersburg." *Southern Historical Society Papers* 14 (1886), 522–42.

Watson, Samuel J. "Religion and Combat Motivation in the Confederate Armies." *The Journal of Military History* 58 (January 1994), 29–55.

Weinberg, S. Kirson. " The Combat Neuroses." *The American Journal of Sociology* 51 (March 1946), 465–478.

Weitz, Mark A. "Drill, Training, and the Combat Performance of the Civil War Soldier: Dispelling the Myth of the Poor Soldier, Great Fighter." *The Journal of Military History* 62 (April 1998), 263–289.

Wiley, Bell Irvin. "Southern Reaction to Federal Invasion." *The Journal of Southern History* 16 (November 1950), 491–510.

Winschel, Terrence J. "Part I: Heavy Was Their Loss: Joe Davis's Brigade at Gettysburg." *Gettysburg Magazine* 2 (July 1989), 5–14.

_____. "Part II: Heavy Was Their Loss: Joe Davis's Brigade at Gettysburg." *Gettysburg Magazine* 3 (January 1990), 77–85.

Woodworth, Steven. "The Meaning of Life in the Valley of Death." *Civil War Times* 42 (December 2003), 54–59, 86–88.

Index